Shouting in a Cage

I0085510

COLUMBIA STUDIES IN MIDDLE EAST POLITICS

COLUMBIA STUDIES IN MIDDLE EAST POLITICS

Marc Lynch, Series Editor

Columbia Studies in Middle East Politics presents academically rigorous, well-written, relevant, and accessible books on the rapidly transforming politics of the Middle East for an interested academic and policy audience.

The Arab Uprisings Explained: New Contentious Politics in the Middle East,
edited by Marc Lynch

Sectarian Politics in the Gulf: From the Iraq War to the Arab Uprisings,
Frederic M. Wehrey

*From Resilience to Revolution: How Foreign Interventions Destabilize the
Middle East,* Sean L. Yom

*Protection Amid Chaos: The Creation of Property Rights in Palestinian
Refugee Camps,* Nadya Hajj

Religious Statecraft: The Politics of Islam in Iran, Mohammad Ayatollahi Tabaar

*Local Politics in Jordan and Morocco: Strategies of Centralization and
Decentralization,* Janine A. Clark

Jordan and the Arab Uprisings: Regime Survival and Politics Beyond the State,
Curtis Ryan

Friend or Foe: Militia Intelligence and Ethnic Violence in the Lebanese Civil War,
Nils Hägerdal

Lumbering State, Restless Society: Egypt in the Modern Era, Nathan J. Brown,
Shimaa Hatab, and Amr Adly

*Classless Politics: Islamist Movements, the Left, and Authoritarian
Legacies in Egypt,* Hesham Sallam

SHOUTING IN A CAGE

Political Life After Authoritarian Co-optation in North Africa

SOFIA FENNER

COLUMBIA UNIVERSITY PRESS *NEW YORK*

Columbia University Press
Publishers Since 1893
New York   Chichester, West Sussex
cup.columbia.edu

Library of Congress Cataloging-in-Publication Data
Names: Fenner, Sofia, author.
Title: Shouting in a cage : political life after authoritarian
co-optation in North Africa / Sofia Fenner.
Description: New York : Columbia University Press, [2023] | Series: Columbia studies
in Middle East politics | Includes bibliographical references and index.
Identifiers: LCCN 2022045536 (print) | LCCN 2022045537 (ebook) |
ISBN 9780231208581 (hardback) | ISBN 9780231208598 (trade paperback) |
ISBN 9780231557504 (ebook)
Subjects: LCSH: Wafd al-Miṣrī. | Political parties—Egypt. | Ḥizb al-Istiqlāl (Morocco) |
Political parties—Morocco. | Cooptation—Egypt. | Cooptation—Morocco. |
Egypt—Politics and government—2011– | Morocco—Politics and government—1999–
Classification: LCC JQ3898.W3 F46 2023 (print) | LCC JQ3898.W3 (ebook) |
DDC 306.20962—dc23/eng/20230103
LC record available at https://lccn.loc.gov/2022045536
LC ebook record available at https://lccn.loc.gov/2022045537

Cover design: Chang Jae Lee
Cover image: © Shutterstock

Contents

[v]

CONTENTS

PART THREE
Life Goes On: How Co-opted Opposition Survives

Acknowledgments

I cannot name the people who truly made this book possible, for fear of repaying their generosity and trust with even more trouble than I have already caused. In Oman, M., M., F., and S. taught me my first lessons in finding a way when choices are limited. In Morocco, N. welcomed me into her life and enriched mine. R. showed me how to be both a good scholar and a good friend. And without one particular interlocutor, who knows who he is, this project simply would not have been possible. In Egypt, so many people shared their thoughts, stories, and prayers that I cannot mention them all. My special gratitude goes to A., A., M., A., A., F., N., A., A., O., and S. for their companionship, hope, realism, and generosity. I would like nothing more than to figure out how to be of use to them. I also owe an older gentleman in Tahrir on June 6, 2012, an eternal debt of gratitude, although I do not know his name.

I have been blessed with exceptional teachers throughout my life. My thinking and my writing will always bear the traces of Ray Morris, Libby Sinclair, Liz Gallagher, Gretchen Orsland, Bob Mazelow, Brian Culhane, Lindsay Aegerter, and Gray Pedersen. Without Noha Forster, Samira Selle, Sultan al-Farsi, Dina Nouayem, and Nadia Harb, I would have given up on learning Arabic years ago. Greg Bell and Jere Bacharach have provided just the right amount of empathy and wisdom over the years; Jere and his wife, Barbara Fudge, offered warm welcomes in both Cairo and Seattle. Several scholars in Egypt helped me find my way, although they bear no responsibility for my heterodox conclusions: Asem Dessouki, Adel Asmat, and Hazem Kandil, who deserves special thanks for hooking me on Egyptian politics nearly two decades ago. Sadly, the eminently thoughtful Dr. Kamelia Shukry passed away before this book was completed. I was looking forward to sharing it with her, and it will be forever poorer because I could not incorporate her reactions.

Any graduate student would count herself lucky to have had one phenomenal committee chair. I had two. Their impeccable political scientific instincts are matched only by their instincts for mentorship; I will carry their voices with me for the rest of my life. Lisa Wedeen taught me to accept my own confidence, to truly value education, and to always reach for exactly what I meant to say. Dan Slater introduced me to a world of concepts and then let me run wild among them. Their families—Don Reneau, Tracey Lockaby, and Ria and Kai Slater (not to mention Bella and the dearly departed Max)—welcomed me into their homes and became my Chicago family. My third committee member, Michael Dawson, reminded me why I cared about all this in the first place, and gave me permission to let that care shine through.

During my early days at Chicago, I was inspired by an especially brilliant cohort of advanced graduate students who showed me how to participate in an intellectual community: Daragh Grant, Rohit Goel, Chris Haid, Diana Kim, Erica Simmons, and Nicholas Rush Smith. Many of these role models became friends, joining a supportive community of peers who combine formidable intellectual firepower with kindness and sincere curiosity: Andrew Leber, Melissa Beresford, Anjali Anand, Eric Hundman, Sarah Parkinson, Emma Stone Mackinnon, Manuel Viedma, Lindsay Conklin, Emily Coyle, Milena Ang, Lissie Jacquette, Yasmeen Mekawy, and Eva Bitran.

Financial support for this project was provided by grants from the University of Chicago and the American Institute for Maghrib Studies, as well as fellowships from Fulbright–Institute of International Education and Mellon/American Council of Learned Societies. Special thanks are due to Kathy Anderson for walking me through every major step of graduate school with patience and skill. In 2007 John MacAloon gave me a chance I desperately needed and for which I will always be grateful. The staff of the National Center for Documentation in Rabat, the Moroccan National Archives, the National Library of Morocco, the Library of Congress, and al-'Alam gave me access to much of the book's primary source material. Their efficiency, graciousness, and care are inspiring. They are in no way responsible for my interpretations.

An earlier form of this manuscript was selected for the Project on Middle East Political Science's Junior Scholars Book Development Workshop in 2017. The current manuscript is much stronger than the version I presented then, thanks to input from Adria Lawrence and Tarek Masoud (my discussants), Amaney Jamal, and Marc Lynch. Adria and Tarek have been generous proponents of the project ever since. I am eternally indebted to Marc for believing in this book and shepherding it into its current form. And I remain thrilled to be working with Caelyn Cobb, who has made the final stages of this process much less stressful than I imagined they would be. I am also grateful to Jillian Schwedler and the participants in the CUNY Graduate Center's Society and Protest Workshop, several meetings of the Chicago Comparative Politics Workshop, and two anonymous reviewers for their feedback and ideas. Matt Buehler provided reassurance and advice at all stages of the project. If any of my students is reading: this work is better because I showed it to other people.

At Bryn Mawr (and in the Tri-Co), Marissa Golden, Joel Schlosser, Osman Balkan, Alison Cook-Sather, and Seung-Youn Oh helped me figure out how to be a faculty member and a scholar at the same time. Alicia Walker was an unwavering source of support as I wondered who I was and what I wanted. Sylvia Houghteling brought humor, light, and great textiles into the tough moments. My Bryn Mawr students, especially Dalia Mahgoub, Ayesha Islam, Claire Knight, and Jamila Ghazi, never failed to hassle me about how the book was going. And my research assistant, Hannah Stanley, has offered me unending logistical and emotional support. Without her calming presence, I am not quite sure what would have happened.

At Colorado College, I have been welcomed, sustained, and supported by a department of friends: Elizabeth Coggins, Dana Wolfe, Christian Sorace, John Gould, Corina McKendry, Joe Dzerdinski, Tim Fuller, Juan Lindau, Eve Grace, Jiun Bang, Maria Sanchez, and Douglas Edlin. Whether we are troubleshooting classroom dilemmas, shopping for eye cream, or urban hiking, I always know I have a team behind me. Beyond my department, Purvi Mehta, Jane Murphy, Diana Norton, and Florencia Rojo have listened to, advised, and trusted me over the past three years.

Family has played a role not only in this book's content but in its creation. My grandparents, John and Dorothy Fenner and David and Sofia Miriam

Mitchell, have provided unwavering support of many kinds throughout the years. John, Dave, and Dottie are gone now, but I know they would have been the book's most eager readers. My brother, Alex, set a good example by both starting and finishing his terminal degree while I worked on mine. By bringing Therin, Wesley, Sidney, Calliope, Rye, and Strider into my life, he has brought me a kind of joy that I could not previously have imagined. My Egyptian family—Talaat, Kamelia, Islam, Adel, Ibrahim, and Aya, along with many aunts, uncles, and cousins—protected me, accepted me, and loved me in ways I will never be able to repay.

This has not been an easy process. Many of the people mentioned above kept me going when I could not see a way forward. Several others deserve special mention here. Britney and Joe Waranius housed me, kept me sane, and provided heroic examples of perspective and resilience. Rachel Plattus and Eli Feghali reminded me of the many forms change can take. The members of Team Floor (Cliff Cheney, Emma Alpert, and Jared Malsin) taught me about the transformative power of friendship in the face of adversity. Zoe Reese, Laura Chirot, and Yuna Blajer de la Garza never, for one second, held my long silences against me. Each one of them is a treasure.

Anny Gaul read drafts, coaxed me through stressful emails, reminded me that I was doing my best, and fed me tidbits of food history during the final years of this project. Her book, a cultural history of the tomato in modern Egypt, will soon be essential reading across a dizzying array of disciplines. Amy Gais showed up right when I needed her, with the right words of wisdom, every time. Her upcoming book, on the freedom of conscience, is as sparkling and perceptive as she is. As this project drew to a close, Charlotte Blum came into my world and saved my life. I hope she never writes a book about it.

Twenty years ago, in a similarly semipublic forum, I told my parents, Elisabeth Mitchell and David Fenner, how proud I was to be like them. That statement is even truer now than it was then, our relationship enriched by years of supporting, challenging, and enlightening one another as we each try to cross borders and bring people together in our own ways.

As I will argue in these pages, authoritarianism spawns not just major tragedies but tiny ones as well. My losses are no great thing in comparison to others'; the grief I live with is just one drop in an ocean of agony. This book is dedicated to my friend Mohamed Talaat, as a promise that I will never forget the world we conjured in that dusty ministry hallway.

Note on Transliterations, Names, and Titles

I use the *International Journal of Middle East Studies* system of transliteration, with four exceptions. First, Moroccan and Egyptian words that include locally specific sounds are rendered as closely to their actual pronunciation as possible (i.e., *balṭageyya*, not *balṭajiyya*). Second, I defer to people's own transliterations of their names (thus, Abdelouahed El Fassi, not ʿAbd al-Wāḥid al-Fāssī). Third, for all other names I omit diacritics, except for medial or final ʿayn. And finally, words and names that have established themselves in English with unfortunate transliterations (*sharia*, Gamal Abdel Nasser) are left in their most recognizable forms, except in book or article titles. The result is chaotic—but, I hope, accessible to a range of audiences.

Anyone identified in the text using only a first name is someone for whom I have created a pseudonym. These pseudonyms, and the vagueness with which I describe my interviewees in citations, may frustrate the reader, but they are essential. While the Wafd and the Istiqlal are both legal parties and members are unlikely to face state sanctions for their party activities, several interlocutors expressed a preference for anonymity vis-à-vis their fellow party members during the consent process. Because these are people who often know each other well, anonymizing them from one another requires an unusual degree of obscurity about names and titles. I have erred on the side of honoring not just the letter but the spirit of their requests, even if at some cost to analytical clarity.

Introduction

CO-OPTATION LIES AT the heart of authoritarian politics. For rulers, it is one of a handful of bedrock survival strategies: regimes bring their opponents into the political fold as a way of defusing threats and disarming rivals. For those opponents, co-optation presents a permanent political quandary. Activists debate the relative merits of participation and rejection under uncertain conditions, always aware that they may be making the wrong choice. These debates are divisive and deeply felt: they crack open movements, ruin relationships, and stall alliances. Despite co-optation's evident centrality, however, the concept remains curiously undertheorized. Too often, scholars reduce co-optation to a straightforward exchange of benefits for quiescence: once an opposition group has "sold out," it becomes docile, more concerned about protecting its newfound benefits than pursuing political change. *Co-opted* becomes a synonym for *weak, pointless,* or *finished.*

The empirical record, however, tells a different story. Not all co-opted organizations become complacent regime allies, and even seemingly domesticated opponents can turn on their co-optors. Co-opted groups nominate regime leaders for reelection (Egypt's Wafd Party, 1999) and announce that those same leaders have lost their right to rule (2011). They parrot regime positions (Democratic Party of Indonesia, 1976) and become focal points for democratic uprisings (1998). They oppose regime attempts to change constitutional rules (Morocco's Istiqlal Party, 1970, 1992) and champion such changes, however imperfect (1962, 1996, 2011). Co-opted groups call for the dissolution of parliaments in which they sit (Wafd, 1986, 1990), withdraw from cabinets in which they hold powerful positions (Istiqlal, 1962, 2013), and denounce electoral manipulation even when it benefits them (Morocco's Socialist Union of Popular Forces, 1998). Co-optation does damage opposition, but it is no guarantee of docility. How can we account for co-optation's power *and* for its limits?

I offer a new theoretical framework that explains both how co-optation damages opposition and how opposition nevertheless manages to survive. I argue that co-optation is best understood not as a secret material transaction but as a public discursive contest (see figure I.1 for a diagram of the argument). When an opposition group is co-opted, an interpretive dilemma arises: why would a party participate in a system it claims to reject? The dominant transactional story ("they sold out") is just one possible interpretation; there are others, including those put forward by the co-opted themselves. Co-optation damages opposition because transactional interpretations are far more persuasive than other alternatives. To understand why, we must look closely at how co-opted parties explain their own co-optation. In this book, I focus on the experiences of two such parties in North Africa: the Wafd Party in Egypt and the Istiqlal Party in Morocco.

In official and unofficial sources, both parties narrate their own co-optation using Romantic metaphors:[1] as costly but necessary steps toward a

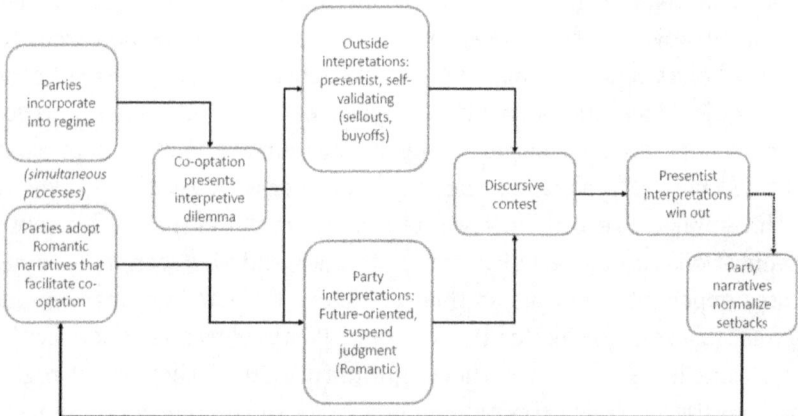

FIGURE I.1 Diagram of the argument.

future in which democratic goals will be realized. The parties' choices, therefore, can only be evaluated from the standpoint of that imagined future, when the decision to participate in the system *will be* revealed to *have been* the correct one. Parties resolve the seeming contradiction of co-optation by insisting that, as viewed from the future, there is no contradiction at all: co-optation is not in tension with democratic change, it *is* democratic change.

Romantic narratives that rely on imagined futures, however, fare poorly in competition with other accounts. The future has not happened yet, and there is no guarantee that the future parties imagine will ever materialize. By contrast, transactional arguments—the party must have sold out—are essentially self-validating in the present, especially in authoritarian regimes, where secret, unverifiable deals are the stuff of everyday politics. As parties continue to insist on their unprovable Romances, observers increasingly read such claims as rank hypocrisy.

Co-optation thus neutralizes opposition not by limiting the actions or aspirations of incorporated groups—as dominant theories suggest—but by making those actions and aspirations ring hollow. Parties' Romantic interpretations must compete with transactional ones, and, for systematic reasons, Romances usually lose. Neither Istiqlal nor the Wafd has abandoned its criticisms of authoritarianism or forsworn confrontational action, but few observers consider such objections sincere. That perception of insincerity isolates the parties from elite and mass allies, including voters, potential coalition partners, and social movements. In the words of one Wafd member, the parties are left "shouting in a cage. There's no echo."[2]

The Wafd and the Istiqlal are testaments to co-optation's power to transform threatening opponents into political afterthoughts. That, however, is only half the story. Despite the damage wrought by decades of incorporation, however, neither party has ceased to exist. Moreover, they occasionally shift into a more assertive, oppositional mode with little apparent warning. What accounts for these parties' survival and their intermittently oppositional behavior?

To answer these questions, I return to the power of ideas to structure political life. I trace party resilience back to the way in which party members construct their parties as families, both literally and figuratively. The familial networks and norms that suffuse the Istiqlal and the Wafd are often criticized as dysfunctional, undemocratic, and patrimonial. I find, however, that embedding party organization in the family—itself an ideological construction more than a biological fact—actually helps co-opted parties survive under authoritarian conditions. Familial norms carve out space for political activities that would otherwise be repressed, offer a conceptual vocabulary that deters fragmentation, and facilitate the recruitment of new members on filial rather than programmatic grounds. The resulting influx of new generational perspectives creates a permanent (if shifting) constituency for change within co-opted parties. It is when that constituency gains the organizational upper hand that we see docility evolve into confrontation.

Throughout the book I focus on the power of language to structure political reality. My claims about language are embedded in—but also, I hope, illustrate—two basic insights. The first is that discursive choices have real political consequences even when language is not deployed sincerely. Party members may not mean what they say, but what they say has consequences whether they are "lying" or not. Second, how we use language makes some courses of action more thinkable and others less so. When we describe a party as a family, we facilitate actions consistent with family relationships and impede those better suited to, say, a sports team or a political science department. I take both these insights from conceptual metaphor theory in linguistics, which (in its various forms) argues that metaphorical language entails logical corollaries and evokes specific norms regardless of speakers' awareness or intentions.[3] Readers who already ascribe to similar tenets will find here amendments and extensions of existing literary, historical, and linguistic theory. Those who are skeptical of such claims will find, in the same pages, a defense of the explanatory power of discourse.

In particular, I am interested in the role of *narratives*: that is, stories with a beginning, a middle, and an end bound together by a plot. Narratives engage with both time and morality, making them rich forms of discourse that can encompass entire metaphorical universes. Following Hayden White's classic theory of emplotment and building on David Scott's postcolonial analysis of Romance and Tragedy, I analyze how the Wafd and the Istiqlal emplot their tales of co-optation. Part 2 thus deals extensively with Romance since both parties have chosen Romantic emplotments: the democratic journey for Istiqlal and the war for political reform for the Wafd. In the book's conclusion, I turn to Tragedy, arguing that it offers more fruitful way of emplotting our *scholarly* interpretations of co-optation.

The Cases

Those familiar with Egypt or Morocco might reasonably wonder why I would take as my subject two hobbled, only vaguely oppositional political parties. After decades of upheaval in the region, to focus on stodgy, disappointing legal parties rather than the vibrancy of the street (or the horror of the battlefield) might seem like missing the point. Such a reaction, however, highlights precisely why the question of co-optation is so analytically and politically urgent. The Wafd and the Istiqlal were not always so irrelevant: co-optation has made them that way.

During the colonial era, the Wafd and the Istiqlal were powerful, well-organized nationalist movements. Supporters and critics alike expected that these two parties would dominate political life after independence. Those expectations, however, were never realized: the Wafd was banned by a new military regime and Istiqlal outmaneuvered by a monarch. Having aspired to rule in parliamentary systems, both parties suddenly found themselves opposing authoritarian regimes. Both were eventually co-opted into formal politics, and both have suffered significant declines in relevance as a result. Understanding the work done by co-optation requires that we look beyond today's parties to recover a lost sense of political possibility: for decades, these two parties were the dominant thinkable alternatives to incumbent authoritarian regimes. Their transformations make them paradigmatic cases of co-optation—a fact that has not gone unnoticed by scholars, who have drawn on the Wafd and the Istiqlal to build existing theories of co-optation as a benefits-for-loyalty exchange.[4]

Such theories, however, remain unable to account for these parties' variable trajectories: both retain a latent capacity for opposition and a tendency to reassert their relevance in times of political upheaval. In this the Wafd and the Istiqlal are representative of a broader class of political movements: those that grew up under colonialism but then failed to take (or hold) power at independence. While many scholars have studied anticolonial movements that became ruling parties, less attention has been paid to those that became opposition parties.[5] Usually nationalist, leftist, or (occasionally) Islamist, these groups managed to gain popularity and build organizational structures during the later years of colonialism. By independence, such movements were often too powerful to be repressed by young authoritarian regimes—so rulers turned to co-optation instead. Understanding how co-optation was able to weaken these movements (and how they neverthe-less survived) is critical to understanding contemporary political landscapes from Burma and Indonesia to Cameroon and Sudan.

This research is the product of more than two years of fieldwork con-ducted entirely in Arabic: eighteen months in Egypt between 2010 and 2014 and eleven in Morocco between 2012 and 2019. In Egypt my research included oral history interviews with Wafd members (elite and otherwise), ethno-graphic observation of party events, and participant observation as a stu-dent at the Wafd's Political Studies Institute.[6] In Morocco I complemented ethnographic observation and interviews with party members in four cit-ies (Rabat, Salé, Casablanca, and a northern town) with extensive archival research. I consulted documents at the National Archives, the National Cen-ter for Documentation, and the Tangier American Legation Institute as well as in Istiqlal's own party archives and those of its Arabic-language newspa-per, *al-ʾAlam*. Wafd documents are harder to come by (for reasons I discuss), but I was able to consult early editions of the party's newspaper at the Amer-ican University in Cairo and the Library of Congress in Washington, D.C.

Reading a Parallel Demonstration of Theory

Comparative History Beyond Controlled Comparison

Historical, interpretive, and ethnographic work often (sensibly) confines itself to a single country, city, or organization; this book asks the reader to hold two complex historical trajectories in her head simultaneously, in all of their detail and ambiguity. What is the logic of this comparison? How should a reader evaluate its effectiveness? Let me begin by emphasizing what this book is *not*: a controlled comparison. Despite the striking similarities and key differences between the two parties' trajectories, years of attempt-ing to shoehorn the Wafd and the Istiqlal into a Millian structure were fruitless—except insofar as my repeated failures redirected my attention from outcomes to processes. *How* were these parties neutralized? *How* have they managed to remain resilient despite that neutralization?

This book is best read as a "parallel demonstration of theory." In 1980 Theda Skocpol and Margaret Somers laid out three major approaches to com-parative history in the social sciences: macro-causal analysis (i.e., controlled comparison), contrast-oriented comparative history, and parallel comparative history.[7] As scholars doing qualitative work have (had to) become more defensive against charges that their work is unscientific and cannot test hypotheses, the latter two approaches have received far less attention than the first. But for the analysis of *processes*, parallel comparative history is ideal: it aims not to test hypotheses but to show how "an explicitly delineated hypothesis or theory can repeatedly demonstrate its fruitfulness—its ability to convincingly order the evidence—when applied to a series of relevant historical trajectories."[8]

By choosing two cases thought to support existing theories of co-optation, I demonstrate that my theoretical approach is better able to "convincingly order the evidence"—that is, to make sense of what we see. I argue in the next chapter that existing theories not only fail to convincingly order the evidence but—more importantly—lead us to ask questions that are theoretical dead ends. Most theories of co-optation strive to explain opposition actions: "Why did the Istiqlal boycott the 1992 constitutional referendum but not the 2011 one?" "Why did the Wafd participate in the 2011 uprising?" As I demonstrate—and as my attempts to impose a controlled comparison on these two cases made extremely clear—such questions rarely lead to theorizable answers. I turn my attention instead to questions of process, adopting what Simmons and Smith call an "ethnographic sensibility" even when my work is not explicitly ethnographic.[9] This book aims to give scholars (and activists) a conceptual and theoretical framework through which to understand how co-optation works, how it reshapes politics, and how it breaks down. How successful I am depends on the extent to which a reader can *make sense* of a co-opted group's behavior using the tools I offer here.

The differences between these two parallel cases allow me to explore and elaborate how co-optative processes play out in different political environments. Istiqlal offers us the rare opportunity to observe a co-opted opposition party assuming limited executive power. The possibility of cabinet participation raises tantalizing questions—"Are we living in a democracy?" "What are we gaining?" "What are we giving up?" "What will happen next?"—in an unusually public way, casting the central dilemmas of co-optation into sharp relief. The Wafd presents a more conventional case, in which a co-opted opposition party is almost completely excluded from ruling structures under a ruling-party regime. The Wafd also gives us a glimpse of how experiences of severe repression (which Istiqlal has never experienced) affect subsequent co-optation.

The paired cases are doing two other kinds of work, no less important for their practicality. First, they made the project feasible under unexpectedly turbulent political conditions. When I began my research on opposition groups in Egypt in 2007, I expected to be documenting their continued failure, not dealing with the aftermath of regime changes, uprisings, and coups. Morocco and Egypt are authoritarian regimes, in which all manner of concerns—curiosity, the pursuit of knowledge, career advancement—must always be weighed against the risks (to ourselves and others) of running afoul of authorities. In uncertain times, these risk calculations can be extremely unreliable. My ability to do research in Egypt evaporated in 2014, a very minor casualty of the 2013 military coup. While some research from afar remained possible for a time, in recent years the risks have increased. With activities like picnicking in a park or carrying a camera now punishable by indefinite detention, I find further probing irresponsible. Having a second case allowed the project to continue. The deeply contextualized study of authoritarianism is possible, but it requires us to take steps and make choices that might not seem intuitive to scholars of freer locales. We may not be able to coup-proof our polities (or our lives), but we should, to the extent possible, coup-proof our projects.

Second, these cases are paired because comparing similar but slightly different cases is a powerful strategy for generating ideas about complex phenomena. Those of us born before the advent of personal computing may once have played with a toy called a stereoscope: a plastic gadget the shape of a pair of binoculars that displayed a three-dimensional image to the viewer. Dutch literary critic Maarten Asscher finds in the stereoscope a powerful metaphor: by aligning two slightly different two-dimensional images, a single three-dimensional image is created.[10] Traveling to Morocco after years of studying Egypt allowed me to see both cases with greater depth and clarity; it helped me *generate* ideas, not just demonstrate or prove them.

Why No Shadow Case?

It has become customary, especially in single or few case studies, to include one or more "shadow cases." Briefer and less comprehensive than their main case counterparts, shadow cases usually serve one of two purposes: either to demonstrate a theory's validity beyond the cases in which it was generated or to provide additional variation on the dependent variable. Such cases can be helpful and even admirable, representing as they do the fundamental comparative desire to speak beyond our specializations and create midrange theory. For two reasons, however, this book does not include shadow cases.

First, the goals of shadow cases—especially variation on the dependent variable—are not the standards by which a parallel demonstration of theory should be assessed. The persuasiveness of my theoretical argument relies on its ability to make sense of the empirical patterns we observe in my two cases: the actions parties take, the way they narrate those actions, and the consequences that ensue. As such, a good parallel demonstration of theory must equip readers to assess its internal validity. Throughout the book, I aim to provide you, the reader, with enough historical, contextual, and textual detail to do precisely that.

Second, and more importantly, one of this book's theses is that processes we think we understand may surprise us. When examined closely, we find that what seems like the obvious truth is simply one of several ways of making sense of the world. The dynamics I analyze here only become legible through granular engagement with data spanning decades—something that simply cannot be done in several paragraphs or a short chapter. Shadow cases, by necessity, require brevity. As such, they privilege certain kinds of explanation: those that hew closely to a dominant interpretation or to conventional wisdom; those that take rhetoric at face value; and those that (as I argue in chapter 3) have a self-justifying component. I simply cannot replicate the argument I present for the Wafd and the Istiqlal in a brief shadow case.

How, then, should readers assess my argument? Is it falsifiable? Without a doubt. The most direct route to falsification would be to demonstrate that co-optation does *not* work the way I describe in my two cases. Is it generalizable? That is an empirical question, and one that I prefer to replace with another query: is it useful? It may well be that my theory holds fully only for holdover parties, not for the other party types I outline (see chapter 1 and figure 1.2). Matt Buehler's *Why Alliances Fail*, for example, convincingly argues for a completely different version of co-optation operating within palace parties.[11] Getting cases right does not require us to abandon midrange theorizing; it simply refigures it as a more collaborative exercise.

Even short of the full framework, *elements* of my analysis may be of use to other scholars of co-optation. For example, genre may prove a fruitful lens through which to analyze parties' rhetoric across many cases. But usefulness is not simply a question of how far a theory can successfully travel. Scholarship must aim to get the facts right and to make sense of them, but to do so for every instance of a broad political phenomenon is an impossible task. We must consider what we contribute even when we are wrong or our findings limited. What kinds of questions do our errors or oversights inspire in others? What kinds of refutations do we invite? How do we perpetuate or disrupt the terms of ongoing conversations? I invite readers to consider not just whether this book's argument is convincing but what it might offer even if (or when) it is not.

The Chapters to Come

This book unfurls in three parts. Part 1 (chapters 1 and 2) lays the historical and conceptual groundwork for the remaining two parts, which take up the questions of how co-optation neutralizes opposition (part 2, chapters 3 and 4) and how opposition nevertheless manages to survive (part 3, chapters 5 and 6).

Chapter 1 offers histories of Istiqlal and the Wafd with a particular emphasis on their trajectories after independence. Moroccan, Egyptian, and international scholars have produced deeply researched accounts of these parties' origins—but such accounts usually end with the withdrawal of colonial forces. By bringing both parties' stories up to the present, I provide historical data otherwise unavailable in English and highlight past moments of political possibility: times when events might have unfolded differently. I also develop a new typology of opposition parties under authoritarianism and explain my focus on what I call "holdover" parties.

In chapter 2 I argue that dominant accounts of co-optation fail to explain the empirical patterns established in chapter 1. I weigh co-optation's two senses—incorporation and neutralization—and advocate for a return to the incorporative one. Co-optation is *not* effective by definition: co-opted parties exhibit both docility and defiance. We must therefore define co-optation as the process of incorporating opponents into formal regime structures while remaining agnostic about any potential consequences. What co-optation does, I argue, is an empirical question, not a definitional one.

With this foundation in place, I turn to the question of whether and how co-optation damages opposition. I find that it does—but not in the way that existing theories predict. The co-opted parties considered here have not abandoned confrontational actions or altered their programmatic commitments. In many ways they are no less oppositional than they were prior to co-optation. What has changed is their relationship to other political actors: they have become isolated, unable to recruit elite or mass allies. Such isolation is not the result of material payoffs; its roots lie in discursive dynamics instead. As I mentioned, co-optation presents an interpretive dilemma: why participate in a regime you despise? All sorts of political actors—party members, potential allies, critics, scholars—must try to square this circle, and co-optation's power lies in the competition among their various interpretations. Co-opted parties tend to rely on Romantic narratives (e.g., "this is the first step on the long road to democracy"), which are systematically less persuasive than transactional accounts (e.g., "the parties must have sold out"). As sellout interpretations take hold, co-opted parties are increasingly dismissed as corrupt hypocrites, unreliable allies, and untrustworthy representatives.

Chapter 3 traces this process by examining Istiqlal's "democratic journey," a Romantic tale of suffering, setbacks, and eventual vindication that structured the party's discourse for more than thirty years. The "democratic journey" reconciled contemporary co-optation with a democratic future, but it could not compete with transactional counterinterpretations. Chapter 4 identifies similar dynamics in Wafdist discourse. Although the Wafd favored martial metaphors over journey tales, the two parties' narratives were structurally similar and did similar political work. Counter to existing theory, which posits that parties submit to co-optation when they lose hope of ever changing the system, I show that optimism suffused both parties' discourse both at the moment of co-optation and for decades after. I also explain why Romantic narratives underperform their transactional competitors and document the increasing isolation of both parties.

In part 3 I ask how parties survive co-optation. How, despite all they have lost, are the Wafd and Istiqlal still around? And why are they still able to shift from docility to defiance with little apparent warning? I trace parties' resilience and their latent oppositionality back to an unexpected source: the idea of "party as family." In doing so, I complicate common criticisms of opposition parties as patrimonial and therefore dysfunctional and undemocratic. I find, by contrast, that embedding party behavior in familial norms actually protects opposition and lays the groundwork for dramatic political confrontations.

In chapter 5 I describe how the idea of "party as family" orders intraparty interactions. Although dense networks of "actual" family ties suffuse both parties, metaphorical kinship binds even members who are not related to one another. Correct party behavior is structured by familial norms, including "familial connectivity" (first outlined by Suad Joseph):[12] the idea that family members are not distinct individuals but extensions of oneself. I identify three ways in which familial norms protect opposition under authoritarian conditions: creating valuable political space, facilitating recruitment despite repression, and deterring fragmentation. Chapter 6 then explores how these processes interact with generational change to produce dramatic volte-faces. Transactional theories struggle to explain why parties would (so to speak) bite the hands that feed them, but both Istiqlal and the Wafd have done precisely that in recent years: the Wafd joined protests against Hosni Mubarak's rule in 2011, and Istiqlal defiantly withdrew from the cabinet in 2013. Generational recruitment and unity imperatives mean that co-opted parties are always driven by internal divisions; there is always a new constituency, with a new worldview, waiting for the balance of power to tip in its favor. Party-as-family contains these differences, but it also normalizes them, protecting intraparty dissent and competition.

The conclusion takes a step back to consider what my analysis means for both activists and scholars. My overarching argument is that co-optation works through discursive dynamics: what damages opposition is not benefits offered but interpretations advanced. Scholars who write about the subject are therefore not dispassionate observers who have no effect on the processes they document; they are *participants* in co-optation. If we insist that opposition parties are hypocritical sellouts, we are not so much observing their neutralization as actively enacting it. How are we to reconcile that reality with our interest in describing events as they are? I return to theories of emplotment, especially to the generative work of David Scott, to argue that we should narrate co-optation in a way the co-opted cannot: as Tragedy. The co-opted seal their own fates, in a sense; the same narratives that facilitate their incorporation also, in the end, neutralize them. But to depict the co-opted as making a bad choice is to ignore the fact that authoritarianism offers no good choices in the first place. Its "endemic uncertainty" confounds strategy, leaving opposition activists to debate decisions whose consequences they cannot possibly know.[13] Only by reimagining their struggles as Tragedy, I argue, can we observe co-optation without perpetuating it.

PART ONE

Co-optation in History and Theory

ONE

The Wafd and the Istiqlal

THE HISTORIES OF the Wafd and the Istiqlal are simultaneously well-known and overlooked. Both have been studied extensively as anticolonial movements, and both, in their current guises as lackluster "opposition" parties, are familiar to any student of Egyptian or Moroccan politics. Rarely, however, are these two phases—prominence and decay—told as part of the same story. In this chapter I connect the dots, placing the contemporary Wafd and Istiqlal in the context of what they once were and, just as importantly, what they might have been. Neither party has always been weak; indeed, for much of their early lives both were prime contenders for political dominance. By tracing the successive periods of expectation and disappointment that have characterized these parties' histories, I argue that co-optation has fundamentally reshaped Egyptian and Moroccan politics by turning central characters into minor ones. How and why this has happened are questions I take up in the rest of the book; the histories presented in this chapter are (to the extent possible) causally agnostic. They lay contextual groundwork for more detailed examinations of specific moments and puzzles in the chapters to come.

In particular, the trajectories described here are the empirical foundation upon which the conceptual analysis in chapter 2 is based. During the research process I often found that claims about co-optation rested on erroneous or incomplete versions of party history. When more detail and context are included, new patterns appear. Therefore, even readers familiar with the region may find valuable surprises here—vanishingly few English-language works have seriously tracked the Wafd and the Istiqlal since independence. Throughout the chapter I define co-optation as the incorporation of opposition actors into the formal structures of an authoritarian regime. As I more exhaustively explain in chapter 2, defining co-optation as incorporation allows us to *study* co-optation's consequences rather than assume them.

To structure complex but parallel narratives, I divide each case into six stages: anticolonial mobilization, authoritarian onset, repression or exclusion, co-optation, and life after co-optation (both before and after the 2011 uprisings). The anticolonial history sets the stage, establishing why it was that people expected (or hoped, or feared) that the Wafd and the Istiqlal might well come to power at independence. The next stage—failure to seize power—explores how the Wafd was outmaneuvered by the Egyptian army and the Istiqlal by Morocco's king. In both cases, authoritarian rulers first tried to repress their party rivals: the Wafd was banned and Moroccan parliamentary life frozen. In the 1970s, however, both parties began the process of incorporation into formal authoritarian political life. After co-optation, expectations of the Wafd and the Istiqlal rose again—would these parties transform a facade of parliamentary democracy into the real thing?—and again proved to be misplaced. Both parties bled support and political relevance, eventually bringing them to their current states.

After laying a historical foundation, I lay out a tripartite typology of nonruling parties under authoritarianism. I have chosen the Wafd and the Istiqlal because they represent a specific subset of opposition groups, which I call holdover parties. I explain why holdover parties—and especially these two holdover parties—are critical cases for any robust account of co-optation.

The Wafd

The Wafd as Anticolonial Nationalist Movement

In the spring of 1919, after more than three decades of British colonial rule, a group of prominent Egyptians made their way to the Paris Peace

Conference to demand independence. Led by lawyer Saad Zaghloul, this delegation—*wafd*, in Arabic—hoped to meet with British authorities to discuss Egypt's future. But Zaghloul was denied a meeting and promptly deported to Malta, sparking major anti-British demonstrations across Egypt. While these protests succeeded at gaining pro forma independence, Egypt would remain under significant British control for another thirty years. The 1919 Revolution ushered in a nominally parliamentary system in which power was divided among British authorities, a hereditary monarch (King Fu'ad), and elected representatives. This system had many flaws—gridlock and unrepresentativeness chief among them—but it is the closest Egypt has ever come to an extended experience with parliamentary government, and it was in this environment that Saad Zaghloul's delegation became a national movement.

The 1919 uprising was not directly orchestrated by the *wafd*, who had traveled to Paris without any organizational backing. As they became symbols of the nationalist struggle, however, the Wafdist Movement grew quickly. A network of local committees sprung up to support Wafd-aligned candidates in the inaugural 1923–1924 elections; they succeeded in securing an overwhelming Wafdist majority, with nearly 90 percent of the seats in parliament. A majority, however, was no guarantee of stable government, and a series of showdowns with the palace forced new elections in 1925, 1926, and 1929. The impromptu networks created at the beginning of the decade became the organizational backbone of the Wafd.[1]

At this early stage, the Wafd's electoral might was overwhelming: its stock of nationalist credibility was unparalleled, its organizational edge over rival parties was significant, and its leader, Zaghloul, was widely respected. As historian Marius Deeb puts it, the Wafd was simply *"the* national party."[2] One British administrator went even further. "My experience," Robert Lindsay wrote to the Foreign Office in 1929, "leads me to think that every Egyptian of any intelligence is at heart an Arabist, a Nationalist, a Wafdist . . . one must come to the conclusion that the Wafd will never finally be broken."[3]

Of course, the precise breadth of the Wafd's original coalition is a matter of historical and political debate (as are, we shall see, the same features of the early Istiqlal Party). Urban historians sometimes overestimate the importance of largely urban phenomena—like interwar political parties— that may not have made much difference to the everyday lives of "ordinary"

Egyptians in the countryside. Colonial Egypt, like colonial Morocco, was a predominantly agricultural society with minimal communications infrastructure; in the 1920s, even in urban areas, more than 80 percent of Egyptians were illiterate.[4] In no sense—despite common Wafd and British claims to the contrary—was *every* Egyptian a Wafdist, or even paying attention to the political struggles in which the Wafd was engaged. Yet that is not to say, as leftist and Nasserist observers sometimes do, that the Wafd's electoral strength was a fiction or built entirely on landlords coercing the votes of their tenants. I wish to take sides in the debate over the Wafd's breadth in only one way: by arguing that an observer in the interwar period might reasonably have expected the Wafd to rule an independent Egypt in the future.

It is in comparison to its contemporaries that the Wafd's coalitional breadth was truly remarkable. During the 1920s other political parties (many of them splinters from the Wafd itself) could mount only meager challenges to Wafdist electoral hegemony. Instead of winning elections, these parties depended on the palace to appoint their members to so-called minority governments that overruled Wafd majorities in parliament. The Wafd of the 1920s had durable if tumultuous alliances with several labor syndicates and was able to contain the spread of communist ideology within the labor movement after a brief heyday between 1921 and 1924.[5] While Wafdist governments may never have followed through on their promises to workers, the party retained the ability to mobilize even those workers who did not necessarily share its programmatic commitments: in the January 1950 elections the "largest communist movement in the country instructed its members to vote Wafdist."[6] In an atmosphere of national struggle against foreign rule, non-elites repeatedly threw their votes and occasionally their bodies behind the Wafd: as a popular joke put it at the time, "if the Wafd nominated a rock, we'd elect it!"[7]

Indeed, while the party is often remembered—and critiqued—as representing large landholders, this description is not entirely accurate. The Wafd's primary social base was in fact an urban–rural coalition of city-dwelling professionals (loosely, *effendiyya*) and rural landlords of medium-sized estates.[8] Medium landholders were those who held between ten and two hundred feddans of agricultural land—far more than the average peasant—but were usually resident rather than absentee. Sons of medium landholding families often migrated to cities and joined the professional class, especially as lawyers, and it was on these family connections that the Wafd's urban–rural coalition was built.[9] While there were always some large landholders in the party's leadership cadre, the Wafd was in no sense the party of large landowners as a class.[10] The party most deserving of that title was the Liberal Constitutionalists, who not only drew a greater percentage of their leadership from large landholders (those holding more than two hundred feddans) but also criticized the Wafd's support of universal male suffrage and other populist policies.[11] Such positions won the Wafd popular support, especially early on, when differences among social classes were subsumed under the (not unreasonable) expectation that all Egyptians had something to gain from independence. Saad Zaghloul was particularly adept at deploying the term *"fellahīn"*—usually translated as "peasants"—in such a way that it included not only actual peasants but all "authentic" Egyptians as members of a single national category.[12]

It was in the 1930s that the Wafd began to acquire the reputation for wealth and corruption that would follow it to the present day. Saad Zaghloul died in 1927, and his successor, Mustafa Nahhas, was unwilling or unable to curb party bigwigs' preference for lavish spending and patronage politics.[13] The party brought into its leadership ranks several large landholders, including Egypt's political "boy wonder," Fu'ad Sirag al-Din.[14] Wearing a tarboosh and often seen with a thick cigar dangling from his lips, Sirag al-Din was a walking stereotype of an entitled *basha*. He hailed from one of the country's biggest landholding families and married into another; in a country in which someone with two hundred feddans was considered a large landowner, he owned more than eight thousand.[15] The politically savvy Sirag al-Din was not particularly interested in meaningful social reform and tended to side with party elders against more egalitarian young Wafdists. The Wafd had a great deal of credibility, but Egyptians' stores of forbearance were not endless.

Moreover, the Wafd of the 1930s had serious competitors for the loyalty of its core coalitional base. The Muslim Brotherhood, founded in 1928, and the fascist Misr al-Fata (Young Egypt) both appealed to the urban professional class that had long been a Wafdist stronghold.[16] In an attempt to keep pace with these two rivals, the Wafd's old guard grudgingly accepted the formation of a paramilitary youth group, the "Blue Shirts," in 1936. The Brotherhood and Misr al-Fata both had similar organizations (the Scouts and the Green Shirts, respectively); all three clashed in pitched street battles. In the end, the Blue Shirts proved too difficult to control, presaging deep generational divides between entrenched party elders and younger, more "radical" elements;[17] the group was disbanded. Misr al-Fata and the Brotherhood had a long way to go before they could rival the Wafd at the ballot box, however, and the specter of a Wafdist takeover remained eminently thinkable. When King Fu'ad fell gravely ill in 1934, the British Foreign Office worried that the situation "could make the Wafd take power and establish 'a republic or a virtual dictatorship.' "[18]

Despite its tarnished public image and a new crop of organizational competitors, the Wafd continued to outperform its rivals at the ballot box. The British imposed direct rule and refused to tolerate majority (i.e., Wafdist) governments during World War II, but when elections were finally held in 1950, the Wafd pulled off another solid victory. As Gordon explains,

> The Wafd polled 54.5 of the popular vote, down from 58.3 in 1942, but captured 229 of 319 seats, attaining an absolute majority. . . . *Al-Misri*, Egypt's largest daily and pro-Wafdist, proclaimed the victory a "people's revolution." For ten days, despite repeated entreaties by Nahhas to disperse, Wafd supporters paraded the streets between the new prime minister's Garden City villa and parliament. When Nahhas opened the new parliament on January 16, he and other ministers were forced to abandon their vehicles and wade through the throng.[19]

Gordon's description is illuminating. Even after years of exclusion from any executive power, the Wafd still dominated electoral politics, its media organizations remained the most widely circulated in the country, and it could still bring significant numbers of citizens into the streets (indeed, it struggled to keep them *off* the streets).

Outmaneuvered at Independence

The 1950 elections turned out to be parliamentary rule's last hurrah. The Wafd-led government, perhaps hungry to secure unwavering popular support, took increasingly confrontational stances vis-à-vis the British. Thanks to a series of ill-advised escalations, the Wafd unexpectedly abrogated the treaty governing British–Egyptian relations. The British moved to secure strategic positions, but the Wafd struck back: on January 25, 1952, Interior Minister Sirag al-Din ordered Egyptian police units at a Suez Canal base to resist incoming British troops. Dozens of Egyptian policemen were killed in the firefight that followed.[20] In response, anticolonial riots broke out in Cairo, burning most of the city's central commercial district to the ground. Responsibility for the Cairo fire remains a point of historiographical and political controversy, but, as Nancy Reynolds argues, "it is clear that many groups, including the British, the King, the Wafd, the Muslim Brothers, and Ahmad Husayn's Socialist Party, thought they had much to gain from fostering some urban chaos in January 1952."[21] Shared responsibility notwithstanding, it was the Wafd that paid the political price: King Farouq dismissed the last elected Wafdist government and installed a minority cabinet in its place.

Despite the upheaval of January 1952, it initially seemed as though parliamentary life might right itself once again. Wafd governments had been dismissed and replaced with minority cabinets before. This time, however, the situation was different. Elections were scheduled for May 1952 but then indefinitely postponed. The Wafd seemed to have abandoned its usual oppositional routine: "In contrast to previous years when the party had been out of power," Terry explains, "the Wafd leaders did not embark upon any provincial tours to gather mass support, or, in populist fashion, to put the party's case directly before the people."[22] Mustafa Nahhas, now in his seventies, left for vacation in Switzerland. The Wafd "refused to see the forest for the trees": while fighting the British and the palace, the party's leaders had ignored political mobilization happening somewhere else entirely: in the ranks of the army.[23]

On July 23, 1952, only hours after a new minority government had been sworn in, a group of junior military officers overthrew King Farouq and declared Egypt an independent republic.[24] The Free Officers, led by future president Gamal Abdel Nasser with senior general Mohammed Neguib in the role of respectable figurehead, founded the July Regime that would rule Egypt until 2011. In the summer of 1952, however, it was not clear whether the new military order was anything more than a temporary state of affairs. Nahhas quickly returned from Geneva—reportedly his first trip on an airplane—and was called, along with Fu'ad Sirag al-Din, into meetings with the new Revolutionary Command Council (RCC). The RCC was already thinking seriously about land reform, and its members wanted to know what the

Wafd's position on such reforms might be—and, more specifically, exactly how much land Sirag al-Din owned.[25] The RCC, dangling the possibility of a return to parliamentary life, encouraged the Wafd to "purge" itself of its supposedly corrupt leadership.[26]

Initially it seemed that the Wafd might acquiesce, sacrificing its leaders to preserve its right to operate under the new order. The new parties law announced in the fall of 1952 banned members of ancien régime governments—essentially, the entire Wafd elite—from participating in politics. In early September 1952 Sirag al-Din stated that the Wafd agreed in principle with the idea of land reform and then resigned from the party.[27] Later that month the Wafd released a platform describing itself as a "socialist, democratic political organization aiming to achieve independence and unity."[28] Nahhas also resigned in the hope that his departure would keep the party legal.[29]

But the Wafd's concessions were in vain. In January 1953 the RCC announced that all political parties would be disbanded and their assets confiscated, and that parliamentary life would not resume for at least three years. In his memoirs, Mohammed Neguib suggests that the party ban was little more than a ban on the Wafd: no other party represented any significant organizational threat to the young July Regime.[30] Although Neguib and his allies floated the possibility of an elected constitutional committee in the spring of 1954, they could not overcome the combined opposition of Abdel Nasser, the armed forces, and workers willing to strike to block elections. The corrupt stagnation of the interwar period had seriously damaged the reputation of parliament and parties, and it was all too easy for Abdel Nasser and his allies to paint elections as a return to aristocratic rule.

Repression

Neguib's eventual dismissal and the ban on political parties met little public outcry. Parliamentary rule (hampered and incomplete though it was) had not served the people of Egypt well during the interwar period, and party politics was commonly associated with corruption, unrepresentativeness, and incompetence.[31] But while the Wafd was fair game for critique, the RCC went out of its way to avoid making a martyr out of Nahhas. The former prime minister was elderly, ill, and still closely associated with the glories of the 1919 Revolution. Nahhas was tried before a revolutionary court, but the trial was kept out of the media, and he was eventually confined to his home rather than jailed.[32]

It was Fu'ad Sirag al-Din—younger, more dynamic, and far wealthier—who bore the brunt of the campaign against the Wafd. His was the longest of the July Regime's revolutionary trials, lasting some forty-five sittings. He was imprisoned several times (under both Abdel Nasser and Anwar Sadat) for a total of more than three years.[33] Sirag al-Din and other Wafd leaders were also slapped with "political isolation" sentences, which prevented them from exercising an array of political rights (voting, running for office, or holding high state positions).

That the RCC took care to ban Sirag al-Din from political life even when elections were suspended highlights the Wafd's continued status as a latent political alternative. Abdel Nasser was reportedly reluctant to try Sirag al-Din, fearing that the charismatic Wafdist would use the sittings as an opportunity to arouse public sympathy.[34] When asked in 1956 whether he thought that future rulers might sell the recently nationalized Suez Canal back to foreign interests, Egypt's military president reportedly replied, "What's the worst that could happen? That I go? That the revolution ends? That our regime ends? So who will come after us? Fu'ad Sirag al-Din, of course. And I am confident that Fu'ad Sirag al-Din's nationalism would not permit him to return the Canal to a foreign company."[35] Admirers of Sirag al-Din cite this response as a testament to the *basha*'s nationalist credentials. Others suggest that Sirag al-Din had British support and might have been reinstalled by foreign intervention.[36] Either way, the statement suggests that the banned, discredited, and largely dismantled Wafd remained a thinkable (although not necessarily desirable) alternative.

Without political parties, formal politics became the realm of a series of "administered mass organizations" that rallied and structured support for the regime.[37] A parliament was reconvened in 1957, but all its members belonged to the government-backed Arab Socialist Union. Public rallies or meetings organized by anyone other than the regime were unthinkable; even private gatherings were subject to surveillance. Party politics seemed dead, and for a quarter of a century—at least to outside observers—so did the Wafd.

Co-optation

Abdel Nasser died in 1970, his reign permanently scarred by Egypt's defeat in 1967. His successor, fellow Free Officer Anwar Sadat, would take the country in a new direction, both politically (up to a point) and economically. Sadat set aside administered mass organizations and unambiguous state socialism for a pluralistic facade and economic neoliberalism. His motivations are the subject of extensive historical debate, much of which is probably irresolvable, depending as it does on insights into Sadat's personal psychology. At any rate, it is difficult to argue that Sadat wanted to co-opt the Wafd: while he took steps to open the political system, he also employed extraordinary measures to keep the Wafd, specifically, out of formal politics.

Sadat began modestly, allowing the Arab Socialist Union to divide itself into three "platforms," widely known by their Arabic name, manābīr (singular, minbar): a "right" minbar, a centrist minbar identified with the government, and a "left" minbar.[38] In March 1976 these manābīr were allowed to become fully independent organizations, and in November of that year they were granted the title of "parties" (aḥzāb). The right minbar became the Liberal Party while the left became the National Progressive Unionist Rally, usually known by the first word of its Arabic name, Tagammuʿ. The center minbar became the Egypt Party, with a Sadat loyalist as its president. It was not until a series of protests in January 1977 tarnished the Egypt Party's public image that Sadat created the National Democratic Party (NDP), naming himself as its president.[39]

The new party system was based on Law 40 of 1977, which laid out a series of demanding requirements for the formation of additional parties. The law required that any new party must have twenty supporting members in the faux-legislative People's Council. After meeting this challenging standard—the People's Council was stocked with regime loyalists—any aspiring party had to submit an exhaustive application to the Party Affairs Committee, which was similarly composed of high-ranking regime officials, including the minister of the interior. Fu'ad Sirag al-Din and other former high-ranking Wafdists would have been prevented from starting a new party because of their political isolation sentences, but Sadat had, perhaps unwittingly, solved this problem for them in 1971. In an attempt to sideline his main rival, Ali Sabri, Sadat's Corrective Revolution lifted the isolation on former Wafdists as part of a broader turn away from Nasserist policies.

Fu'ad Sirag al-Din seized the opportunity to refound the Wafd. On January 5, 1978, Ibrahim Farag (another high-ranking member of the original party) delivered to the Parties Committee ten copies of the party platform and bylaws and the personal information of 591 founding members, including, to the great surprise of Egypt's political class, twenty-two sitting members of the People's Council.[40] On February 4, after six sessions, the Parties Committee determined that the New Wafd Party—bearing the exact same name as any prior party was prohibited—met the criteria for legalization.[41]

Sadat responded to this unexpected development by changing the law. He issued an immediate presidential decree (qarār jumhūri) reinstituting the political isolation of Fu'ad Sirag al-Din and Ibrahim Farag and called for a national referendum on the isolation of former Wafd leaders. Sadat then introduced new legislation, the Law for the Protection of the Home Front, which imposed political isolation on all those who had held either cabinet posts or high party positions prior to 1952. He was careful, however, to include exemptions for current loyalists who had once belonged to other interwar parties.[42]

In light of these setbacks, the Wafd's ruling committee decided on June 2, 1978, to dissolve the party.[43] Sirag al-Din failed to send the paperwork finalizing the dissolution to the Ministry of the Interior, however, allowing the party to claim in court that it had merely suspended its activities and therefore retained the right to unilaterally resume them at any time.[44] In September 1980, as Wafd-affiliated lawyers fought the new restrictions in court, Sirag al-Din was arrested along with hundreds of other intellectuals and politicians. He would not be released until after Sadat's assassination in 1981, and the judicial wrangling over the party's status would last another three years after that. The New Wafd managed to wrest legal status from the courts only shortly before the 1984 parliamentary elections.

As the legal process dragged on, the Wafd set about reanimating its party structures and reviving its popular base. The party's ability to sway more than twenty members of the People's Council had taken many by surprise, and hopes at the time were high. New president Hosni Mubarak had made moves toward increased pluralism, at least rhetorically, and it was too early to know that those moves were insincere. Local scholars wondered whether Egypt was seeing the dawn of a two-party system on the British or American model.[45] "Few doubted his estimates," Terry writes, "when Sirag al-Din suggested that in freely held elections the Wafd would get 30 percent of the vote, the Central Party [the Egypt Party] 40 percent, the independents 15 percent, and the parties of the left and the right about 15 percent."[46]

The 1984 elections, however, were not freely held, and as table 1.1 shows, the Wafd fell far short of 30 percent of the vote. What was striking, however, was not that Mubarak's well-entrenched authoritarian regime managed to take the overwhelming majority of the seats; it was that the Wafd won any at all. Besides the ruling NDP, no other party—not even Tagammuʿ or the

TABLE 1.1
Wafd Party Parliamentary Election Results, 1923–2020

PARLIAMENTARY ELECTION YEAR (FOR LOWER HOUSE WHEN BICAMERAL)	WAFD SEAT TOTAL	AS PERCENTAGE OF TOTAL SEATS
1923–1924	188	87.44
1925	86	40 (still the largest single party)
1926	150	69.77
1929	198	83.89
1931	Boycott	0
1936	169	72.84
1942	240	90.9
1945	29 partial boycott	10.98
1950	225	70.53
1964	Banned	0
1969	Banned	0
1971	Banned	0
1976	Banned	0
1984	58	12.66
1987	35	7.64
1990	Boycott	0 (some Wafd members took seats but were expelled from the party)
1995	6	1.32
2000	7	1.54
2005	6	1.32
2010	6 partial boycott	1.15
2011–2012	38	7.48
2015	36	6.38
2020	26	4.58

Source: Data through 1995 from Matthias Ries, "Egypt," in Elections in Africa: A Data Handbook, ed. Dieter Nohlen, Michael Krennerich, and Bernard Thibaut (Oxford: Oxford University Press, 1999), 337–344.

Liberals, originally *manābīr*—cleared the 8 percent threshold for parliamentary representation under the party-list system revised the previous year. The Wafd was the only opposition in parliament, and it had won fifty-eight seats.

The 1984 elections are a point of controversy among observers of the Wafd. In advance of the vote, the Wafd and the Muslim Brotherhood—Egypt's two oldest surviving political movements and on-again/off-again enemies for decades—entered into their only successful electoral alliance. The Muslim Brotherhood was illegal, and the 1983 electoral system (party-list proportional representation) did not allow for independent candidates. The standard explanation is that the Wafd was legal but lacked a popular base, while the Brotherhood had a strong base but lacked legal status. The two complemented each other, allowing them—in this conventional view—to overlook significant ideological differences.[47] This view may correctly capture the parties' motivations, although there is no way to prove its accuracy conclusively (the deal seems to have been hammered out in secret by Fu'ad Sirag al-Din and Brotherhood supreme guide Omar al-Tilmissani).[48] However, assuming the Wafd to have a weak base and the Brotherhood a strong one is, to some extent, to read later developments onto earlier ones. As I have suggested above, in the early 1980s serious observers thought the Wafd might represent a viable alternative to the NDP; twenty years later, when much of the relevant scholarship on the Wafd–Muslim Brotherhood alliance was written, the hopes of the 1980s seemed naive and misplaced.

Vote totals from the 1984 and 1987 elections suggest a robust Wafdist base. In 1984 the Wafd list won 778,131 votes, translating into fifty-eight seats, of which eight were filled by Brothers and fifty by Wafdists (a poor repayment if the bulk of the list's votes were coming from Brotherhood supporters).[49] In the 1987 elections, the Brotherhood jumped ship, allying instead with the Liberal Party (which had taken a turn toward Islamism) and the opposition Socialist Labor Party to form the Islamic Alliance. Presumably, voters who had only chosen the Wafd in 1984 to support the Brotherhood would thus have chosen the Islamic Alliance in 1987. But although the Wafd lost ground in terms of seats, winning only thirty-five, its vote totals remained essentially the same: 746,023.[50] Turnout did increase between the two elections (from just over 41 percent to just over 50 percent[51]), but the Wafd did not collapse without the Brotherhood. If the 1984 voters were mostly Wafdists, then the party's popular base was not nearly so weak as is commonly asserted; if they were not, then the Wafd was able to attract more voters in its second Mubarak-era election than it had in its first—a promising sign.

Whatever the 1984 alliance yielded in terms of added votes, however, the Wafd paid dearly for it as an organization. While the party could never have been accurately described as "secular," it was ecumenical, committed to the union of "the crescent and the cross" that adorns the party flag. Copts had always made up an influential handful of the party's top figures. In protest against the decision to ally with the Brotherhood—whose commitments to the rights of religious minorities have always been ambiguous at best—a number of prominent Wafdist intellectuals left the party, among them Farag Fouda.[52] Fouda had just published a moving defense of the Wafd's role in contemporary Egyptian politics, *The Wafd and the Future*, in 1984. Less histrionic than Sirag al-Din's usual rhetoric, Fouda's articulation of the Wafd's position might inspire even those who cared little about the pre-1952 party. His departure from the party was a real setback.

Life After Co-optation, 1984–2011

By the late 1980s it was becoming clear that Hosni Mubarak would not follow through on his initial promises of political liberalization. An electoral system originally built to handle three regime-loyal *manābir* now included both a revived Wafdist opposition and a growing Islamist contingent. Together the Wafd and the Islamic Alliance held 20.7 percent of the seats in the 1987 parliament, holding the ruling NDP to just over 75 percent. The 1972 constitution could only be amended with the support of a two-thirds majority of the legislature, and opposition representation was creeping upward.[53] Under judicial pressure to revise the electoral law—Egypt's Supreme Constitutional Court had ruled both the 1984 and 1987 parliaments unconstitutional because of the electoral systems used to produce them[54]—the regime seized an opportunity to permanently disadvantage its opponents. The regime scrapped party-list proportional representation entirely, replacing it with a system of two-member districts that privileged independents. This reform worked well for the NDP's emerging business allies and very poorly for opposition parties.

Most opposition groups—including the Wafd—chose to boycott the 1990 elections. That decision seems to have been a miscalculation.[55] The regime took advantage of the absence of opposition to run an unusually clean vote, and the Wafd was locked out of parliamentary life for five years.[56] In 1993 the party encouraged a boycott of the referendum to confirm Hosni Mubarak's third term in office, calling instead for the direct election of the president. After this period of rejectionism, however, the Wafd approached the 1995 parliamentary elections as an opportunity to right itself and continue its campaign for clean elections and an empowered legislature. The day of the vote, the party's newspaper ran a banner headline: "Truth above force" (al-ḥaqq fawq al-quwwa).[57]

The next day the headline was dejectedly reversed: "Force above truth."[58] Although the Wafd and other parties complained (rightfully) of fraud and voter intimidation, the party's final showing was a severe disappointment: the Wafd took only six seats, barely 1 percent of the legislature. The causes of this electoral decline are many: the 1990 electoral law disadvantaged opposition parties, the Wafd had been out of the public eye for five years, and all forms of public contention were restricted by the regime's ongoing campaign against Islamists. Meanwhile, the elderly Fu'ad Sirag al-Din was ailing, raising difficult questions about the future of the party that he had embodied for so long.

Sirag al-Din died in 2000, only a few months before new parliamentary elections were scheduled to take place. His successor and former aide, lawyer Noman Goumaa, was controversial from the start. The Wafd had few rules concerning term limits or constraints on the party executive; when Sirag al-Din was in power, suggesting such things would have been impertinent. But few Wafdists were ready to grant Goumaa—who was rumored to have ties to the Mubarak regime[59]—the same prerogatives.[60] Nevertheless, there were few institutional structures in place to contain Goumaa's ambition. He emulated Sirag al-Din's unilateral decision-making style, committing the Wafd to run in the 2000 elections despite internal discussions of a boycott and the disarray attending Sirag al-Din's death. As Goumaa put it for the party's official history, the Wafd had only two choices: run as best it could or "boycott and be forgotten and cut off from the streets."[61] The Wafd fielded a respectable number of candidates (indeed, 63 percent of all opposition candidates), but the results were again disappointing: just 7 seats out of 454.

Goumaa's troubles only continued. He began to clash with Ayman Nour, the Wafd's brightest rising star. Goumaa eventually expelled Nour, who went on to found a new party, al-Ghad (Tomorrow), taking with him a handful of educated, dynamic young Wafdists. When Mubarak opened presidential elections to multiparty competition in 2005, the Wafd initially signaled that it would not participate, citing concerns about electoral integrity. But after Nour announced that he would run, Goumaa abruptly changed his position, purportedly at the request of the party's high committee.[62] Goumaa—like Nour—campaigned on an end to Egypt's state of emergency, calling for a "'parliamentary republic' where the elected legislature 'supervises the executive.'"[63] State television and private newspapers refused to run Wafdist campaign ads until the party removed its slogan, "We are suffocating."[64] The ultimate outcome—a Mubarak victory—was never in any doubt, but Goumaa's third-place finish (2.8 percent), behind Ayman Nour (7.3 percent), was an embarrassment.

The party continued to flounder in the 2005 parliamentary elections, held just three months later. After the usual rumors of a boycott or an opposition alliance, the Wafd ran on its own and won only six seats. The Wafd's High Committee lost whatever patience they had left and ousted Goumaa from the party presidency. He filed a legal complaint, claiming that only the larger Wafd General Assembly could remove him. The General Assembly then convened to do exactly that, nominating party elder Mustafa al-Tawil as interim Wafd president. Mahmud Abaza was then elected as the party's new leader.

Goumaa and his supporters did not give up easily, however. In late March 2006 they entered the Wafd's Cairo headquarters and occupied the building. When Abaza's supporters tried to enter, violence broke out: eight people were shot, fifteen others injured in other ways, and the building was set on fire.[65] Goumaa was arrested when the police arrived, putting a more decisive end to his literal battle for control of the Wafd. Why people would risk their lives to control a party that held less than 1 percent of the seats in parliament and seemed to be going nowhere fast is a persistent concern of this book.

Abaza's rule as party president (2006–2010) was less eventful, although not without its own controversy. As we shall see in chapters 5 and 6, Mahmud Abaza came from one of Egypt's most powerful extended families and was routinely accused of favoritism in his administration of the party.[66] When his term was up in the spring of 2010, with the Wafd in financial trouble, he found himself running against El-Sayyid el-Badawy Shehata, a wealthy pharmaceutical magnate. The 2010 Wafd elections remain a point of pride for the organization: with supervision by judges and other public figures, the vote is understood to have been a free and fair one, and when Abaza was defeated, he graciously stepped aside.

The Wafd During and After the Arab Spring

In early December 2010, just a few weeks before Mohammed Bouazizi set himself on fire in Tunisia, Egypt held parliamentary elections—scheduled, as usual, in multiple rounds. The Wafd had been embroiled in debates about boycotts and alliances for months, but these proposals all fell through. The party would enter the elections on its own.

For unknown reasons, the Mubarak regime decided to rig the 2010 contest with even less pretense than usual. Astonished by the scale of manipulation, both the Wafd and the Muslim Brotherhood—two organizations that rarely boycott elections or work in parallel—pulled out of the elections after the first round. The Wafd asked any members who had won seats in the first round to refuse to take them and expelled anyone who failed to comply. Perhaps still sensitive about its failed 1990 boycott, the Wafd selected a "shadow government" and emphasized that it was still committed to political engagement: "The Wafd shadow government affirms that the Wafd's withdrawal from the latest elections for the People's Council is not a withdrawal from political life, nor a withdrawal from its responsibilities and commitments to the Egyptian people to struggle for their legitimate right to a better life and to work to establish real democracy."[67] While the repercussions of the botched elections were still shaking the Egyptian political scene—the Brotherhood lost eighty-seven of its eighty-eight seats, a major change in its status—an unprecedented and unexpected uprising broke out in Tunisia. While Tunisia is much smaller than Egypt, the two countries' shared characteristics did not go unnoticed: both were republics; both were ruled by aging, increasingly corrupt men with ties to big business; and both were facing the prospect of power being handed from an elderly father to a much younger son—potentially dooming both countries to decades of further authoritarian rule. Criticisms of Ben Ali's wife, of the abuses of the security services, and of the looming danger of *tawrīth* (inheritance) were all complaints that resonated in Egypt.

The story of the 2011 uprising is obviously not primarily a story about the Wafd. It is, however, a story in which the Wafd plays a role—not the role usually assumed, and not a completely inconsequential one. Unlike the two parties to which it is usually compared, the Nasserists and Tagammuʿ, the Wafd authorized its members to participate in protests *as Wafdists*, not just in their "personal capacities," on January 23, 2011. At that time, no one knew what the planned protests on January 25 would look like, or how they would turn out. A Wafd contingent appeared at a protest outside of the Supreme Court that morning, and Wafdists marched down the Nile Corniche toward Tahrir Square later in the day. After the first day's stunning turnout, the Egyptian flag became the uprising's central motif. But on that first day the green crescent and cross of the Wafd could be seen among the crowds—a faint echo of the original uprisings, ninety-two years earlier, that had brought the party into being (see figure 1.1).

Members of the Wafd leadership were undoubtedly involved in talks with the regime, but apart from several hours on February 3, the party refused to publicly abandon the demonstrations or participate in the regime's haphazard attempts to right itself. On January 29, el-Badawy called for a national

FIGURE 1.1 Wafd members demonstrate on January 25, 2011. *Nile Corniche, Cairo.* *Photo credit:* Nadia el-Awady.

unity government (two days later, Mubarak announced a new cabinet with no opposition figures whatsoever). Critics of the party focus on the Wafd's reluctance to openly call for the ouster of Mubarak; el-Badawy only declared he had lost his right to rule on January 31. But as one young Wafd activist told me in early 2014, "We didn't ask for Hosni Mubarak to go because it didn't matter. The difference was eight months and he would leave. If we had done that [i.e., agreed to a dissolved parliament and a new constitution under continued ceremonial Mubarak rule, with the promise that neither Hosni nor Gamal would run in scheduled September 2010 presidential elections], where would we be now?"[68] With the remnants of the transition crumbling around us, it was clear that his apathy vis-à-vis Mubarak did not signal apathy about regime change.

While the tale of Egypt's failed democratic transition is not primarily a story about the Wafd, it is one in which the Wafd's role must be taken seriously—in part because the events of 2011–2013 demonstrated precisely how important holdover parties can be. Even as regimes change, organizations with some bare minimum of structural advantage can play pivotal roles. In the fall of 2011, as protesters battled the police along Cairo's Mohamed Mahmoud Street, Egypt prepared for yet another parliamentary election. A new crop of parties had sprung up, imbued with the spirit of Tahrir and in some cases headed by prominent activists with no history of collaborating with the regime. Yet when the votes were counted, the Wafd outperformed every other non-Islamist party, winning some thirty-eight seats. There is a tendency to blame Egypt's subsequent polarization on the Brotherhood, but as Wickham accurately notes, one of the things that doomed Egypt's democratic experiment was the "tendency of nearly all the country's main political actors, regardless of their ideological orientation, to invest more time and energy in the competition for short-term partisan advantage than the pursuit of common goals"—a tendency "just as pronounced among many groups in the secular camp as it was in the Brotherhood itself."[69] Despite the Islamists' reputation for insularity, when Mohamed Morsi was elected president in 2012, "he did in fact reach out to several other presidential contenders and other prominent opposition figures to join the government in various capacities, and such overtures were rebuffed."[70] Two Wafd figures in a position to know confirmed to me that the Wafd was offered the prime ministership and turned it down, citing a party policy against taking appointed rather than elected posts.[71]

In late November 2012, under pressure from Egypt's maverick judiciary, which was threatening to invalidate the constitutional drafting committee and cast the transitional roadmap into chaos, President Morsi announced a constitutional declaration putting his decisions above judicial review. The Wafd joined more than thirty opposition organizations—a reflection of the intense proliferation of parties that had occurred since 2011—to launch the so-called National Salvation Front (NSF). The NSF was an uneasy coalition of liberals, leftists, and nationalists, but it managed to hold long enough to support the June 30 protests and the army's seizure of power on July 3, 2013. During this time the NSF often met in the Wafd's headquarters—no other component party had enough room.

Some supporters of the 2013 coup have revised their positions over time, acknowledging President Abdel Fattah al-Sisi's abuses while nevertheless maintaining that Morsi would have been worse, had he been given the opportunity. The Wafd generally does not belong in that category: its criticism of Sisi has been muted and its appeals to nationalism (the new regime's legitimating ideology) loud. The Wafd backed Sisi over opposition candidate Hamdeen Sabbahy in the 2014 presidential elections and even joined the state-created "For the Love of Egypt" list in advance of the fall 2015 parliamentary vote. Indeed, el-Badawy announced publicly that the list had been "selected by sovereign state agencies" and then joined the list anyway.[72] The Wafd held its ground, winning thirty-six seats—far more than its peers, Tagammuʿ (two seats) and the Nasserists (1 seat). The Wafd's current president, Bahaa Eldin Abu Shoka, is a close ally of Sisi's.

Nevertheless, a few cracks in the Wafd's support for the regime are visible. The Wafd is fundamentally a nationalist party and as such takes territorial integrity seriously (indeed, some Wafdists still believe that Egypt is the rightful ruler of the territory that is now Sudan and South Sudan). Sisi's government committed to selling two islands in the Gulf of Aqaba, Tiran and Sanafir, to Saudi Arabia in 2017. This deal was widely unpopular, and the Wafd challenged it publicly, claiming that the islands are Egyptian and selling them should be put to a popular referendum.[73] That the Wafd has risked open opposition to defend two small islands but not to decry the loss of rights and freedoms reflects its nationalist, rather than liberal, identity.

Thus, over the course of nearly a century, the Wafd has experienced several transformations: from an electorally dominant nationalist movement to a banned organization, from a banned organization to a promising opposition party, and from promising opposition to "cartoon party" (*ḥizb kartōnī*).[74] The Wafd's is unquestionably a story of decline. But it is also a story of resilience. Despite Abdel Nasser's ban, the Wafd was able to re-form; despite its history of collaboration with the regime, it was the Wafd—not the new revolutionary groups—that captured the largest non-Islamist vote in 2012. What this book aims to explain is both sides of this story. Why has the Wafd fallen so far? And how has it nevertheless managed to survive? As we shall see, the history of the Istiqlal, although different in its particulars, raises precisely the same questions.

Istiqlal

Istiqlal as Anticolonial Nationalist Movement

What would become the Istiqlal Party began its life as a secretive anticolonial organization in Morocco's spiritual capital of Fez. Its members were a handful of intellectuals educated in the *salafi* modernist Islamic tradition, among them the "golden-tongue[d]" Allal al-Fassi.[75] They were part of a loose network of activists motivated, in part, by successive decisions by the French aimed to separate "Arab" and "Berber" Moroccans for legal, educational, and military purposes.[76] These included the establishment of a "Berber" civil service college at Azrou, the broader trend of "free schools," and the infamous "Berber ḍahir" in 1914.[77] Primarily (but not exclusively) "urban, young, aristocratic, and Arab," such activists banded together to form a *zāwiya*, borrowing the word and the organizational form from Sufi brotherhoods.[78]

In 1933 members of the *zāwiya* formed the Bloc for National Action (*kutlat al-ʿamal al-waṭani*, or the Kutla). As Adria Lawrence has argued, at this early stage Moroccan and specifically Kutla resistance to colonialism was more focused on reform than on outright independence.[79] The political landscape started to diversify: multiple parties formed out of the Kutla, calling for reforms to Protectorate administration and the local promotion of alternatives to French education. Despite the limited nature of nationalists' demands, however, the French response was uncompromising. The Kutla was banned, spinoff parties were forced to operate in secret, and leading activists (including al-Fassi) were arrested.[80]

As reforms continued to founder, an explicitly separatist nationalism soon emerged.[81] On January 11, 1944, the Istiqlal Party came into formal existence with the signing of the Manifesto for Independence (*wathīqat al-istiqlāl*). Referencing a national history reaching back thirteen centuries, the short document announced the formation of the Istiqlal Party and its first demand: "the independence of the Maghreb and its territorial unity under the aegis of His Majesty, King of the country, our Lord Muhammad bin Yusuf (may God support him and render him victorious)." Fifty-nine activists signed the statement; some of them were then promptly imprisoned by French authorities.[82] The Kutla, for its part, had not been particularly interested in the monarchy; the manifesto represented Istiqlal's assessment that the sultan could be a powerful symbol of national unity.[83] The new party chose Ahmed Balafrej as its head, with Allal al-Fassi—then exiled in Gabon—in the "purely honorary" role of *za'īm* (leader).[84]

Istiqlal began to branch out from its historical roots in the Islamic intellectual centers of Fez, incorporating "broader sectors of the urban bourgeoisie and the new urban proletariat" by engaging in a range of social activities:[85] publishing a newspaper (*al-ʿAlam*, 1946); establishing the first in a series of women's organizations, the Sisters of Purity (also in 1946); organizing picnics; and sending speakers to weddings and religious holidays.[86] Its membership grew rapidly. Whereas the party had claimed only some three thousand members when it released the 1944 Manifesto of Independence, by 1952 it boasted more than one hundred thousand.[87] Given Morocco's patchwork of colonial authorities—Spanish, French, and multinational— the country's nationalist movement was always far more fragmented than Egypt's. Istiqlal had serious competitors, from Abdelkrim al-Khattabi's armed republican rebellion in the northern Rif to the rival Party of Shura and Istiqlal. Nevertheless, Istiqlal remained the preeminent nationalist organization, even if its popularity and its elite—like those of the Wafd— were primarily urban in nature.

As Istiqlal's popularity and social reach expanded, the relationship between Sultan Muhammad V and the nationalist movement grew steadily closer. The sultan was the scion of the Alawite dynasty, which had reigned in the area since the seventeenth century. Rather than abolishing the monarchy, French authorities had buttressed it, reinforcing its control over religious affairs while creating a parallel French system of administration for other matters. But on April 9, 1947, Muhammad V made a speech in Tangier signaling that his years of (occasionally grudging) cooperation with the French had come to an end: he was now aligned with the movement for independence. Istiqlal, recognizing in the sultan a powerful national symbol, was increasingly supportive of the monarchy as an institution—even though members of its forerunner, the Kutla, had not been. But by building up the sultan as a symbol of Moroccan identity, Istiqlal was supporting a political actor it was ultimately unable to control. Despite Allal al-Fassi's cultural capital, Istiqlal lacked a single, charismatic leader; forced to operate in secret and plagued by French repression, the party's collective leadership had outsourced the role of inspiring national hero to the sultan.[88]

French authorities, for their part, were unwilling to tolerate a less compliant monarch. In late summer 1953 Muhammad V and his family were exiled to Madagascar. Public outrage was widespread and feverish—anecdotes still circulate of Moroccans seeing the sultan's face in the moon—and Istiqlal was quick to make its position clear. Allal al-Fassi, then in Egypt, released a strongly worded statement broadcast on nascent radio technology and reprinted by newspapers. Although al-Fassi had previously shied away from explicitly endorsing armed resistance, his "Call from Cairo" suggested his position had changed.[89]

Outmaneuvered at Independence

Faced with rising dissidence, the French began negotiations for a transfer of power. Istiqlal and other political forces sent representatives to a conference at Aix-les-Bains in 1955, but the French ultimately handed power to the sultan (henceforth styled the "king"). On November 16, 1955, Muhammad V returned from exile, declared the country independent, and made it clear that he intended to reign *and* rule despite Istiqlali opposition. As Miller describes the moment, "implicit in his words was the message that the Sultan himself, the elected head of the *umma*, would be the supreme leader. Yet he faced a formidable competitor in the Istiqlal, who had played the part of the master architect of independence; with its sprawling network, its armed militants, its local cells, in every city and town and throughout the countryside, it was a state within the state that had to be absorbed."[90] In retrospect, it may seem inevitable that the king would become the pre-eminent executive authority in independent Morocco. The regime set about establishing a network of support in rural areas, relying on tradi-tional notables who opposed the Istiqlal.[91] With rural support and the reins of the administrative state, the king had a clear advantage. In the 1950s, however, questions still swirled about the balance of power between the monarch and elected institutions. The king established a cabinet almost immediately, in December 1955, and appointed a proto-parliament, the National Advisory Council, in 1956. Istiqlal, however, was underrepresented (relative to its political prominence) in both bodies, holding just under half of the twenty-one cabinet seats and only ten of the seventy-six council seats. Istiqlal remained committed to a (symbolic) monarchy, but it also pushed for a strong parliamentary system in which elected governments would have constitutionally protected executive powers.

Thus the "struggle for power between Mohammed V and the Istiqlal now became the principle motif of the new state's political life."[92] Rather than explicitly denouncing democracy, supporters of a strong monarchy played up the fear that Istiqlal intended to become an authoritarian ruling party like China's Chinese Communist Party or Kenya's Kenya African National Union. Istiqlal's repeated demand that cabinets be "harmonious" (*munsajima*)—that is, that they be formed from members of the same (or like-minded) parties—was recast as a specter of incipient authoritarianism, and worries persisted about Istiqlal's hegemonic aspirations.[93] Yet the conflict at base was one over "ministerial responsibility": "The party wished as a minimum to be consulted on the appointment of all ministers, and, opti-mally, to place an Istiqlali prime minister empowered to designate his own ministers. Second, the Istiqlal demanded that the ministers be given full responsibility for executing the programs of their departments . . . and that the prime minister be given effective control over the implementation of governmental policies."[94] Contemporary Moroccan political observers might find much they recognize in these demands: multiparty cabinets with lim-ited authority have proven disastrous for political accountability. When something goes wrong, Moroccans must determine whether to blame the king, the *makhzen*, the prime minister, or the minister directly in charge of the matter (who might hail from a different party than the prime minister).

Asking that the prime minister be able to choose his cabinet and that the government exercise real authority is not inherently authoritarian. Istiqlal had much to gain from a strong parliamentary system, but that does not mean its demands for one were necessarily insincere.

The king put up a multipronged defense of his authority. Political scientists have tended to focus on one of his tactics: undermining Istiqlal's dominance by encouraging the multiplication of political parties. Inspired by John Waterbury's canonical (but worryingly essentialist) *Commander of the Faithful*, successive generations of scholars have noted the authoritarian benefits that can accrue to a monarch who paints himself as a mediator among squabbling political factions.[95] But none of the new parties was as damaging to the Istiqlal as the party's own split in 1959—a development in which even Waterbury concedes the king had little hand.[96]

Between 1958 and 1959 Istiqlal cracked open, gradually giving birth to a splinter party, the National Union of Popular Forces (known by its French acronym, UNFP). The split is variously described as ideological (right–left), as generational (young–old), as personal (Allal al-Fassi versus Mehdi Ben Barka), and as the inevitable consequence of a diverse nationalist movement deprived of its common colonial enemy. There is some truth to each of these descriptions, but none is sufficient on its own. The eventual UNFP contained both party elders (Ahmed Balafrej) and young activists; while the departure of those elders made space for a new generation of Istiqlali youth (M'hamed Boucetta, Mohamed Douiri) to move into positions of prominence. Ideological divides have also been oversimplified: "Allal al-Fassi, for all his Islamic education, was not...the obscurantist conservative that some have described, nor was Ben Barka the uncompromising leftist so often depicted by French journalists."[97] Whatever the balance of causes, the split left a major mark on the Istiqlal, which has not witnessed any significant schisms since.[98]

Thus by the early 1960s, Istiqlal was no longer "*the* party" in Moroccan politics.[99] It was, however, still the *strongest* party in Moroccan politics, and still committed to parliamentary sovereignty. Istiqlal managed to hang on to most of its membership and popular support during the schism;[100] the UNFP and the palace-encouraged new parties could not compete with the mother movement's organizational muscle. What doomed Istiqlal's aspirations, in the end, was the second prong of the king's strategy: his monopoly over state agencies. During the Protectorate era, the sultan had been restricted to mainly religious and ceremonial duties; control of administration and coercion rested with the French. At independence, however, the king quickly arrogated the colonial administrative system to himself either swallowing up or suppressing other armed forces and building a lasting alliance with a network of local enforcers known as *qā'id*s and *muqaddam*s.[101] The king held the reins of government firmly in his hands, and the parties could do little more than withhold their cooperation until he deigned to grant them access.

Exclusion

The already conflictual relationship between the nationalist parties and the palace further deteriorated after Muhammad V's death in February 1961. The symbolic embodiment of the independence struggle was succeeded by his son, Hassan II, who was even less interested in developing meaningful parliamentary institutions than his father had been. Hassan shelved the constitutive council his father had convened to write the constitution, preferring instead to have a clique of loyalists draft the document behind closed doors. When it was finally unveiled and put to a referendum in December 1962, Istiqlal advocated for a "yes" vote; the constitution was not ideal, but party sources—not for the last time—described a seeming disappointment as a victory. "We discussed [the constitution]" a lead editorial in al-ʿAlam declared, "and came out convinced that we had a duty to achieve one of the demands upon which this party was founded": the establishment of a constitution, no matter its content.[102] Skeptics, still worried about a one-party state, assumed that Istiqlal expected parliamentary majorities large enough to amend the constitution at will.[103]

In advance of the long-awaited 1963 parliamentary elections, such skeptics banded together with palace loyalists to form the first of Morocco's many "administrative parties": the Front for the Defense of Constitutional Institutions. Technically independent of the monarchy but obviously allied with it, the hastily-assembled FDIC (again, known by its French acronym) easily won a plurality of seats, trouncing both the Istiqlal and the UNFP. It was not the last time that a palace-linked party formed on the eve of elections and supported by local administrators would make an improbably strong showing: the same pattern would repeat itself in the 1970s (the National

Conference of Independents, RNI), the 1980s (the Constitutional Union, UC), and the first decade of the 2000s (the Party of Authenticity and Modernity, PAM). The evenly balanced parliament that resulted from the 1963 elections (see table 1.2) was a recipe for gridlock: Istiqlal and the UNFP, acting together, could block regime initiatives but not pass their own. Citing parliamentary paralysis and a border war with Algeria, Hassan II declared a state of exception in 1964, dissolving a parliament that had passed a total of two laws in its brief existence.[104]

Under the state of exception, elections were suspended, parliament's role in policymaking (further) reduced, and cabinets increasingly filled with technocrats, loyalists, and especially military officers at the expense of the political parties.[105] Elections were repeatedly delayed—and rendered irrelevant by the king's assumption of near-total executive power: Hassan II served as his own prime minister from 1961 to 1962 and again from 1965 to 1967. When he finally called elections in 1970, Istiqlal boycotted them. The party also rejected Hassan II's attempt to amend the constitution in 1970, claiming that he was simply "constitutionalizing the state of exception."[106]

TABLE 1.2
Istiqlal Party Parliamentary Election Results, 1963–2016

PARLIAMENTARY ELECTION YEAR (LOWER HOUSE WHEN BICAMERAL)	ISTIQLAL SEAT TOTAL (DIRECT ELECTION EXCEPT WHERE NOTED)	AS PERCENTAGE OF TOTAL SEATS	PARTY RANK
1963	41	28.5	2
1970	8 boycott (4 by direct election, 4 by indirect election)	3.33	2
1977	51 (46 direct, 5 indirect)	19.3	1
1984	40 (23 direct, 17 indirect)	13.3	4
1993	52 (43 direct, 9 indirect)	15.6	4
1997	32	9.9	5
2002	48	14.8	2
2007	52	22.5	1
2011	60	15.2	2
2016	46 (35 constituency, 11 quota)	11.6	3

Source: Data through 1997 from Juan Montabes Pereira and Maria A. Parejo Fernandez, "Morocco," in *Elections in Africa: A Data Handbook*, ed. by Dieter Nohlen, Michael Krennerich, and Bernard Thibaut (Oxford: Oxford University Press, 1999), 630–637.

Istiqlal's activists were largely spared violent repression during this time, although there were repeated tussles with the regime over press censorship, and Istiqlalis active at the time report social pressure to abandon their party activities.[107] Nevertheless, the party stood outside of formal politics—still technically legal, but not participating in any of the regime's institutional structures.

Incorporation

The post-1964 political order was not sustainable. Increasingly dependent on the military, King Hassan narrowly escaped two attempted coups in 1971 and 1972. Shortly after the former attempt, he extended an invitation to the Istiqlal and the UNFP to join the cabinet. Operating in alliance as the National Bloc, the two parties entered into talks with the palace in winter 1971. These talks broke down in February 1972, when the king announced another new constitution without consulting the parties.[108] The National Bloc boycotted the subsequent constitutional referendum (which passed anyway), and Allal al-Fassi publicly turned down a renewed offer of participation in the government in April 1972. Speaking on the steps of the prime minister's office, he explained that "the objective conditions [for participation] which His Majesty had repeatedly mentioned in our conversations . . . were not on offer."[109] While Istiqlal was not enthusiastic about military rule, the threat posed by the coup was not enough to drive it into the king's embrace. Not even a second coup attempt could induce the parties to rejoin formal politics.

Soon, however, Istiqlal's position changed dramatically. Allal al-Fassi died in Romania in 1974. According to Istiqlal sources, he suffered a heart attack while lobbying Romanian general-secretary Nicolae Ceauşescu to support Morocco's claim to the Spanish-held Sahara.[110] Al-Fassi's anointed successor, Marrakeshi lawyer M'hamed Boucetta, was approved as secretary-general by consensus at the ninth party conference; any discussions about alternative candidates were kept safely out of the public eye.[111] As the showdown between Morocco and Spain over the Spanish Sahara escalated, Istiqlal's new leadership threw its support behind the so-called Green March, a multiday mass demonstration to assert Moroccan sovereignty over the disputed area. The Green March is the focus of chapter 3, in which I explain how this event transformed Istiqlali descriptions of political life. Istiqlal read the Green March—which seemed "successful" at the time—as a victory, a concession to its demands, and a sign that political reform was once again possible. Metaphorically, the Green March became the first step in a long "democratic journey."

Armed with a new, optimistic view of politics, Istiqlal avidly participated in local elections in 1976 and national elections in 1977. Although regime-aligned independents formed a majority in the 1977 parliament, and despite complaints about voter intimidation, Istiqlal returned to the cabinet for the first time in more than a decade.

Life After Co-optation, 1977–2011

For many Moroccans, the 1980s were the "years of lead" (sanawāt al-raṣāṣ): times of political imprisonment, disappearances, and torture. Leftists, Islamists, and those suspected of plotting against the king suffered the most, as Hassan II relied ever more heavily on the civilian policing apparatus.[112] Interior Minister Driss Basri worked with local officials to manage elections, suppress dissent, and confront increased syndicate and strike activity.

For the Istiqlal, however, the 1980s were primarily a time of political paralysis. For the first half of the decade, the party remained in government as elections were delayed and internal concerns subordinated to the imperatives of an ongoing war in the Sahara. Although the party had refused to let the Green March silence its internal criticism in 1975, its overwhelming commitment to territorial unity now began to overshadow other issues. M'hamed Boucetta was the minister of foreign affairs, the public face of Moroccan diplomacy as the country lobbied the United Nations and the African Union to recognize its claim to the Sahara. Boucetta was a lifelong diplomat and a committed pan-Maghrebist;[113] for him, as for many Istiqlalis, the carving up of North Africa into Morocco, Algeria, and Mauritania was bad enough, and further division was to be avoided at all costs. Given the overwhelming primacy of territorial integrity in Istiqlali thought and rhetoric, it is not surprising that the party laid low during contentious strikes in Casablanca in 1981. While Istiqlal did raise the issue of rising prices in parliament, strike activity crossed a line.[114] "No strikes during the battle for the Sahara," al-ʿAlam bluntly put it.[115]

[45]

Istiqlal seems to have paid for this position in the 1984 elections. The party's lack of emphasis on domestic issues coincided with the continued expansion of the "Basri system," and its reluctance to endorse workers' mobilization was out of step with the times.[116] Although it is difficult to weigh the relative impacts of Ministry of the Interior intimidation and voter dissatisfaction, the result was an embarrassing performance: the party won just over 13 percent of seats and was left out of the resulting cabinet. Istiqlal now stood alongside the Socialist Union of Popular Forces (USFP), which had done quite well in the 1984 contest, as the nationalist opposition. It would not join a cabinet again until it entered the 1998 Alternance government, fourteen years later.

With elections scheduled for 1989 and 1990 again delayed because of the situation in the Sahara, Istiqlal and the USFP became more strident in their demands for reform.[117] The parties made a joint call for a revised constitution in 1987 and, unusually for Istiqlal, backed a serious national strike in December 1990.[118] In 1991 and 1992 the two parties—operating with several smaller organizations as the Kutla (Bloc)—issued memoranda to the king demanding human rights protections, decentralization, and real executive power for the prime minister.[119] By this point Hassan II was willing to make concessions. His health was declining, and the question of a smooth succession suddenly seemed urgent. A government that incorporated the USFP (now the most threatening opposition party) and the Istiqlal might guarantee some stability during the transitional period to come.

The parties would not settle for just anything, however. King Hassan proposed a minimal constitutional reform package in 1992, putting the document to a popular referendum. It passed with 99.96 percent of the vote, according to the Interior Ministry, but both Istiqlal and the USFP boycotted the referendum.[120] When legislative elections were finally held in 1993, the Kutla parties fell short of a majority and refused two offers to form a minority cabinet in 1993 and 1994. Another attempt at constitutional reform, passed by referendum in 1996, was more to the parties' liking; the Kutla advocated for a "yes" vote. Yet while the 1996 reforms reached further than those offered in 1992, the new document still "ignored fundamental demands related to the powers of the king and the government/prime minister."[121] While opposition had wrested some changes from the regime, most of the Kutla's key demands remained unfulfilled.

In Istiqlal's case, nothing makes this clearer than the 1997 elections. Despite assurances from Basri's Ministry of the Interior, the results showed clear signs of fraud: Istiqlal won just 9.9 percent of the seats, its lowest share ever, leaving the party in fifth place. Boucetta immediately announced that the party rejected the results and would not participate in any institutions built on a fraudulent basis.[122] And yet, just three months later, five Istiqlalis joined an opposition-led cabinet. As I argue in the next chapter, this is just one of many episodes in Istiqlal's history that transactional models of co-optation struggle to explain.

Thus, on the eve of the twenty-first century, as Morocco awaited a new king, Istiqlal was back in the government. The party had a new secretary-general: Boucetta had stepped down after the elections, and Abbas El Fassi was selected as his replacement (again with minimal public contestation, although there were other candidates). Leadership change was in store for Morocco as well: Hassan II died in 1999, and his son, Mohammed VI, came to power promising reforms. It soon became clear, however, that the Alternance had not produced much tangible change. The two USFP-led governments that ruled between 1998 and 2002 did very little: without real executive power, opposition cabinets struggled to implement reform programs or deliver on their electoral promises. As its time "in power" wore on, the USFP bled electoral support. Istiqlal, slightly less damaged by the experience (they did not hold the actual prime ministership), took first place in the 2007 elections. Essentially repeating the USFP's controversial decision, party head Abbas El Fassi accepted the king's invitation to form a government.

During and After the Arab Spring

Abbas El Fassi's prime ministerial term was marked with controversy from the start. Some critics saw family favoritism in his choice of cabinet ministers while others denounced him for taking "dictation" from the palace.[123] Moreover, his ability to actually control policy was just as limited as his predecessors' had been. All of these factors might have caused problems for the Istiqlal in normal times. It was the party's bad luck, however, to be "in power" when protests swept across North Africa in late 2010 and early 2011. Morocco's uprising was not as disruptive as those in Egypt or Tunisia—in part because street protests were already such an entrenched part of ordinary Moroccan politics—but it was a disaster for the Istiqlal. With criticism of the monarch illegal, protesters' ire fell on El Fassi, his ministers, and the party itself. Angry citizens gathered outside the party's headquarters in central Rabat, chanting *"irḥal, irḥal"*—"leave, leave"—the same language reserved for ruling autocrats elsewhere in the region.

None of the country's political parties backed the February 20th Movement, although some individual members of the Istiqlal (and other parties) did participate.[124] Instead of joining the crowds in the streets, the parties rallied around yet another proposed constitutional reform, announced by Mohammed VI just weeks after the demonstrations began. The 2011 constitution contained concessions to several potential sources of opposition: Tamazight was elevated to the status of an official national language, and women were promised "civil and social equality."[125] It was parties, however, that looked like they had the most to gain from the new document. For the first time in Moroccan history, the constitution would mandate that the king select the prime minister from the party that received the most votes in parliament. Article 47, as this stipulation was known, seemed like a huge step forward for parties: no longer would technocrat-led minority governments be a possibility. All the major parties called for "yes" votes on the document, which (like every other constitution ever put to a referendum in Morocco) passed by a wide margin. It was the Islamist Party of Justice and Development (PJD) that benefited most immediately, however. Bolstered by popular pressure for new faces in government, the PJD was swept into power in hastily called parliamentary elections in the fall of 2011. Istiqlal joined the resulting cabinet but would not stay for long.

After all this, Abbas El Fassi no longer had a future as Istiqlal's leader. The old model of "forced consensus" (*al-tawwāfuq al-ijbārī*) could not be defended after the Arab Spring; later that year, Istiqlal held its first competitive election for party leadership. In the lead-up to the sixteenth party congress in 2012, a public horse race ensued. The two leading candidates were Abdelouahed El Fassi (Allal al-Fassi's son) and Hamid Chabat, the mayor of Fez. With the support of Istiqlal's youth wing, and despite opposition from the party establishment, Chabat edged out Abdelouahed El Fassi. The former mechanic was an unconventional choice for the party: his origins were humble rather than aristocratic, and he worked his way into the party hierarchy through

Istiqlal's affiliated labor union. Chabat immediately clashed with the PJD leadership, and within a year he had withdrawn Istiqlal from the cabinet.

Even Chabat's more confrontational style, however, did little to revive the party's electoral fortunes. Local elections in 2015 and a national contest in 2016 yielded disappointing results, reinforcing divisions between pro- and anti-Chabat coalitions. Those divisions were further exacerbated by the regime's violation of Article 47 in 2016. That article, included in the 2011 constitutional reforms, had stated that the party with the most votes would form the government (presumably under its party head). The PJD won the 2016 elections, but the monarchy wanted to be rid of Prime Minister Abdelilah Benkirane. The palace stalled the cabinet formation process, hoping to force Benkirane to step aside and leaving Morocco without an elected government for months. Istiqlalis hotly debated joining a defiant Benkirane cabinet, but an alliance of palace-backed parties were set on sidelining both Benkirane and Istiqlal.[126] In the end, they succeeded: Benkirane stepped aside, leaving his second-in-command, Saad Eddine el-Othmani, to form a cabinet.

The showdown over the 2017 cabinet reminds us that macro-level political concerns still factor into Istiqlal's decisions about cabinet participation. As it became clear that Benkirane was being forced aside, Istiqlalis were sharply divided about participation: some were in favor of joining the Othmani government while others were sharply opposed. The difference was not motivated by differing opinions of Benkirane himself; his relationship with the Istiqlal has been tense, and even Istiqlalis against participation had little positive to say about him. In my conversations with them, however, they repeatedly stressed that the Moroccan people had chosen Benkirane when they voted for the PJD, and that democratic norms require that the people's wishes must be respected.[127] Thus, even in 2017, a debate about whether to join the cabinet was still in some sense a referendum on the state of Morocco's democratic transition (or lack thereof). The broader conversation about the ultimate shape of Moroccan politics was not over.

Chabat's time in power, however, was. Increasingly paranoid and demagogic, he lost the party's 2017 elections by a wide margin, 234 votes to 924. The victor was Nizar Baraka, Allal al-Fassi's son-in-law and very much a part of Istiqlal's aristocratic elite. Baraka, a former finance minister, lacks Chabat's blustery personal style and his history of labor activism. Indeed, Baraka is generally understood to be a close ally of the palace: he had to resign from a state council in order to take the secretary-generalship and has done little in that position to challenge the regime. Benefiting from the stunning collapse of the PJD, Istiqlal won eighty-one seats in the 2021 legislative elections and joined a loyalist-led cabinet as a junior partner. How co-opted parties can shift rapidly from confrontational leaders to docile ones (and vice versa) is another of this book's concerns.[128]

Why These Parties? A Tripartite Typology

As is clear from even these brief histories, the Wafd and the Istiqlal differ in fundamental ways from other parties also classed as "opposition." For example, while the UNFP/USFP has experienced intense repression, Istiqlal has operated in relative safety. The Wafd and the leftist Tagammuʿ party (the original "left" *minbar*) have completely different organizational histories. And neither the Wafd nor Istiqlal share trajectories with "administrative" (FDIC, PAM) or ruling parties (NDP). It may seem intuitive that co-optation would work differently for diverse parties, but mainstream theories of co-optation tend to lump them all together as "opposition." Some accounts even argue that ruling and nonruling parties co-opt opponents in the same way.[129]

The starting point of my case selection is the idea that co-optation may, in fact, work differently for different kinds of opposition party. Existing typologies usually focus on parties' programmatic orientation or legal status.[130] But these approaches are ill-suited to the project at hand. Programmatic distinctions, usually based on unidimensional spectra, consistently erase nationalist parties or recast them as "right-wing" or "liberal," misrepresenting their ideological status and the nature of their support.[131] Legal/illegal distinctions fail to capture the behavior of illegal but permitted groups (like the Egyptian Muslim Brotherhood) and import co-optative outcomes (like legal incorporation) into typologies intended to help study co-optation.

I propose instead that we differentiate parties based on the timing of their foundation and the actors responsible for creating them. I begin by setting aside ruling parties, which are widely agreed to do unique work to support authoritarianism.[132] I distinguish among three types of nonruling organization: holdover, challenger, and palace parties (see figure 1.2). Challenger parties are those created "from below" by non-regime actors after the onset of authoritarian rule. Palace parties, meanwhile, are created by incumbents (or with the tacit encouragement of incumbents) to play a supportive role in parliament.[133] Some of the best extant work on co-optation is on palace parties. Buehler, for example, expertly considers the co-optation of individual politicians into palace parties in the Moroccan case—a process that, although run by the same regime, differs sharply from the dynamics I describe here.[134] Holdover parties—those created by non-regime actors prior to the onset of incumbent authoritarian rule—have received relatively little distinct attention. Istiqlal and the Wafd are prime examples of holdover parties: both were founded prior to the regimes that eventually co-opted them and by actors outside the eventual authoritarian elite.

Holdover parties are particularly apt cases through which to study co-optation. Substantively, their co-optation represents a complete remaking of a country's political landscape. They confront emerging authoritarian regimes not as a handful of dissidents but as fully formed organizations with impressive organizational, electoral, and social-service apparatuses. They cannot simply be nipped in the bud. They must be actively dismantled or redirected—a process that is both vital to authoritarian survival and legible to observers. Whereas challenger parties might be crushed (or co-opted)

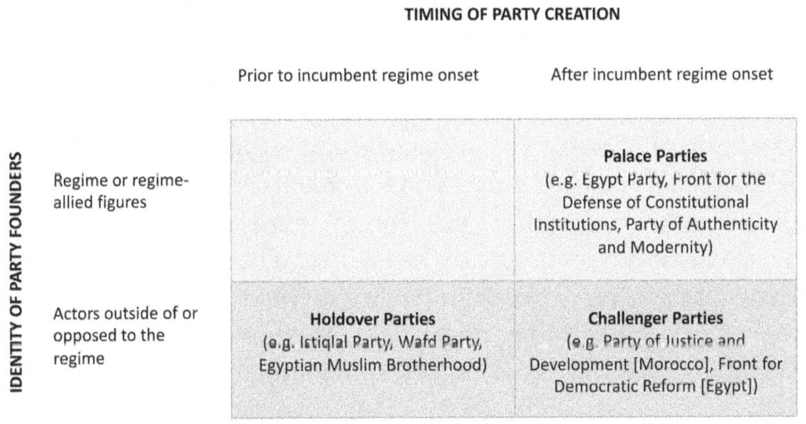

TIMING OF PARTY CREATION

	Prior to incumbent regime onset	After incumbent regime onset
IDENTITY OF PARTY FOUNDERS Regime or regime-allied figures		**Palace Parties** (e.g. Egypt Party, Front for the Defense of Constitutional Institutions, Party of Authenticity and Modernity)
Actors outside of or opposed to the regime	**Holdover Parties** (e.g. Istiqlal Party, Wafd Party, Egyptian Muslim Brotherhood)	**Challenger Parties** (e.g. Party of Justice and Development [Morocco], Front for Democratic Reform [Egypt])

FIGURE 1.2 A typology of non-ruling parties under authoritarianism.

before scholars know much about them, the co-optation of holdover parties leaves clear public traces. Holdover parties may not be the sexiest or most appealing opposition groups, but they do provide an unparalleled window onto crucial processes of authoritarian survival.

I have chosen to focus specifically on the Wafd and the Istiqlal because they are widely considered open-and-shut cases of "successful" (from a regime standpoint) co-optation. At independence, vulnerable young authoritarian regimes saw these organizations as real rivals, but over time they have both been incorporated and, to a significant extent, neutralized. Because of their transformations, the Wafd and the Istiqlal are commonly invoked as straightforward examples of incorporation's crippling effect on opposition.[135] Such accounts, as I argue in the coming chapter, fail to comport with patterns of party behavior even in these two cases. The Wafd and the Istiqlal are crucial cases for any theory of organizational co-optation precisely because they have figured so prominently in prior accounts.

Moreover, I focus on these two parties because—despite contemporary impressions to the contrary—they are substantively important both to their home polities and as representatives of the broader class of colonial-era movements that failed to come to power at independence. While ruling parties born of anticolonial struggle have received considerable scholarly attention, their less successful counterparts have been largely ignored. Yet these organizations—unappealing though their ideologies and histories of collaboration may be—have repeatedly shown their relevance. From Morocco and Egypt to Burma and Indonesia, such movements have tended to reassert themselves in times of political upheaval. Indeed, they can emerge from co-optation to become the pivots upon which entire polities turn. Consider, for example, the roles of the Wafd and the Egyptian Muslim Brotherhood (also a holdover organization) during and after Egypt's 2011 uprising. The Wafd and the Brotherhood did not lead the protests, but the former's unwillingness to make a deal with the floundering regime and the latter's organizational muscle did contribute to the eventual outcome. In the first post-Mubarak parliamentary elections, the Brotherhood's Freedom and Justice Party outperformed all other Islamist groups; the Wafd, while coming in a distant third, outperformed all other non-Islamist groups. Despite their histories of collaboration and quiescence, these two groups handily defeated new parties launched by revolutionary activists and imbued with the spirit of Tahrir Square. Incorporated holdover parties rarely represent the leading edge of politics, and their complex histories can make them difficult to cheer for. But their orientations and trajectories still have an outsized impact on the political landscape. Even in a state of decay, they are often their countries' broadest and best-organized political alternatives. Citizens may not think highly of such parties, but, to paraphrase an unfortunate former secretary of defense, societies do politics with the organizations they have, not the organizations they want.

TWO

Conceptualizing Co-optation

THE PAST TWENTY years have witnessed a wave of scholarly interest in authoritarian politics.[1] As part of this research agenda, the role of repression in sustaining authoritarianism has received careful theoretical attention. Moving beyond the assumption that repression always contributes to authoritarian stability, scholars have argued that a reliance on repression may alter the very nature of regimes and endanger their reproduction.[2] Different coercive institutions have been disaggregated from one another and their respective roles in supporting autocratic rule examined.[3] Detailed work has highlighted the coercive dimensions of activities, from discourse to social spending, that do not initially seem repressive.[4] Even repression's seemingly paradoxical capacity to both suppress and encourage mobilization has been embraced as a puzzle rather than ignored.[5] No longer can a scholar assert that a regime's stability depends on repression without carefully specifying which mechanisms are at work and acknowledging the existence of ambiguous effects.

The other major hypothesized pillar of regime durability, co-optation, has not received the same careful theoretical treatment. Burgeoning literatures on authoritarian institutions, electoral authoritarianism, and authoritarian distribution all claim to be dealing, at least in part, with co-optation.[6] Far from being overlooked by scholars, co-optation seems to be everywhere. Indeed, it increasingly threatens to become a residual category for all regime-stabilizing practices that are not explicitly coercive, from social spending and infrastructure projects to party legalization and cabinet appointments. Despite all this attention, however, our understanding of co-optation remains one-dimensional. The central premise that has been abandoned in studies of repression—that it always supports regime stability—is alive and well in studies of co-optation. The idea of co-optation as a practice or process, vulnerable to destabilization and failure, is too often replaced by the idea of co-optation as outcome: the neutralization of threats against the regime.[7]

This state of theoretical affairs is lamentable precisely because co-optation's effects *are* so variable and ambiguous. Even working with a narrow definition of co-optation—bringing opposition groups into authoritarian elections—the range of behaviors exhibited by co-opted groups is striking. Such groups may support regime leaders for reelection (Wafd, 1999) or announce that those leaders have lost their right to rule (Wafd, 2011). They may oppose regime attempts to change the rules of the political game (Istiqlal, 1970, 1992) or champion such changes, however imperfect (Istiqlal, 1962, 1996, 2011). These colorful histories call into question the notion that co-optation automatically produces docile, unthreatening opposition. They suggest that there is life after co-optation: continued political agency and possibility, and a range of behaviors that demands explanation.

Our current understanding of co-optation as effective by definition leaves us unable to explain co-optation's profound but variable effects not only on the co-opted but on politics more broadly. Co-optation has two senses, one relating to incorporation and the other to neutralization. *Incorporation* is the act of bringing opponents into the formal structures of a political regime.[8] When nonruling parties are granted legal status, participate in authoritarian elections, or take positions in authoritarian cabinets, they are incorporated. Groups are *neutralized*, by contrast, when they are rendered unthreatening (or less threatening) to authoritarian incumbents. Neutralization can have many causes, not all of which are related to incorporation (severe repression, for example, can often neutralize an opponent). In this book I pose several key questions made possible by the separation of these two senses: How does incorporation neutralize the co-opted? How do incorporation and neutralization reshape co-opted organizations' structures and practices? When and how does incorporation break down? And when it does, will neutralization persist?

In this chapter, I undertake three major tasks. I begin by defining co-optation in its incorporative rather than neutralizing sense. I then review existing models and compare their predictions to the empirical patterns of co-opted party behavior outlined in chapter 1. I find that the empirical record comports poorly with existing theories: we simply do not see the forms or patterns of neutralization that our dominant theories of co-optation predict. Finally, I trace the patterns of neutralization that we *do* see and outline a new theory of co-optation that can better account for those patterns. My approach takes party actions not as discrete dependent variables needing to be explained but rather as windows onto processes of neutralization that are both unstable and profound in their effects.

Defining Co-optation

As currently understood, *co-optation* suffers from two distinct forms of confusion. The first is a confusion between two possible senses of the word: one connected to incorporation, the other to neutralization. The original definition of "to co-opt," derived from the Latin *co-optare*, is "to elect into a body by the votes of its members."[9] This meaning is the root of the first, incorporative sense of the term: co-optation has something to do with bringing a new actor into a system. As a 1651 text put it, speaking of a religious notable, "he suffrd himself to be coopted into the College of Cardinals"[10]—that is, rather than being elected to the College by the members of a larger body, he was selected by the members of the very body he was to join. While this meaning may sound archaic to contemporary ears, it is still commonly used in organizational bylaws. In recent decades, however, the word's incorporative sense has been eclipsed by its more common, ordinary-language meaning. In everyday speech (at least in American English), a co-opted group is one that has "sold out," been "bought off," or been otherwise rendered unthreatening, weak, or irrelevant.[11] This second sense, in which to co-opt is to neutralize, exists ineradicably alongside co-optation-as-incorporation.[12] As a result, co-optation is often understood to be effective by definition: an opponent brought into an authoritarian system is co-opted (that is, incorporated), while an opponent who is neutralized is also described as "co-opted." Unsurprisingly, incorporation is then argued to inevitably produce (or reflect) neutralization.

The second confusion plaguing discussions of co-optation accounts for a great deal of the conceptual stretching that has rendered our understanding of co-optation so thin. If to co-opt is to neutralize, then all manner of neutralizing activities can be classed as "co-optation," regardless of whether they resemble one another or the word's other, incorporative sense. In recent years, distributive practices such as patronage and social spending—which might easily produce neutralization through non-incorporative mechanisms (e.g., "performance legitimacy," material interest, programmatic appeal)—have been lumped in with more traditionally incorporative activities (holding multiparty elections, recruiting individuals into a ruling party) as instances of co-optation.[13] Thus, an outcome—neutralized opposition, commonly proxied by regime survival—is used to define what counts as co-optation. That co-optative processes might rightly share other features (i.e., an incorporative component), or that they might not (always or only) produce neutralization is rendered invisible by the very definition of our concept. The questions I ask here—when and how incorporation produces neutralization—can only be asked if we distinguish between these two senses. Throughout the book I use the term *co-optation* to mean *incorporation*, remaining definitionally agnostic about co-optation's effects. As Michael Lacy, who offers a similar conceptualization in the context of American government relations with indigenous communities, puts it, "this definition of co-optation differs markedly from popular usage, which typically identifies co-optation with one of its possible results, the neutralization of a threat to the power holder."[14]

Incorporation is not, in my understanding, a dichotomous variable. Groups count as incorporated if they participate in the formal structures of a regime, but that participation can be shallow or deep. A group that has legal status but boycotts elections would be shallowly incorporated; a deeply incorporated group might be one that is legal, participates in elections, and holds seats in a cabinet. Shifts from shallow to deep incorporation can be more consequential than shifts from a state of unincorporation to one of shallow incorporation, and scholars should remain attentive to movement between any two points on the spectrum.

Whereas incorporation has multiple degrees, neutralization can take multiple forms, which are rarely disaggregated in existing scholarship. Gross proxies like regime survival fail to specify precisely *how* opposition has been rendered unthreatening. What constitutes successfully neutralized opposition? Is it potential opposition that never becomes opposition? Opposition that retains antiregime commitments but agrees to be silent? Or opposition that gives voice to alternative visions of politics only through approved channels? Is it opposition that performs compliance when the regime demands, or opposition that can perform contestation for international audiences? What about opposition that remains critical, noisy, and confrontational—but also weak, isolated, and unpopular? As I suggest below, specifying the form that neutralization takes is key to mediating among various models of authoritarian co-optation.

Evaluating Existing Models of Authoritarian Co-optation

Two Models of Co-optation

Existing models of co-optation tend to fall into (or combine) two general categories: transactional models and acculturation models.[15] Transactional accounts understand co-optation as the exchange of benefits for political support. Per such models, co-optation produces an equilibrium in which opponents have not fundamentally changed their commitments but agree to limit their opposition as long as they continue to receive benefits from the regime. Acculturation models, by contrast, posit that incorporation fundamentally alters the commitments of the incorporated, encouraging them to identify with the dominant regime and thus moderating any radical commitments or alternative aspirations. Much existing work combines these two mechanisms to present a model of co-optation that works through both transaction and acculturation, but I separate them here because they have starkly different implications for how incorporated groups should behave.

Transactional models describe co-optation as the exchange of some form of bounded, commodity-like benefit for an opposition group's very oppositionality—its willingness to make confrontational claims or challenge a regime's hold on power.[16] Benefits may be material, influential, or legal, and they may accrue to individual leaders or to an organization as a whole. For Jennifer Gandhi and Adam Przeworski, incorporated groups modulate their opposition in order to access limited policy concessions. They find, as does

Gandhi elsewhere, that the simple existence of a parliament—which suppos-edly proxies a concessions-for-quiescence exchange—extends regime dura-tion.[17] For Ellen Lust, incorporated groups contain their opposition in order to protect benefits that regimes provide to incorporated opponents but not to extrasystemic ones.[18] These benefits might include material perks, policy influence, proximity to power, or legal protections (the right to open a headquarters or publish a newspaper, parliamentary immunity, etc.). Incorporation produces neutralization because incorporated ("included") opponents are hesitant to risk their access to benefits by mobilizing along-side extrasystemic ("excluded") actors.[19]

Transactional models have clear logical implications for the behavior of co-opted parties. Taken literally, Gandhi and Przeworski's model is of little use in predicting individual instances of incorporated party behavior. Many authoritarian regimes with parliaments have those parliaments for long periods of time, during which opposition parties might display a range of behaviors. The presence of a multiparty parliament (a constant) thus can-not explain variation in party behavior across decades. The spirit of their argument, however, can be applied at a more granular level. Transactional models suggest that as long as benefits continue to flow, parties should con-tinue to moderate their oppositionality in order to remain incorporated. When benefits cease to flow (or drop below a certain threshold), parties should jump ship, so to speak: they should withdraw from co-optative incor-poration and thus be freed to engage in more confrontational behavior. Transactional co-optation is a constant equilibrium, in which benefits must outweigh the costs of foregone contention. Thus, when transactional co-optation breaks down, it should leave no scars: parties should, ceteris pari-bus, return to being as threatening to an incumbent regime as they were prior to incorporation.

Yet when parties do withdraw from incorporative arrangements, they are usually much the worse for wear. They do not simply bounce back to their prior levels of threateningness and viability. This empirical reality may explain why so many theories of co-optation include both transactional and acculturational components. Acculturation models suggest that the act of participating in a regime's formal structures fundamentally alters the pref-erences of opposition over time, slowly inuring them to the political status quo. This approach has been championed by a large literature on the incor-poration of Islamist groups, which—somewhat quixotically—is concerned with whether the incorporation of Islamists into electoral authoritarian regimes will acclimate them to liberal democratic practices.[20] Although this research agenda does not explicitly address theories of co-optation, it offers some of the most sophisticated work on the topic. Rather than assuming that incorporation inevitably reflects or produces any single outcome, scholars investigating the so-called inclusion-moderation hypothesis have examined and debated the effect of incorporation on groups' goals, structures, and repertoires. Some have found evidence that participation can indeed moderate radical positions—that is, can induce programmatic change. The posited mechanisms vary: Carrie Rosefsky Wickham focuses on exposure to actors of other political persuasions, while Jillian Schwedler points to the imperatives of competition for votes.[21]

More traditional acculturation models, including Lust's, emphasize how, over time, "legal opposition elites [come to] see themselves as an integral part of the regime and become committed to maintaining it," in part because they "often develop close relationships" with state elites.[22] In these models, co-optation works by actually altering the preferences of incorporated groups. Therefore, if groups were to see a decrease in benefits, their new, pro–status quo preferences might not disappear immediately. Not only should we expect incorporated groups to become less confrontational over time, we should also expect something of a "hangover": neutralization that persists even after incorporation has finished. That neutralization, crucially, should take the form of explicit programmatic changes—the public disavowal of violence or revolution, for example.

In the discussion that follows, I demonstrate that both transactional and acculturation models fail to account for empirical patterns of opposition behavior in the specific cases at hand: the Wafd and the Istiqlal. Although these are only two cases, they are cases that any robust theory of co-optation should be able to explain. The neutralization of well-organized, mass-based opponents is exactly the kind of process that makes co-optation substantively important (not to mention the fact that a number of the theories outlined above rely on these two cases in their own analyses). Neutralization has unquestionably occurred in both cases. It has not, however, taken the form that existing models predict: neither party has displayed significant, unidirectional programmatic change or restrained from confrontational actions in patterns that might map on to proffered benefits.

Comparing Theoretical Expectations to the Empirical Record

Discrete, public political actions—boycotts, strikes, protests, cabinet participation, demands[23]—are the backbone of empirical studies of co-optation.
They serve as powerful dependent variables: proxies that (seemingly) allow
scholars to observe both opposition commitments and the extent to which
opposition threatens incumbent regimes. Both acculturation and transactional accounts, however, struggle to account for empirical patterns of incorporated party action. I suggest two reasons for this predicament: first, the
neutralization that incorporation produces is *not* primarily programmatic
change or restraint from confrontational action; and, second, actions are
not nearly so workable a proxy for either opposition preferences or regime
stability as scholars usually assume. In this section, I compare patterns of
party action to those predicted by acculturation and transactional models.

Figures 2.1 and 2.2 present timelines of major actions and positions taken
by each party since the onset of incorporation (1984 for the Wafd; 1956 for
the Istiqlal). Actions usually understood as confrontational or oppositional—
boycotts, "no" votes on regime initiatives, refusals to join the cabinet,
demonstrations—are written in bold. Actions usually understood as docile
or cooperative—"yes" votes, joining the cabinet, refraining from protest, and
so on—are in normal text. These timelines are combined with charts indicating the number of parliamentary seats held by each party over time
(figure 2.2 also includes the number of cabinet seats held by Istiqlal; the
Wafd has never been in a post-1952 cabinet). Since cabinet and parliamentary
seats are the usual vectors through which benefits are theorized to be
transmitted, these figures allow us to consider how time (acculturation)
and benefits (transaction) map onto patterns of opposition behavior. I consider how acculturation models fare first.

EVALUATING ACCULTURATION MODELS

As the figures demonstrate, neither party has shown a gradual turn away
from confrontational actions over time. Istiqlal members took cabinet seats
in the 1950s, the early 1960s, the late 1970s and early 1980s, from the late
1990s to 2013, and in 2021—but refused offers to participate in the cabinet
in the early 1970s, the early 1990s, and 2016. The party joined contentious

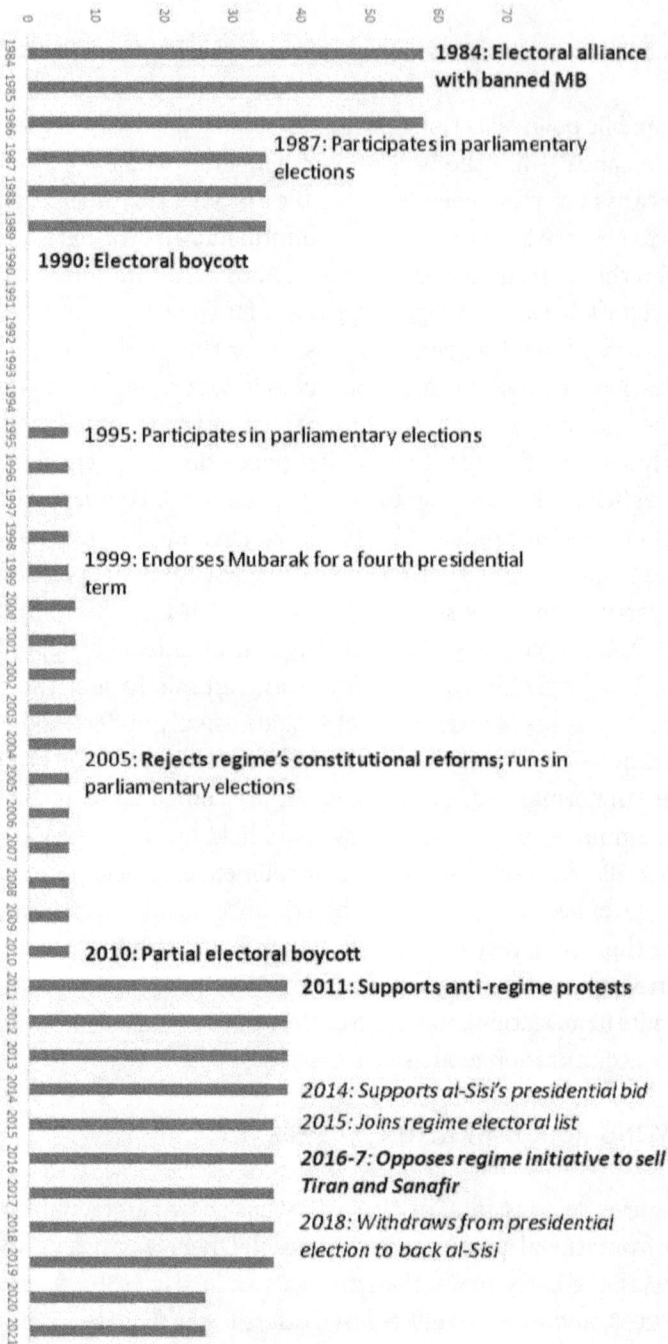

FIGURE 2.1 Wafd parliamentary seats and party actions, 1984–2021.

0 10 20 30 40 50 60 70 80 90

1955 1957 1959 1961 1963 1965 1967 1969 1971 1973 1975 1977 1979 1981 1983 1985 1987 1989 1991 1993 1995 1997 1999 2001 2003 2005 2007 2009 2011 2013 2015 2017 2019 2021

■ cabinet ▥ parliament

1962: Supports regime's constitution

1965: Supports strikes in Casablanca

1970: Rejects constitution; boycotts elections
1972: Declines cabinet participation
1973: Declines cabinet participation

1975: Cooperates with regime on Green March

1977: Returns to elections and cabinet

1981: Opposes contentious strikes

1990: No-confidence motion in government, participation in strikes

1992: Rejects constitutional reforms
1993: Declines cabinet participation
1994: Declines cabinet participation (again)
1995: Affiliate union backs general strike
1996: Supports constitutional reforms

1998: Joins *Alternance* cabinet

2011: Rejects participation in protests;
backed constitutional reforms
2013: Withdraws from cabinet

2021: Joins loyalist cabinet

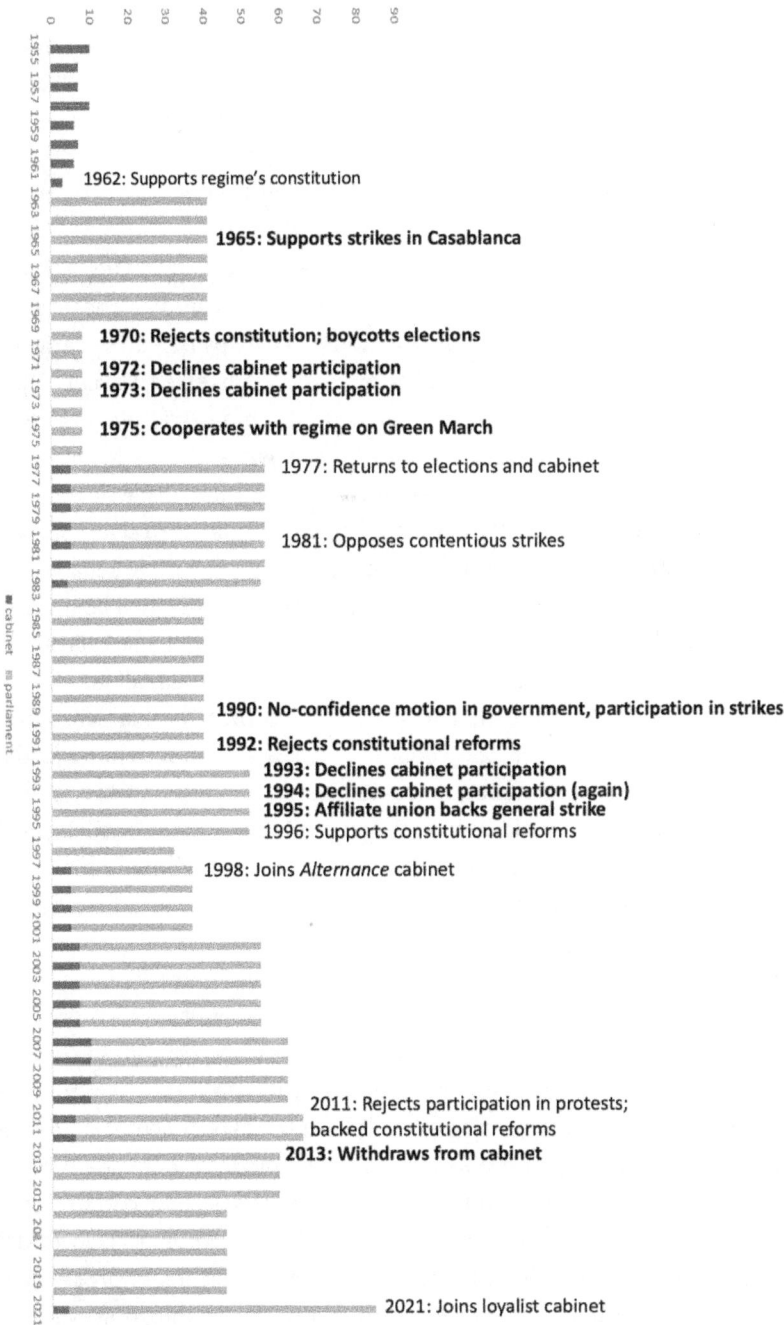

FIGURE 2.2 Istiqlal cabinet, parliamentary seats, and party actions.

strikes in the 1960s and 1990s but hung back from them in the early 1980s. Istiqlal only boycotted one national parliamentary election, in 1970. The Wafd, for its part, boycotted parliamentary elections in both 1990 and 2010, and, after thirty years of incorporation, participated in illegal antiregime protests in 2011—not at all the pattern of behavior that acculturation models would predict.

A careful reader might object that a shift in party position vis-à-vis the regime, per transactional or acculturation models, would not necessarily produce an observable shift in party actions.[24] Perhaps Istiqlal became less willing to participate in extra-institutional actions (strikes, boycotts, protests, etc.) over time but remained convinced that these actions could be justified in particularly dire circumstances. Thus, while the party had a low threshold for participation in strikes in the 1960s, it may have developed a higher threshold by the 1990s (i.e., acculturated to authoritarianism) and only participated in the contentious strikes of the latter decade because economic and political conditions were much worse than they had been thirty years earlier. This objection is fundamentally correct—but it also raises questions about the usefulness of actions as proxies for neutralization. Lust astutely recognizes this problem and attempts to control for it (at least cross-nationally) by arguing that the economic crises she considers in Jordan, Egypt, and Morocco were of roughly equal severity.[25] She supports this claim with quantitative economic indicators and evidence that the societies in question faced similar problems (a fall in real wages, high unemployment) and that governments pursued similar policies (international assistance, structural adjustment) in response.[26]

However, asserting comparability (for purposes of control) across space is one thing; doing so across time within the same country is a more complicated endeavor. Crises or situations of grievance are difficult to compare in part because prior events shape the meaning of later ones. As William H. Sewell Jr. points out in his critique of what he calls "experimental time," successive moments of decision-making are anything but independent of one another.[27] For example, the Wafd's approach to electoral boycotts over the last twenty years has been shaped by the party's botched 1990 boycott. After much debate, the Wafd chose to sit out the 1990 elections in protest over authoritarian reforms to Egypt's electoral laws. The regime, however, took advantage of the boycott to run an unusually clean election, leaving the Wafd shut out of parliament and the regime's international image largely unscathed. The failure of the 1990 boycott—not just that it cost seats (which could matter for many reasons, not all of them about foregone benefits) but the fact that it occasioned no change in regime policy or alterations to the electoral law—is often mentioned by Wafd members when they are asked about the party's reluctance to boycott in subsequent elections. As one high-ranking Wafd official put it, admitting that the 1990 boycott had been a mistake, "if we had been in a normal country [dawla ʿādeyya], there would have been some sort of reaction [from the regime] to our boycott."[28] The disappointing result suggested that Egypt's was not a "normal" regime, in which confrontation might lead to change—and that realization factored into every subsequent discussion about a boycott. The 1990 boycott and the 2010 boycott are not at all independent events that can be compared without somehow controlling for the effect of one on the other. Multiple "variables" could change between any two moments: potentially the party's commitments but also its sense of the political landscape and the available stock of historical precedents. The empirical challenge of acculturation models that use actions as a proxy for neutralization is the difficulty of determining whether it is acculturation or changed political opportunity structure—or both—that is driving party actions.

Acculturation could, in theory, also be studied more directly through an analysis of parties' stated political commitments. The inclusion-moderation literature has employed this approach, looking for evidence of change in Islamist groups' positions on key issues—the rights of minorities, women's role in society, and so on—as a result of their acculturation to "democratic" norms. What might such an approach tell us about the Wafd and the Istiqlal? How have decades of incorporation altered the explicit political commitments of these two parties?

One of the most striking arguments against simple acculturation models is the extent to which both parties' major stated goals—goals that often conflict with the institutional structures of incumbent authoritarian regimes—have remained consistent over time. That this consistency has gone largely unnoticed (or actively denied) by observers stems in large part from inattention to the specificities of nationalism as a postcolonial oppositional ideology. Nationalism has received considerable attention in the colonial era, and its impact on ruling parties has been well studied.[29] Yet while both the Wafd and the Istiqlal are first and foremost nationalist parties, in journalistic and (American) scholarly sources they are rarely described as nationalist in anything but their origins. The Istiqlal is variously referred to as "conservative" or "loyalist," and the Wafd as "right-wing," "liberal," or even, in the polarized environment of post-2011 Egypt, "secular." Moreover, as opposition parties in authoritarian regimes, both are often assumed to be "democratic," or at least "anti-authoritarian," in all their commitments. As such, when they concur with authoritarian incumbents on specific policies or issues (the Western Sahara, the monarchy, anti-Islamism, etc.), those decisions are often read as changes: as instances of incorporated opposition conceding to regime demands, abandoning or suppressing any commitments to the contrary in order to maintain a good relationship with (and access to benefits from) the regime.

Understanding these two parties as primarily nationalist, however, suggests that moments of agreement between party and regime should not necessarily be understood as instances of "selling out." In chapter 3, I make this argument with reference to Istiqlal's position on the Western Sahara in the 1970s, which has long been mistaken for an example of Istiqlal's willingness to abandon its democratic commitments. I thus take up another example here. During the uprisings of the Arab Spring, much attention was paid by journalists, scholars, and other observers to the ways in which the Tunisian chant "the people want the fall of the regime" (al-sha'b yurīd isqāṭ al-niẓām) changed as it moved across the region. When the protests reached monarchies with strict lèse-majesté laws, chants often shifted to "the people want the reform of the regime" (al-sha'b yurīd iṣlāḥ al-niẓām) or "the people want the end of corruption" (al-sha'b yurīd inhā' al-fasād).[30] In Morocco, some participants in street movements like February 20 were willing to at least entertain the idea of regime change, but the country's political parties were not. One could read this contrast as a sign that the parties, Istiqlal included, were either unwilling to risk their benefits (per transactional models) or had been in the halls of power so long that they no longer saw the regime as something that needed to fall (acculturation). In either case, it would seem that incorporation was responsible for Istiqlal's unwillingness to call for the end of the monarchy.

If Istiqlal was interested in toppling the Moroccan monarchy, however, it has assiduously concealed that goal for some eight decades. While its forerunner, the Kutla, was not monarchist, Istiqlal's two most famous anticolonial texts, the 1944 "Independence Manifesto" (wathīqat al-istiqlāl) and Allal al-Fassi's 1953 "Call from Cairo," both demand the establishment of a constitutional monarchy. Even the most scandalous rumors about tensions between Istiqlal leaders and the monarchy concern private denunciations of individual rulers, not indictments of the monarchical system as a whole.[31] A commitment to the monarchy is part of Istiqlal's long-standing interpretation of Moroccan nationalism, which acknowledges the country's diversity and looks to a monarch to hold the nation together where language, ethnicity, and traditions cannot.[32] To the extent that this position has changed since the 1930s, it changed *before* independence, when Istiqlal decided to back the sultan, not since the party's incorporation.[33]

The contemporary logic of Istiqlali monarchism strongly echoes that originally outlined by Allal al-Fassi in his most famous work, *Self-Criticism* (*Al-naqd al-dhātī*), which is still commonly read and referenced by Istiqlal members.[34] Al-Fassi argues that the king is the guarantor of "progress and continuity," who will "keep the balance among the members, classes, and institutions [*hī'āt*] of the nation."[35] The monarch should be "a figure above all the parties and all the political issues that might be discussed by public opinion, as the safeguard of the continuation of authority [*sulṭa*]."[36] Moreover, al-Fassi argues, the king should not be accountable to the people because accountability has led to revolutions (*thawrāt*) in Morocco's past.[37] Contemporary Istiqlalis also reference the importance of a monarch who can unify the nation.[38] While the idea of king as unifier and arbiter has been widely discussed as a strategy employed by the monarchy to weaken political parties, it is also a long-standing part of Istiqlal's program for political reform.[39] Istiqlal's stated support for the monarchy should not automatically be assumed to signal acculturation. In party explanations, the symbolic work done by a king is a prerequisite for both democratic politics and the continued existence of Morocco as a polity—itself a nationalist goal par excellence.

In the Wafd's case, the party's willingness to cooperate with or support regime crackdowns on Islamist opponents might spark doubts about the sincerity of the Wafd's supposed commitments to the "liberal" values of pluralism and free association. In the 1990s and again in the aftermath of the 2013 military coup, the Wafd's stated interest in democracy and pluralism did not extend to its Islamist peers. This might be surprising for a "liberal" party, but it is not surprising for a nationalist one. The Wafd has occasionally treated the Muslim Brotherhood (MB) as an ally, but those moments have been deeply controversial, demonstrating the deep-seated resistance to pan-Islamist ideologies that has long been a part of Egyptian nationalism. In 1984 the MB's general guide, Umar al-Tilmissani, and the head of the Wafd, Fu'ad Sirag al-Din, agreed on an electoral alliance that would allow a small number of MB candidates to compete on the Wafd's electoral lists. The reasons for this alliance are obscure and contested, but its consequences were clear.[40] A number of influential intellectuals who had flocked hopefully to the party in 1978 resigned in protest, including prominent writer Farag Fouda, who was assassinated by Islamists just eight years later. For a party whose crescent-and-cross symbol had been a symbol of interreligious (or at least Islamo-Christian) Egyptian nationalism since 1919, the alliance with the Brotherhood was seen by many as a rejection of core Wafdist values.

The Wafd has long allied itself with articulations of Egyptian nationalism that firmly reject any ideology—from pan-Arabism to pan-Islamism—that suborns Egypt to some other national unit. Ahmed Lutfi al-Sayyid, one of the founding fathers of Egyptian nationalism, famously rejected any suggestion that Egyptians belonged to a larger Arab nation (or, if he is read uncharitably, a larger human community). During the 1910–1912 uprising against invading Italian forces in Libya, Lutfi al-Sayyid opposed sending military, financial, or even humanitarian assistance, arguing that such a gesture might send the message that Egyptians shared an Arab identity with Libyans threatened by war and colonial expansion.[41] As Farag Fouda put it in 1984, explaining the Wafd's position, "the only identity that matters to us is that Egyptians are Egyptians";[42] "we want a country in which a Copt is closer to the heart of an Egyptian Muslim than an Indian Muslim is."[43] The Wafd's vehement rejection of Islamism and pan-Arabism is a long-standing commitment. As a party vice-president described Islamists to me in 2013, "they refuse to sing the national anthem. To them, the nation is just a piece of dirt (ḥiṭat turāb)."[44] Contemporary Wafdist sources often describe Egyptian Islamists as traitors to the nation or foreign agents—not members of the proper Egyptian political community within which rights and freedoms should be guaranteed.[45] Thus, when the Wafd approves of anti-Islamist crackdowns, it is not conceding anything—this is an issue on which the party and successive military rulers have long agreed.

A final source of the impression that the Wafd and the Istiqlal have undergone significant programmatic change stems from the tendency to read the history of the left onto non-leftist opposition parties. The Istiqlal and (at least the pre-2013) Wafd do seem committed to parliamentary life and free elections, but this could be a retreat from a thicker, perhaps more social justice–oriented understanding of popular sovereignty. For hardcore Communist parties, for example, the embrace of elections as the hallmarks of democracy—or the embrace of democracy at all—would represent significant programmatic change.[46] The same is not true for the Istiqlal and the Wafd, however. Both have long articulated visions of an ideal political system that are based on Anglo-American proceduralist principles. A directly elected president with limited powers, a powerful parliament with multiple political parties, and freedoms to associate and organize were key commitments of the old, pre-1952 Wafd that have been carried through to the new party. The refounded Wafd was careful not to completely disown the egalitarian achievements of the Nasserist era, insisting that the July Regime had both "good and bad" and that its promotion of social justice was admirable, "though we may find its means objectionable."[47] Yet distributive justice was never a key part of the party's platform and thus cannot be said to have dropped out over time. Indeed, the countries to which Wafdists were willing to look for models of democratic politics set a fairly low bar. Asked in 1977 about the regime's argument that multipartyism could not be tolerated during the ongoing conflict with Israel, Fu'ad Sirag al-Din answered, "I don't really see the connection. Our enemy has political freedom, a multiparty system, and beat us twice, and the no-party system didn't keep us from being defeated twice. Parties would stand by the government in these times. We cannot have democratic life without parties, and parties cannot do the work they are supposed to do unless they are founded without restriction or condition."[48] That an Egyptian nationalist party would suggest that Israel's multiparty system was the kind of "political freedom" to which they aspired should indicate that the Wafd's commitment has always been primarily to elections and a powerful parliament rather than to thicker, more distributive, or more radical notions of democracy.

A similar argument can be made for the Istiqlal.[49] Allal al-Fassi's *Self-Critique* encourages Moroccans to draw upon parts of various political systems, taking the best and the most appropriate elements from each. Citing Montesquieu and Maurice Duverger and considering the merits of "popular democracies," the American and British systems, continental European polities, and the Soviet regime, al-Fassi argues that "we must benefit from all of human experience—there is in this world no regime that is completely illegitimate [*bāṭil*] nor one that is entirely correct."[50] "Great flexibility," he writes, "is a necessity in political thought."[51] Al-Fassi is keen on popular participation, but his enthusiasm is limited to conceptualizing voting as a duty and encouraging people to be engaged in public affairs, no matter how humble their backgrounds or limited their education.[52] He rejects fascist systems, "which settle for representing interests instead of representing individuals."[53] What he would commit to, and what successive Istiqlal documents demanded, was a constitutional monarchy with an elected parliament. While the Istiqlal did evince a commitment to popular mobilization on the Sahara issue, they nevertheless continued to emphasize the way in which regular elections were the hallmark of popular participation in governance.[54] While the extent to which notions of democracy have shifted among the Istiqlal's leftist peers is an open and important question, an alternative notion of democracy has not fallen away from Istiqlal's rhetoric; it was never there in the first place.

This study is not primarily about what members of these parties do or do not "actually" believe. Parties' public statements, however, do represent consequential political actions in their own right. I suggest that an analysis of these statements should begin by recognizing nationalism, not democracy, as each party's fundamental guiding political commitment, and by remaining attentive to the ways that nationalist opposition in the postcolonial world is prone to programmatic overlap with nationalist authoritarian incumbents. Not all instances of agreement count as acculturation.

EVALUATING TRANSACTIONAL MODELS

The question of whether these two parties' actions track onto the extension and retraction of benefits is a thornier one. Let us return to figures 2.1 and 2.2. In Istiqlal's case, there does not seem to be any clear congruence between the number of parliamentary seats held—which, to recap, is a common proxy for benefits—and the party's willingness to engage in confrontational behavior. In the case of the Wafd, declining seats seem to coincide with increased docility toward the regime (contra the transactional expectation), with the notable exception of the 2010 election boycott and the 2011 uprising. Could the Wafd's confrontational behavior during this period have something to do with lost benefits?

The most common explanation for the Wafd's boycott and its participation in the January 25 uprising is that the sheer amount of fraud in the first round of the 2010 elections soured the party on the rigged electoral process and, ultimately, on the regime itself. This account would initially seem consistent with transactional models of co-optation. If exclusion from parliament lessens access to benefits (whether rentier or influential), it might seem intuitive that a badly rigged election would precipitate withdrawals from incorporation. There may be some truth to this argument for the MB, which ended up losing eighty-seven of its eighty-eight seats in the 2010 elections: the door to parliamentary participation—and any attendant benefits—was effectively slammed in the Brotherhood's face. Yet it accords less well with the Wafd's experience. At the end of the first round, the Wafd had already improved upon its 2005 performance, gaining six seats (it had won only six total in 2005) with races still to run. Wafdists estimate that the party walked away from between eleven and sixteen potential seats when it chose to boycott.[55] Moreover, the Wafd had long complained of gross electoral fraud and bemoaned its meager representation in parliament; 2010 was hardly a surprise in this respect. As one party vice-president told me, the reaction to the 2010 election "was about the people, not the parties; the parties always knew it [the electoral process] was fraudulent," but in 2010 the fraud was so blatant that even ordinary citizens felt it.[56] Another vice-president told me what was stunning about the 2010 manipulation was not its ultimate effect on seat totals but the sheer "gall" (*fugr*) of it. NDP candidates were winning districts they would have won anyway; what was frustrating was the impossible margins of victory they were claiming, and it was that insult that truly rankled.[57] Thus, a simple benefits explanation hardly suffices to explain the Wafd's position in 2010 and 2011.

In Istiqlal's case, there does appear to be some congruence between the number of cabinet seats the party held and its willingness to engage in confrontational actions. Istiqlal's participation in the unrest of the 1960s and 1990s does coincide with periods in which the party was not in the cabinet.[58] Yet this congruence raises more questions than it answers. Cabinet participation has an odd dual status in action based studies: it is both an independent variable (it represents incorporation and access to benefits) and a dependent variable (agreeing to participate in the cabinet represents an act of cooperation with regime preferences; refusing a cabinet offer is a confrontational move). Here again we are confronted with the conceptual and operational intertwining of incorporation and neutralization: if cabinet participation represents both, then claims that cabinet participation pro-duces neutralization are tautological.

Transactional accounts, moreover, have little to say about refusals to join the cabinet or other forms of what seems, from a benefits perspective, like opposition self-denial. Such incidents are surprisingly common. Istiqlal rejected offers of cabinet participation in 1972, 1973, 1993, 1994, and 2016–2017. The party also withdrew from two cabinets, in 1965 and 2013. The Wafd, for its part, called for the dissolution of a parliament in which it had won thirty-five seats after the 1987 elections. Other parties exhibit similar behav-ior: USFP candidates refused to accept seats that they had won through obvious manipulation in 1997, for example.[59] A proponent of transactional models might suggest that refusals are simply what happens when opposi-tion is not offered enough benefits; what the regime is offering does not out-weigh the costs of forgoing opposition in order to become more deeply incorporated.

Yet establishing what, a priori, will count as "enough" benefits proves tricky, and such arguments often infer post hoc that if a party is incorpo-rated, it "must" have been offered the right benefits. Consider the long debates over Istiqlal's cabinet participation during the 1990s. For nearly a decade, the parties of the Democratic Bloc negotiated semipublicly with the palace about whether and under what conditions they might join a so-called Alternance cabinet.[60] King Hassan II made three major overtures, in 1993, 1994, and 1997–1998. The first two were refused and the third accepted. Is it possible to explain this pattern using a transactional approach? Was the last offer accompanied by a better package of benefits or concessions?

Starting in 1987 and continuing with memoranda to the king in 1991 and 1992, Istiqlal and the USFP laid out broad demands for political reform. The bloc repeatedly cited several major goals: more human rights protections, the amendment of article 35 (which relates to the king's ability to declare a state of exception), increased powers for local governments, and better over-sight of public funds.[61] Their central demand was one that Istiqlal had been calling for since the late 1950s: that the powers of the king and the govern-ment be clearly delineated, with the government empowered to actually make and implement policy.[62] The parties also repeatedly expressed clear preferences about the proposed Alternance cabinet itself: first, it should result from an electoral victory (that is, it should not be created by royal appointment of minority opposition party members), and, second, it should not include Driss Basri, the interior minister who had supervised both electoral fraud and political repression since 1979.

In August 1992 Hassan II announced a set of constitutional reforms that "ignored most of the suggestions of the opposition" and "hollowed out" the ones it did acknowledge.[63] With the exception of the small Party of Progress and Socialism, the bloc boycotted the resulting referendum—but, unsurprisingly, the constitution passed anyway. When long-delayed parliamentary elections were held in 1993, the bloc won 106 of 333 seats; the USFP and Istiqlal both made major gains over their 1983 performances but lost out to a palace party (the National Conference of Independents) for first place. The disappointing constitution and the lack of an opposition majority seriously hampered Hassan II's first attempt to install an Alternance government. Hassan's insistence that he retain loyalists in five "sovereignty ministries"— including Driss Basri at the Ministry of the Interior (MOI)—did not help either.[64] It is hardly surprising that the Istiqlal and the USFP turned down the king's 1993 offer—and his subsequent 1994 offer, which gave up four of the sovereignty ministries but would have kept Basri at the MOI.[65] What is surprising, from a transactional perspective, is what happened next.

Hassan II's second attempt to appease the bloc with constitutional reform was more meaningful: another set of amendments in 1996 improved on the 1992 document in several ways. Yet the foundational issue of the king and the prime minister's respective powers remained unresolved. As Moroccan constitutional scholar Muhammad Nabil Muleen put it, the 1996 constitution was a "Machiavellian tactic" to "burnish the image of the regime without giving up one bit of real power." He adds, albeit with the benefit of hindsight, that "the Bloc swallowed the bait"[66]; both the Istiqlal and the USFP supported the new document.

Had the Alternance followed immediately on the heels of the new constitution, however, the transactional approach might have some traction: appeased by a (slightly) better constitution, the parties consented to cooperate with the palace. However, the bloc still insisted that Alternance could only follow a clean election that produced an opposition majority—a problem that the 1997 legislative elections were supposed to solve. The bloc and Basri's MOI made a "gentlemen's agreement" (mīthāq sharaf) that the election would be free from fraud. But as results began to come in, it quickly became clear that there had been administrative meddling on an almost unprecedented scale. Istiqlal was the hardest hit, knocked back to fifth place with only thirty-one seats (just under 10 percent of the lower house). As journalist Muhammad al-Taʾiaʿ observed, Istiqlal, the oldest party in Morocco, did about as well as the Social Democratic Party, which was formed just a few months before the election.[67] Istiqlal president M'hamed Boucetta immediately denounced the results, proclaimed that the party would not participate in any resultant bodies, and called an emergency general conference—the first in Istiqlal's history—to debate a response. That conference, convened in December 1998, reiterated Boucetta's complete rejection of the vote.[68]

Given Istiqlal's "catastrophic" performance, the bloc was left with only 102 of 325 seats, far short of a majority and even fewer than they had had in 1993.[69] While the USFP—perhaps not entirely without the assistance of the MOI[70]—had managed to secure a plurality, an opposition government still would not represent a parliamentary majority. Yet when Hassan II summoned USFP head Abderrahmane al-Youssoufi to the palace on February 4, 1998, and offered him the post of prime minister, al-Youssoufi accepted. The eventual Alternance government had not four "technocratic" sovereignty ministries (as offered in 1993), or one (as offered in 1994), but five.[71] Two weeks later, Istiqlal held its regularly scheduled thirteenth party conference. Boucetta resigned and Abbas El Fassi was selected as his replacement. Al-Youssoufi, after refusing to renegotiate informal understandings he had (supposedly) worked out with Boucetta, offered El Fassi five ministerial posts. El Fassi took the offer back to Istiqlal's executive committee, which reportedly agreed to join the cabinet by a margin of one vote.[72]

Thus, after nearly a decade of insisting that an Alternance government would have to reflect a fairly elected parliamentary majority, that the government would need to have clear executive powers, and that Driss Basri could not be a part of it, Istiqlal joined a forty-one-member cabinet whose powers were not clearly defined, after an election that the bloc had lost (even if the USFP had won) and that had clearly been tampered with by Driss Basri, who would remain minister of the interior. A transactional account that pays close attention to parties' stated demands would struggle to make sense of this outcome. Cynics, skeptics, and materialists may still point out that perhaps the relevant transactions were personal and secret. Questions such as, "What did King Hassan give al-Youssoufi?"; "What did al-Youssoufi promise

El Fassi?"; or "How did El Fassi buy off the executive committee?" are common responses in both Moroccan political discourse and international scholarship. While titillating and perhaps accurate, however, they do not lead to much in the way of social scientific theorizing: secret transactions are unverifiable and therefore run the risk of becoming post hoc "just so" stories. As I discuss in the following chapter, it is these just-so stories, not the transactions they supposedly describe, that account for most of the damage done to incorporated opposition.

In this section, I have suggested that the mechanisms posited by acculturation and transaction models of co-optation fail to concord with patterns of opposition behavior. In doing so, I hope to have highlighted the methodological and conceptual challenges inherent to any study of co-optative processes that takes party actions as its primary dependent variable. Problems of experimental temporality, comparative control, the dual independent/dependent variable status of crucial indicators, and the obscurity attending situations in which party leaders can make consequential decisions in secret: these are real challenges. Moreover, even if we were able to set aside these methodological obstacles, the neutralization of the Wafd and the Istiqlal has simply not followed the patterns that existing models suggest. We see neither unidirectional change in party behaviors and commitments nor a pattern that corresponds to observable, verifiable patterns of benefit extension and retraction.

But What About the Viagra?

Under the protection of [parliamentary] immunity as it exists in Egypt, parliamentarians engage in relatively minor infractions and large-scale fraud and embezzlement. Parliamentarians have been accused of illegally importing large quantities of Viagra.

—LISA BLAYDES, *ELECTIONS AND DISTRIBUTIVE
POLITICS IN MUBARAK'S EGYPT*

Accounts of transactional politics in the region often come worryingly close to stereotype. Scholars emphasize mostly male politicians' interests in fancy cars and sexual enhancement drugs;[73] there seems sometimes to be palpable relief that politics can be explained by baser desires rather than, say, ideological commitments. But my suggestion that we need to move past transactional models is not to say that transactional politics are not taking place. Material benefits change hands in most countries' elections, and Morocco and Egypt are no exception. Side payments, bribes, vote-buying, and rent-seeking behaviors do occur. I suggest, however, that these transactions are neither driving party actions (because, as noted above, patterns of benefit provision do not map onto patterns of action) nor producing neutralization (because neutralization, I argue, does not primarily take place in the space of contention between party and regime). It is also important to note that my ethnographic observation of both parties has revealed little evidence of robust flows of patronage coming from parliamentary participation. Istiqlal's leaders—all of them, including the party's chief executive—hold other jobs because politics, whether the party is winning or losing, is no way to support a family. As one member of parliament put it, "anyone who works in politics also needs to have a career."[74] Lower-level Wafd members show few signs of being able to leverage party connections to gain benefits—indeed, some complain about how little their Wafd connections help them when they try to secure employment for younger relatives.[75]

Of course, these parties may still attract voters with material inducements—and governments do seem to lure individuals with perks and cash. Buehler, for example, demonstrates how material clientelism in the countryside allows Moroccan palace parties to co-opt members of other parties.[76] Samer Shehata, for his part, provides an in-depth account of the distributional politics involved in Egyptian vote-garnering through a case study of the (ultimately unsuccessful) reelection campaign of one Wafdist member of Parliament, Mounir Fakhry Abdelnour, in 2005.[77] For Shehata, as for Lust and Lisa Blaydes, access to services forms the backbone of politicians' appeals to voters at election time.[78] It is worth noting, however, especially in the case of the Wafd, that the party's best electoral performance came in the year—1984—when it had no record of providing services (at least since 1951) and a deeply confrontational relationship with the incumbent regime. Transactionality can be a feature of electoral life without being the sole driver of all party behavior. As one Istiqlali interlocutor explained, "Moroccan elections are all about money. But politics isn't just about elections."[79] I am far more concerned with the question of membership—why people join parties—than I am with the question of why people vote for them. These two parties were, after all, originally *movements* and have retained many movement-like characteristics. Their organizational structures and activities extend far beyond electoral campaigns, and it is in non-electoral spaces that the resources for mounting a threat to the regime are—or are not—gathered.

"Shouting in a Cage": Neutralization in the Wafd and the Istiqlal

To say that neither the Wafd nor the Istiqlal has demonstrated the kind of neutralization that existing models expect is not to say they have endured co-optation unscathed. Quite the opposite—one of the most common reactions to this project is bafflement. Why I would bother examining two such unimportant parties? Indeed, as one interlocutor put it, "that sounds like studying the vice presidency." Although these two parties have not been domesticated—as transactional and acculturational accounts imply—they have been isolated: separated from potential allies among other parties, civil society, and the masses. They have also, in part through isolation, been rendered irrelevant: what they do and say is not understood as influential or consequential. What has happened to these parties is not that they have given up critiquing power or calling for democracy; it is that no one really thinks it matters when they do. Measuring isolation and irrelevance is difficult: both factors are based in public perception, and these parties' pointlessness is often so obvious that people do not bother to mention it explicitly. I will explore the causes of isolation in the next chapter; here I wish only to demonstrate that an overall decline in relevance has occurred. I rely on two metrics: electoral results and popular discourse.

Both parties have lost electoral ground over time. Authoritarian election results, of course, reflect a range of factors beyond a party's ability to attract support (i.e., its connection to mass elements): repression, voter intimidation, and outright fraud also play a role. Even under authoritarianism, however, elections are capturing *something*, even if it is only the regime's ability to tamp down party activity or a party's ability to buy votes. I approach election results as a driver as much of a reflection of party relevance: people use elections to judge the relative popularity and functionality of various groups, assessing the importance of each one to political outcomes.

Istiqlal has lost significant ground in terms of vote share over time. In Morocco's first post-independence election (in 1963), the party won a full 30 percent of the vote despite reports of fraud and manipulation in favor of the palace-backed FDIC.[80] In the 1977 vote, Istiqlal outperformed all other parties with 21.6 percent of the vote; by 1983, that total had dropped to 15.3 percent and Istiqlal down to fifth place. In the three most recent parliamentary elections (2007, 2011, and 2016), the party's vote share has settled around 10 percent. But early electoral results actually underrepresent the organizational strength of the anticolonial Istiqlal—and thus the extent of its decline. Douglas Ashford, who had access to Istiqlal records in the early 1960s, estimated that the organization had between 1.6 and 2 million members in the late 1950s, of whom approximately 250,000 were "active" and "well-informed."[81] Even counting the smaller membership total, some 14 percent of the population belonged (however passively) to the party. The current Istiqlal could only dream of such a wide reach. Three waves of the World Values Survey between 2001 and 2010 found that only between 3 and 6 percent of Moroccans would choose a generic Istiqlal candidate in a hypothetical election; the percentage rose to 10 only when the options "I don't know" and "I wouldn't vote" were removed, forcing respondents to select a party.[82]

The Wafd's decline, whether one measures from its interwar heyday or from its return in the 1980s, has been even more dramatic. The Wafd won 80 percent of the vote in the 1923 election and was still winning absolute majorities at the close of the parliamentary experiment in 1950. The "New Wafd" entered at around 15 percent of the vote, but after the 1990 boycott the party struggled to secure more than 1 percent of parliamentary seats. In 2001 only 1.9 percent of Egyptians said that they would vote for a generic Wafd Party candidate (although, given its polarizing history, a full 15 percent said that they would *never* vote for a Wafd candidate).[83] The party has experienced a slight revival in the years since the 2011 uprising, winning 9.2 percent of the vote in 2011–2012 and slightly over 5 percent in 2015. This resurgence may have multiple causes: the party's organizational capacity, however reduced, is still superior to that of many other non-Islamist parties; the rise of xenophobic nationalism after 2013 fit well with the Wafd's ideological commitments; and the removal of the MB from the political scene has allowed other parties to increase their vote shares.

Another way to observe neutralization is to consider the way in which the parties are perceived on the national stage. Istiqlal once played a leading role in Moroccan politics. Despite the split with the UNFP, the Istiqlal of the late 1950s and early 1960s was unquestionably a central character in the drama of political life. During the 1950s Istiqlal was often referred to as "the party" (al-ḥizb), the definite article marking its primacy and prominence.[84] That usage is entirely gone from urban political discourse; it would make no sense in a contemporary conversation to refer to "the party" without a name or an acronym. This is not simply because there are now more political parties; Istiqlal was never the only self-identified party in Moroccan politics. The difference lies in its relative stature. Whereas Susan Gilson Miller describes the conflict between the king and the Istiqlal in the 1960s as the "principal motif" of Moroccan politics, no possible reading of contemporary Moroccan politics would envision Istiqlal in such a pivotal role.[85] That place has been taken by the Islamists (both legal and illegal) and, more recently, nonparty groups like February 20th or the Hirak Movement. To put it in more colorful terms, consider a December 2014 spread in the Moroccan political magazine *TelQuel* comparing the country's political groups to the warring factions of George R. R. Martin's A Song of Ice and Fire series. *TelQuel* cast Istiqlal as the Baratheons, former rulers who have fallen by the wayside as other actors—the PJD (the Starks) and the PAM (the Lannisters)—battle each other, the February 20th Movement (the Wildlings), and illegal Islamist movements (the White Walkers) for political dominance.[86] As for the Wafd, long gone is the day when it would make sense to speculate, as Egyptian political scientist Abdel Labib Rizq did in the 1990s, that Egypt was headed for a two-party democratic system with the Wafd and the NDP as its two poles.[87] In 2011, while the Wafd's early participation in anti-Mubarak protests is remarkable from the standpoint of existing theoretical expectations, it was not widely noted or considered particularly consequential at the time (in contrast to, for example, the MB's participation, which was closely watched and debated).

To be sure, both the Wafd and the Istiqlal's increasing isolation and irrelevance must be considered in the context of the increasing isolation and irrelevance of political parties more broadly in both countries. The issue of "popular boycotts" of elections and "political apathy" (al-ʿuzūf al-siyasī) are regular topics of political books and pundits' lamentations in Morocco. Although exact levels are difficult to compare because registration and eligibility rules have changed, turnout has been steadily declining over time (with a spike for the 2011 elections; see table 1.2) from 70 to 80 percent in the 1960s and 1970s to under 40 percent in the most recent contest. As figure 2.3 shows, Istiqlal's loss of support as a total percentage of votes pales in comparison to its loss of support as a percentage of Morocco's total population—in large part because fewer and fewer Moroccans bother to participate in elections at all.[88] Despite attempts to increase turnout—opening public channels to parties, decreasing the voting age to eighteen—youth turnout is particularly low.[89] Registration is currently not mandatory, and many young people simply do not bother to register or to pick up their voter cards.[90] Nor do they join parties: a recent study suggested that only 1.6 percent of young Moroccans are members of a political party or an affiliated union.[91] In Egypt, the numbers are hardly better: in 2012, 98.6 percent of World Values Survey respondents said they were not members of a political party.[92]

Popular disillusionment with parties and the turn to nonparty organizations—from Egypt's Kefaya to Morocco's Hirak—has a multitude of

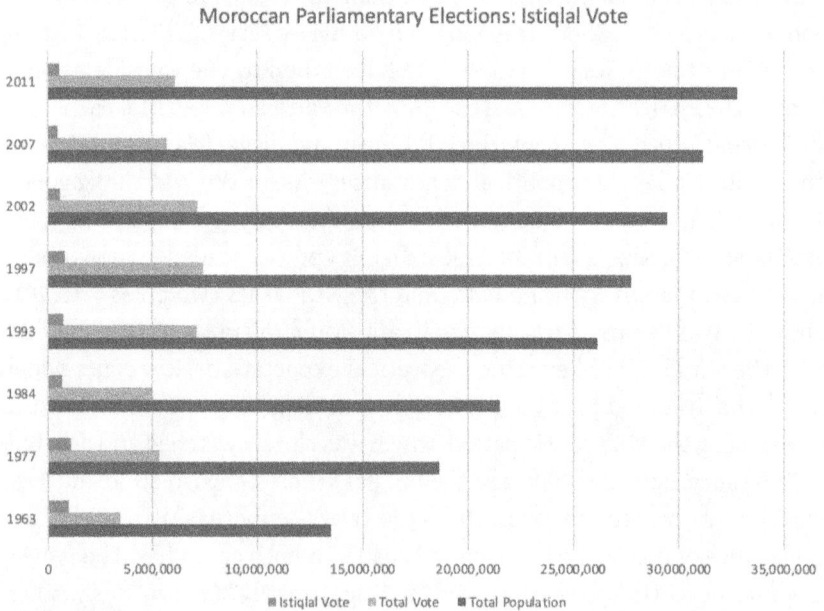

FIGURE 2.3 Istiqlal vote, total vote, and total population, 1963–2011.

causes, many of which are beyond the scope of this study. "NDP independents" in Egypt and hastily constructed administrative parties in Morocco have hollowed out the image of parties as anything other than disposable vehicles for aligning oneself with power. It is important to keep in mind, however, that the decline of parties in general and the decline of these two particular parties are likely to be recursively linked. The July Regime's attempts to discredit the entire notion of party politics were, at their origin, attempts to undermine the Wafd; the repeated hasty construction of palace parties in Morocco has aimed to weaken the Istiqlal. That said, however, it is also true that the Wafd and the Istiqlal have declined even as other political parties have experienced increases in popularity. Parties are not especially well regarded in general, but not all parties are doomed to declining support and relevance.

A New Approach to Studying Co-optation

What I offer here is a new approach to studying co-optation, one that takes actions not as dependent variables needing to be explained but as windows onto processes of neutralization that are vulnerable to destabilization but also profound in their effects. This book does not focus on explaining individual boycotts, protests, or moments of quiescence. Instead, I place those actions in the context of broader dynamics of continuity and change; my approach aims not to predict specific actions but to make sense of them.

My approach works within the typology of nonruling parties introduced in the previous chapter (figure 1.2). I suspect that much variation in co-opted party behavior is in fact due to previously underappreciated differences in party type. I propose disaggregating nonruling parties into three types, defined by the timing of their creation and the identity of their creators. *Holdover parties* (the category that includes the Wafd and the Istiqlal) are those created prior the onset of incumbent authoritarian regimes. *Challenger parties* are those created "from below" by nonregime actors after the onset of authoritarian rule, while *palace parties* are created by incumbents to play a supportive role in parliament.[93]

Although I do not exhaustively defend this hypothesis here, there is reason to suspect that co-optation works differently for these different types of parties. Palace parties lack an extended organizational tradition and are often too short-lived to develop one over time; moreover, they usually do not have strong independent programmatic commitments, instead tending to back regime initiatives. As a result, and much like ruling parties, they are often simply vehicles for the co-optation of individuals qua individuals. Their co-optation is therefore relatively straightforward and most resembles transactional models.[94] For challenger and holdover parties, the picture is more complicated.

Challenger parties are often subject to a great deal of repression. Emerging under authoritarianism, they have little time or space to develop robust organizational apparatuses and need all the help they can get. Such parties might reasonably incorporate to gain legal cover for their activities. It seems likely that challenger parties would respond in a comparatively automatic, Pavlovian manner to regime inducements that contribute to their organizational survival. But since such parties are often centered around narrow ideological commitments (communism or Nasserism, for example), they are unlikely to remain silent in the face of regime actions that violate their core programmatic commitments. When scholars lump the Wafd in with the Nasserists, or Istiqlal in with the PJD, they are reading the experiences of challenger parties onto holdover ones.

Holdover parties, however, merit separate consideration. Formed prior to incumbent regime onset, they are often large, well-organized mass organizations that must be redirected, harnessed, or gradually weakened rather than nipped in the bud. In their dealings with holdover parties, rulers often turn to co-optation as an alternative to repression (as in Morocco) or permit co-optation after repression has failed (as in Egypt). Holdover parties therefore differ in several key ways from their challenger peers: first, they have a literal head start and thus can accumulate generations of organizational tradition long before challenger parties are even founded; second, they do not necessarily have to incorporate to secure their physical survival; and, third, they can often draw upon past experiences in power and accumulated nationalist credibility to claim that they are truly viable alternatives to incumbent regimes. Their incorporation is thus substantively important, meaningfully organizational (unlike that of palace parties) and unlikely to be coerced (unlike that of challenger parties). Moreover, and as mentioned above, it is holdover parties that constitute our classic cases of co-optation. Any new theory must account for their trajectories.

*   *   *

Co-optation is hiding in plain sight. The existing term, which contains within itself both a cause (incorporation) and one potential outcome (neutralization), produces our intuition that co-optation must be a powerful, reliable tool in the authoritarian arsenal. That intuition is, of course, partially correct: as the Wafd and the Istiqlal demonstrate, incorporation can drastically reconfigure political life, turning popular mass movements into insular, family-run organizations. But, as I argue throughout this book, there is nothing inevitable—or irreversible—about the neutralization of the Wafd or the Istiqlal. In the chapters that follow, I aim to render co-optation's effects visible and comprehensible without ignoring their ambiguities.

PART TWO

A Changed Life

How Co-optation Neutralizes Opposition

THREE

Co-optation as Interpretative Dilemma

Istiqlal's Democratic Journey

PERHAPS THE MOST common accusation leveled against co-opted groups is that they have "sold out" or been "bought off"—that is, that they are hypocrites more interested in personal gain than in pursuing their professed political commitments. The quotidian language of selling out and buying off echoes and underlies social-scientific theories that conceptualize co-optation as a transaction: the exchange of some form of bounded, commodity-like benefit for a commitment not to pursue oppositional goals. In the most extreme transactional models, the co-opted were never "really" opposition at all; they were only perk-seekers performing opposition in order to gain access to regime patronage networks.[1]

Implicit in transactional models of co-optation is the idea of neutralization as a process that takes place between opposition and regime.[2] Opposition is neutralized either because it no longer wishes to undertake confrontational actions or because it agrees to suspend such actions in exchange for benefits. Yet, as I argue in the previous chapter, these arguments struggle to comport with the very patterns of behavior they purport to explain. What I propose here is that neutralization, in its most insidious form, occurs in another space entirely: in front of various audiences, including potential mass supporters, pundits, scholars, and other organizations or movements. Co-optation does not neutralize opponents by deterring them from critique or complaint. Instead, it severs links to mass and elite support, rendering even the most strident criticisms moot through the dual curses of isolation and irrelevance.

Istiqlal and the Wafd were once organizations with a proven record of connecting with other political groups and with mass constituencies. Intellectuals and mass supporters alike allied with the Wafd in the 1940s and 1950s and would do so again (albeit on a smaller scale) as the party fought for legal status between 1978 and 1984. Istiqlal, for its part, began its career as an opposition party with a proven ability to mobilize broader constituencies. When the party defended contentious strikes or called for constitutional reform in the 1960s, its positions were politics: closely watched and considered by other political actors. By the first decade of the 2000s both parties were still calling for democracy and still intermittently challenging the regime, but there was, as one Wafd member put it, "no echo. They were shouting in a cage."[3] The loss of an echo—of allies and supporters who can amplify the volume and extend the reach of a party's actions—is the most damaging form of neutralization, and the only form that comports with empirical patterns in the cases at hand: continued (if intermittent) opposition that simply does not seem to affect broader political outcomes.

In this chapter I locate the roots of neutralization in the interpretive dilemma that co-optation creates. All actions are susceptible to multiple interpretations, of course, but co-optation urgently demands interpretive resolution because it seems contradictory: why would a system's opponents agree to participate in it? Outside observers, party members, and ordinary citizens must all find answers to this question; those various answers then compete against one another for prominence.

I argue that co-optation's interpretive dilemma creates severe reputational problems for co-opted parties. Such parties lose credibility in the most fundamental sense: what they say is no longer taken seriously as an indicator of what they believe or intend. Their confrontational statements can be easily ignored as the empty promises of hypocrites; they are not perceived as reliable partners in efforts to challenge the regime. Incorporated parties become less popular, less credible, more isolated, and less relevant. Crucially, the mechanism here is discursive. Co-optation does not neutralize opponents through "material" processes of which discourse is straightforwardly reflective or epiphenomenal: the discourse is what is doing the work. Embedded as they are in history and language, the specifics of these discursive processes will vary somewhat from case to case. Nevertheless, the basic architecture I outline here for Istiqlal should be applicable to other holdover opposition groups (including the Wafd, whose discourse I examine in chapter 4). In this chapter I trace three processes set in motion by co-optation's interpretive dilemma.

First, I argue that there is an elective affinity between co-optation and Romantic emplotments of politics: those that emphasize a hero's suffering en route to an eventual vindication. In existing literature co-optation is often something parties grudgingly accept when they lose faith in the possibility of radical change. I argue, instead, that discourses of hope, possibility, and future vindication are powerful facilitators of incorporation. Istiqlal's turn toward the regime in the 1970s is often described by scholars as a transaction: the party either gave up on its long-term aspirations or agreed not to pursue them in exchange for limited material, influential, and legal benefits. Istiqlal sources, however, narrate the moment quite differently. As they describe it, Istiqlal was not conceding failure but was motivated by a major victory—one that demonstrated that the country was headed for a democratic future. The party publicly "emplotted" Moroccan political life as a Romantic narrative in which Istiqlal would ultimately be vindicated and its sacrifices justified once democracy was finally achieved.[4]

Second, Romantic narratives, which rely for their moral analysis on inherently unverifiable future events, perform poorly in competition with other readings. Their reliance on the future puts them at a logical disadvantage when compared to other sense-making efforts. Observers have an interpretive choice: ascribe to the party's Romantic narrative (which will not be verified until the very end of the story, so to speak) or explain the contradiction of co-optation with reference to hypocrisy, corruption, or greed in the present. While the latter approach may require imagining secret backroom deals or unobserved payoffs, obscurity is so common in authoritarian regimes that the leap of faith required to call parties hypocritical (i.e., the belief that they were "bought off" in secret) is much smaller than that required to suspend judgment until the parties' imagined future finally arrives.

Third, Romantic narratives of incorporation are extremely resilient to negative feedback. Metaphors and other discursive constructions can shape how organizations process inputs from their environments. Romances anticipate setbacks and suffering, providing an easy way to make sense of electoral defeats, declining popularity, and other seemingly negative developments without logically necessitating a change of strategy. Istiqlal relied on its "democratic journey" metaphor to explain all manner of setbacks, discursively erasing the question of whether those setbacks might merit serious consideration or a change of strategy. The harder the going, the more of a vindication the ultimate victory would be; the party's responsibility was to stay the course. The built-in resilience of Romance helps explain why parties are so slow to abandon narratives that, from an outsider's perspective, seem to be causing trouble for party credibility.

Texts and Sources

In laying out my argument, I rely on two distinct types of sources. To explore how Romantic narratives might have an elective affinity with co-optation and how those narratives normalize negative feedback, I draw on Istiqlal's own party documents: newspaper editorials, conference reports, public speeches, and electoral programs. These tend to be collectively authored texts, hammered out by committees behind the scenes of party conferences or approved by party leaders before appearing in al-ʿAlam. They are texts designed for public consumption, both within the broader mass base of the party and beyond it. In the early decades after independence, prior to the emergence of privately owned newspapers, party papers were the only alternative to state-run dailies;[5] al-ʿAlam could expect a wide audience. The paper's flagship editorial, "the opening [statement]" (al-iftitāḥiyya), which used to appear daily but has become more occasional in recent years, always appears on the front page above the fold. From this position, the editorial's headline and opening paragraphs can be read by Moroccans pausing to peruse the day's papers at newsstands, whether or not they eventually purchase a copy.[6]

I am primarily concerned with how Istiqlal read aloud its political choices, not why it made them. I routinely refer to "Istiqlal's" rhetoric, by which I mean the official, public statements of the party and its leaders. This should not be taken to imply that such rhetoric is universally agreed upon, or that the party is some sort of ideological monolith (neither is true). Indeed, I explore Istiqlal's many internal disagreements in some detail in part 3. All I mean to suggest here is that the single, official voice the party presents to outside audiences has political effects even if not all Istiqlalis agree with it.

I also examine competing interpretations of Istiqlal's co-optation from outside the party. I consider readings offered by leftist analysts and activists who have historically been potential allies as well as ordinary-discourse readings from Moroccans uninvolved in party politics. These readings are drawn from works of scholarship and political analysis in both Arabic and French and from articles in political magazines (*TelQuel*, *Wijhat Naẓar*, and *al-Zamane*, among others) widely available in urban Morocco. Like newspapers, such magazines are often displayed on the street for passersby to peruse, contributing to the circulation of interpretations beyond the small subset of people who actually buy a copy. To take just one example, a pedestrian in central Rabat could, in 2014, walk past back issues of *Wijhat Naẓar* laid out by a street bookseller just a few dozen feet from parliament. One issue was adorned with a gravestone bearing several party logos and a headline announcing the "death of the political parties." That issue was published in 2008, but its message was still clearly visible (if a bit faded from the sun) six years later. Whether one agrees with it or not, whether one reads the articles inside or not, the basic idea—"the political parties were once alive, but now they have died"—becomes part of a script that politically informed Moroccans can access and use in conversation.[7]

I also consider the readings offered by Moroccan and foreign scholars. Morocco's (urban) book culture, relatively high availability of translated works, and widespread reading knowledge of French mean that there is more intercourse between international scholarly analysis and local public common sense than in many other countries in the region (Egypt, for example). Morocco's comparatively permissive associational environment has left space for serious intellectual analysis of the country's politics by its own people; many of the arguments that appear in English-language scholarship originate with Moroccan thinkers and observers. Indeed, I want to emphasize that existing scholarship on co-optation has largely taken one set of interpretations and presented them as fact—not as one side in a discursive conflict that itself produces neutralization.

"Ordinary" interpretations—those from people not primarily involved in political life who might presumably vote for, support, or listen to the calls of the Istiqlal—were gathered from more informal interviews over the course my fieldwork. While the Moroccans I spoke with are overwhelmingly urban (albeit from varied socioeconomic backgrounds), these are publicly available scripts: interpretations floating out in public discourse that people can draw on when asked by a foreign researcher what they think about the Istiqlal Party. Such scripts may represent deeply held beliefs, they may simply be the repetition of something heard recently in order to ease the conversation, or they may fall somewhere in between. In this sense, the strict "representativeness" of my sample of interviewees is not particularly important; they are access points to shared discursive moves.[8]

Throughout this chapter, I set aside the ongoing conflict over the Sahara, which has cost far too many lives and dashed far too many aspirations. My concern here is how the issue was read by one extremely partisan organization, and what that reading tells us about co-optation. My focus does nothing to amplify or center the voices of those who have experienced the conflict's effects, but I do not mean it to detract from their own views and analyses—or from the urgency of the situation.

Sincerity and Ideology

When one is making the case that words matter, one must naturally address the concern that those words are being deployed cynically rather than sincerely. Istiqlal members may speak of a "democratic journey," but is that what they actually believe? Do (non)voters really think that Istiqlal members are hypocrites, or are they just saying so? The answers to these questions are essentially unknowable; even if one could ensure that interlocutors were telling the truth as they understood it, psychoanalytic theory has given us real reasons to doubt people's access to their own motivations. In general, the claims I make here do not depend on actors believing sincerely in the discursive tropes they employ. The specific relationships between my arguments and sincerity vary throughout the chapter, so I wish to pause here to foreshadow them.

As far as Istiqlal's democratic journey metaphor is concerned, what matters for neutralization is that Istiqlal has found a way to talk about its co-optation as the fulfillment rather than the abandonment of its democratic principles. As a result, the party is still able to describe itself as committed to democracy; the "democratic journey" allowed Istiqlal to incorporate without a "road to Damascus" moment in which it explicitly abandoned its former positions.[9] This matters because it means that the interpretive dilemma—an explicitly pro-democracy party participating in a nondemocratic regime—remains. Counterintuitively, had Istiqlal publicly acknowledged a major programmatic shift, its credibility might actually be in better shape.

I also suggest that there is an elective affinity between Romantic narratives and incorporation. *Elective affinity* is, of course, Max Weber's term, and in its original context—*The Protestant Ethic and the Spirit of Capitalism*—it does seem to rely on sincere belief. It is a literally religious faith in the tenets of Protestantism, in his view, that spurs believers to industry and self-discipline. To some extent, I am making a similar claim: if Istiqlal members sincerely believe that democratization is a process that will come about through difficult sacrifices that will eventually be revealed as necessary and correct, they—logically—should be more amenable to co-optation. In my conversations with members of the party, the "democratic journey" and other metaphors of gradual movement toward democracy come up regularly and implicitly, even when interlocutors are sharing personal perspectives rather than repeating a party line. Although it is impossible to be certain, these usages suggest sincerity—or at least that the democratic journey has become a baseline assumption rather than a conscious argument.[10]

That said, I rely on an understanding of ideology that does not require sincerity in order to work. This understanding draws on Havel's work on the role of ideology in post-totalitarian contexts, but it is adaptable to a wider range of political circumstances.[11] Havel argues that ideological statements— "workers of the world, unite!"—facilitate behavior that would otherwise be more difficult for actors to justify or accept. The greengrocer's sign "helps [him] . . . to conceal from himself the low foundations of his obedience. . . . It hides them behind the façade of something high."[12] The greengrocer need not feel strongly about international workers' solidarity; all he needs to do is find it less objectionable than telling himself "I have to put up this sign because I am afraid of the consequences if I do not." "Ideology," Havel writes, "facilitated the constitution of power by serving as its psychological excuse."[13] While this may not be an accurate description of *all* the phenomena imperfectly indexed by the term "ideology," it does capture one of the things that ideological constructions can do, even when not deeply believed or sincerely held: facilitate certain courses of action and impede others. It is possible that some opposition activists who choose incorporation believe, on some level, that they are doing the "wrong" thing in cooperating with the regime. And it is possible that while they may not fully believe that Morocco is on a democratic journey, the existence of that narrative makes it ever so slightly easier to lie to themselves about what they are actually doing.[14]

I continue to rely on this quasi-Havelian notion of ideology when I turn to Romantic narratives' ability to normalize negative feedback. Again, I view discourse—and especially metaphor—as a facilitating factor.[15] Even if a party member is not entirely convinced that setbacks are just a natural part of the larger Romantic journey, the availability of the narrative provides discursive resources to those advocating steadfastness rather than a change of tack. Scholars of metaphor and of organizational decision-making have demonstrated that the language we use to talk about reality deeply shapes our experience of it. The assumptions baked into our language are not always explicitly recognized such that we might talk about them being "believed" or "sincere"; they play a role in making outcomes thinkable and sayable that does not depend on belief—or, in some cases, even conscious awareness.

My approach to ideological claims shifts somewhat when I consider how other political actors have interpreted Istiqlal's incorporation. Here my argument is more dependent on those outsiders actually believing that Istiqlal are corrupt hypocrites—but here it is less obvious why people would misrepresent their own positions (being unaware of their motivations, of course, is still a possibility). Scholars, as a general rule, should not be in the business of making arguments they believe are incorrect, so insofar as I am analyzing scholarly discourse, I largely set aside sincerity concerns. As far as Moroccans voters, pundits, and activists are concerned, there is little reason to believe that distrust of political parties in general and the Istiqlal in particular is anything other than sincere. However, if it is not, it is still possible that ideological constructions—the idea that Istiqlalis are hypocrites, for example—are playing a facilitative role similar to that outlined above. Having a ready excuse to throw up one's hands at the slow, fraught process of political reform—"the parties are all corrupt, anyway"—may well be a story people tell themselves to justify their reluctance to take risks for political change.[16]

Romantic Narratives and Co-optation

Istiqlal Returns to the Fold

The 1970s are widely considered an inflection point in the relationship between the Istiqlal Party and Morocco's regime.[17] During the 1950s and 1960s, Istiqlal looked like an opposition party. While it never called for the abolition of the monarchy, the party did oppose many of King Hassan II's initiatives and strongly rejected the marginalization of parties and parliament that attended Hassan's declaration of a state of exception in 1965.[18] Under the state of exception, elections were suspended, parliament's role reduced, and cabinets increasingly filled with military officers, technocrats, and loyalists at the expense of the political parties.[19] Istiqlal, which had since its founding in 1944 called for a constitutional monarchy with a strong role for parties and parliament, stood in clear (if ineffectual) opposition to this authoritarian turn.

In the 1970s, however, King Hassan II reopened the political system to electoral competition and party politics. Although these moves did little more than restore the system to its pre-1965 state, Istiqlal agreed to return to formal politics. The party participated in local elections in 1976, national elections in 1977, and the Parliament and the cabinet that resulted from the 1977 vote. Istiqlal expressed concerns about electoral fraud and continued to advocate for constitutional reforms, but its participation helped to facilitate and lend credence to the king's attempt to wrest political power away from an increasingly unreliable military. In the decades to come, Istiqlal's precise degree of participation in the regime's formal structures would vary. In the 1980s it did so poorly in (rigged) elections that it was left out of the cabinet, and in the 1990s Istiqlal joined with the socialist USFP to negotiate its cabinet participation with an ailing King Hassan. But the relationship between Istiqlal and the monarchy would never seem so confrontational after the 1970s as it had before them.

The Green March

Dominant accounts tend to trace both Istiqlal's incorporation *and* its neutralization back to the November 1975 Green March (*al-masīra al-khaḍrāʾ*), an extended mass demonstration that aimed to bring what was then the Spanish Sahara under Moroccan control.[20] The Green March mobilized some 350,000 civilians to travel into the Spanish-controlled territories south of internationally recognized Morocco. The goal was to force Spain's hand: either Spanish forces would have to fire on unarmed demonstrators or Spain would have to cede the territory. The gambit worked, at least vis-à-vis the European colonizer: Spain's forces declined to engage the demonstrators, many of whom bore copies of the Qur'an (hence the Islamic "green" of the march's name). The Spanish government renounced its claim to the territory within days. While the Green March turned out to be only one skirmish in a decades-long struggle over the Sahara, it seemed decisive at the time.[21] Territorial issues were (and remain) highly salient in Morocco, which had lost "its" southern territories when Mauritania became independent, and which was under threat on its eastern border from a hostile Algeria. To this day, Spain still holds two enclaves (Ceuta and Melilla) on Morocco's northern coast. In such a context, "ordinary Moroccans rallied to the King's side, and a torrent of popular patriotism erased growing doubts about his competency to rule."[22]

Existing accounts in both history and political science thus reasonably consider the Green March a victory for the regime. Problematically, however, they conclude that it must therefore have been a defeat for opposition actors—Istiqlal included—and their aspirations. As Lust argues, "after almost a decade of violence and repression, the parties realized they were unable to topple the King. . . . Consequently, they established their willingness to accept the [1972] Constitution, the King called for new elections, and a political bargain was struck."[23] In this, Lust concurs with Gandhi and Przeworski's claim that it is "when an opposition sees no chance to overthrow a dictator in the foreseeable future" that "they may prefer limited influence to interminable waiting."[24]

Muhammad Radwani concurs, arguing that the Green March and its aftermath was a time when the nationalist parties—Istiqlal first among them—"gave up on their visions and imaginings of modernity," settling instead for the monarchical status quo.[25] In short, the mid-1970s would initially seem like a moment in which opposition groups came to consider far-reaching political change impossible and settled for securing whatever benefits they could. Regardless of the specific nature of the benefits offered, the neutralization of opposition is, in this reading, ensured by the very conditions that also give rise to incorporation. Any incorporated group is by definition also neutralized: it has given up on and will not pursue the kind of far-reaching political change that might threaten an incumbent regime.

Close attention to Istiqlal's public discourse during this critical period, however, reveals another way of talking about the relationship between the Green March and the future.[26] Istiqlalis read the event not as a defeat but as a victory for the party and, moreover, as a victory that could serve as model and preamble for more victories en route to a desired democratic future. After the "march" (*masīra*), a little-used and generically modernist metaphor, that of the "democratic journey" (also *masīra*), became Istiqlal's structuring metaphor for politics.[27]

Party sources describe the Green March as the fulfillment of a long-standing Istiqlali demand. The return of the "violated lands" (*al-arāḍī al-mughtaṣiba*) still held by European powers and the restoration of Moroccan "territorial unity" (*al-waḥda al-turābiyya*) were recurring, central features of Istiqlal's party platforms and leaders' major speeches from independence onward. The successive failures of palace-backed governments on the Sahara were regular targets of Istiqlali critique. As early as 1959, Istiqlal president Allal al-Fassi criticized the authorities (*al-sulṭa*) for their "silence on major national issues," including territorial unity.[28] One of al-Fassi's last public speeches, known as the "Call from Kuwait," alerted Moroccans to (from al-Fassi's perspective) an impending catastrophe: Spain seemed to be preparing to call a referendum on Sahrawi self-determination. Such a referendum, al-Fassi warned, could lead to outright independence from both Spain and Morocco.[29]

Istiqlal's pressure for action on the Sahara outlived al-Fassi, who, ever the diplomat, died suddenly in May 1974 in Nicolae Ceaușescu's Bucharest office. The party offered two public memoranda to the king that same year, urging prompt action to preempt a move toward Sahrawi independence. Even as new secretary-general M'hamed Boucetta and party elder Boubakr Kadiri joined the regime's diplomatic efforts, other party spokesmen kept up their criticism.[30] In the pages of *al-ʿAlam*, one Istiqlal luminary criticized the administration (*al-idāra*) for its "silence" at the United Nations and for its "lateness" and "confusion" in coordinating diplomatic efforts at the International Court of Justice in The Hague.[31] Istiqlal's recommendations grew increasingly specific over time: four days before the king announced the march, an *al-ʿAlam* editorial announced that "before us are only two options": either do nothing or "change our methods," which up to that point had been primarily juridical and diplomatic (i.e., not popular) in nature.[32]

Thus, when the Green March was finally announced, Istiqlal leaders described it not as monarchical initiative but as a concession to their repeated demands. Boucetta noted in an October 23, 1975, interview that the upcoming march was "an important step" but cautioned that "we must not forget that Istiqlal had been demanding for more than a year that the people be enabled to enter into the battle against the colonial forces that are holding our Sahara." Rather than allowing a moment of nationalist fervor to overshadow the party's ongoing oppositional aspirations, Boucetta continued his calls for political reform: as far as domestic politics were concerned, he argued, "nothing has changed, and problems are still waiting for solutions, whether on an economic or a political level."[33] As another party leader put it, it was al-Fassi's death that had helped persuade "officials [*al-masuʾlīn*] to radically change their path and their positions, and to join the caravan of the Moroccan people on the issue of the Sahara."[34] The "caravan" of momentum leading up to the Green March, in this reading, was not the king's invention; it was already in motion when the regime decided to join it.

Moreover, Istiqlal argued that the Green March's success could be parlayed into success in achieving its other political goals, including those relating to parliamentary power. Four days after the king announced (prematurely, as history would prove) that the Sahara had been returned to Morocco, *al-ʿAlam* ran a lead editorial titled "A New Morocco . . . and Elections."[35] The piece draws an analogy between the "popular mobilization" that fueled the Green March and the mobilization of voters needed to ensure the success of the country. The king had announced that elections would be held soon, and Istiqlal's rhetoric on the coming vote echoed its discussion of the Sahara: "holding elections at professional, regional, and national levels is the fulfillment of a demand for which Istiqlal has always called."[36] Party sources framed progress on democracy, like progress on territorial unity, as the regime's adoption of long-standing Istiqlal priorities. As the party's demands were met by popular action on the Sahara, so too might they be met on other issues. Far from abandoning its visions of the future, Istiqlal was finally starting to articulate how, after years of authoritarian retrenchment, those visions might be realized. It was the language of possibility—not defeat or impossibility—that coincided with its co-optation.

The Romance of the Democratic Journey

The apparent success of the Green March ushered in a new way of talking about politics. Istiqlali sources began to consistently characterize Morocco's political trajectory as a "democratic journey." Using three words—*masīra* (march, journey), *masār* (path, trajectory), and *musalsal* (series, chain)—the metaphor conjures up images of step-by-step motion toward a more democratic future. In what follows, I argue that the "democratic journey" is best understood as a Romance in which present sacrifices are justified with reference to a hypothetical future triumph.

The democratic journey has a distinct narrative structure: a beginning, a middle, and an end; and a plot that governs the relationships among those elements. The journey's "inaugurating motif" was the series of perceived successes that followed from the Green March.[37] According to former youth wing leader ʿAbd al-Qadir al-ʿAlami, "most users of the term agree that the journey [*musalsal*] began in 1976 after the Green March and the passage of the law structuring local councils and governing local, professional, and parliamentary elections, after a not insignificant period during which these institutions were paralyzed by the national parties' boycott of them."[38] Al-ʿAlami here reverses the common understanding that Hassan II shut the parties out of power, casting the period from 1965 to 1976 as an opposition-party boycott of formal political institutions—and reclaiming agency for Istiqlal. The journey also had clear "transitional" moments making up its middle: "steps" that must be taken to achieve further successes.[39] Although the language used did not always fit strictly with the metaphor, the idea of a project begun but not finished is common in party materials from the late 1970s. As Boucetta put it in his speech to the party's tenth national conference in 1978, "we have realized some of the pillars of our platform; it is still up to us to complete the process." The 1977 elections, he continued, were a "step" (*khuṭwa*) in the direction of democracy; the struggle to reform the country's institutions would be "the next step in our struggle on the path to democracy."[40] Most importantly, the democratic journey implied a successful end: the realization of a constitutional, monarchical, and—most importantly—democratic regime.[41]

Scholars attuned to matters of historical emplotment in the tradition of Hayden White and David Scott will recognize the "democratic journey" as a Romance.[42] A Romantic emplotment, as originally described by White, is "a drama of the triumph of good over evil, of virtue over vice, of light over darkness, and of the ultimate transcendence of man over the world in which he was imprisoned by the Fall."[43] It is "a drama of redemption," marked crucially by its victorious ending.[44] Endings are critical to all narratives, and they are the elements of historical emplotment least bound by the requirements of "reality"—as White points out, "we cannot say, surely, that any sequence of reality actually comes to an end, that reality itself disappears, that events of the order of the real have ceased to happen."[45]

Narrative endings—especially Romantic ones—fundamentally reshape the very linear temporal progression on which they seem to depend. In his account of "narrative time," Paul Ricœur points out that a story is "governed by its way of ending" and thus "constitutes an alternative to the representation of time as moving from the past forward into the future. . . . It is as though recollection inverted the so-called natural order of time. By reading the end in the beginning and the beginning in the end, we learn also to read time itself backward, as the recapitulating of the initial conditions of a course of action in its terminal consequences."[46] Any reader of novels can surely relate to the experience of finishing a story and reinterpreting the significance and meaning of earlier events in light of the ultimate conclusion. A narrative that stretches into the future, hanging its hopes on an imagined end yet to come, implies that there will one day be a similar reevaluation and reinterpretation. Once the story's ultimate end has been revealed, what seems cowardly, unwise, or hypocritical today may be revealed to have been brave, far-sighted, and eminently principled. This is particularly true for narratives emplotted in the Romantic form, which places great emphasis on vindication and redemption, and therefore on ends. Romantic endings render the present, to adapt Reinhart Koselleck's term, a "future past."[47] For Koselleck, a "future past" is a future once aspired to but that never materialized; I mean the term somewhat differently. A "future past," in my sense, is a way of understanding the present as a time that will eventually be looked back on as the past from the standpoint of a specific future.[48]

Istiqlal's democratic journey rhetoric is shot through with the idea of the present as the future past. The democratic journey was regularly compared not just to the Green March but also to a prior long and ultimately successful "journey": the struggle for independence. Reaching back to the 1940s and

1950s and evoking the party's unrivaled nationalist credentials, a September 1984 al-'Alam editorial argues, "just as the journey to independence [masīrat al-istiqlāl] had thousands of victims, so too does the journey to democracy [masīrat al-dimuqrāṭiyya]."[49] These dual parallels—to the Green March and the struggle for independence—help to highlight the specifically Romantic emplotment of the democratic journey narrative. Both these earlier struggles were eventually successful (or seemed that way in the 1970s). The victims (ḍaḥāyā) of the struggle for independence and the losses and sacrifices involved in resisting French and Spanish colonialism were vindicated and justified by the eventual success of that struggle. Such setbacks were no reason to abandon the campaign; costs were to be expected, but the journey was still worthwhile. Indeed, its high cost made the ultimate victory all the sweeter, transforming it from a victory into a vindication, "a practice of providing evidence to refute a disagreeable or incorrect claim and a practice of reclamation, and indeed, of redemption of what had been denied."[50] Logically, the more Istiqlal suffered in its struggle to reach democracy, the more meaningful its eventual triumph would be. The party's references to sacrifice are particularly striking when one recalls that the detentions, abuses, and deaths that scarred Moroccan politics during the "years of lead" were not primarily directed at the Istiqlal Party. It was the USFP and especially illegal communist and Islamist groups that bore the physical costs of repression while struggling for an alternative future. This fact raises the intriguing question of what, exactly, Istiqlal imagined itself to be sacrificing in the struggle for democracy: perhaps, as I discuss in the coming section, the easy popularity that comes with appealing to more immediate political desires.

As Istiqlal stood on the edge of co-optation into a regime that still fell far short of the party's stated aspirations, party sources described politics not in terms of hopeless resignation to a perpetual authoritarian present but as a future-oriented process of change that required immediate sacrifices. According to Istiqlal's official mouthpieces, co-optation was justified not by benefits received in the present but by successes to be achieved in the future. Judgment must be suspended until an imagined future would arrive to rewrite the past. When Boucetta died in 2017, his generational peer Abdelkrim Ghellab memorialized him in classic Romantic fashion: "Failure and success. . . . History will record the periods of success and ascribe them to those responsible and will record the periods of failure and ascribe them to those who maneuvered, without pity, in favor of their own self-interest, not carrying the burden of the national interest."[51] Four decades after the Green March, and years after explicit references to the democratic journey became rare, Ghellab (who also passed away in 2017) still makes a Romantic moral case for his compatriot. Boucetta may have died without leaving a democratic Morocco, but he—and, by implication, the party—cannot be judged until time transmutes the present into the future's past.

Counterinterpretations, Credibility, and Neutralization

The idea that co-optation can discredit opponents is not a new one; scholars and activists have long noted co-optation's negative reputational effects. For Philip Selznick, those effects stem from the impression of complicity that incorporation can engender. Writing of the Tennessee Valley Authority, he observes that "what is shared [with the co-opted] is responsibility for power, rather than power itself."[52] But what has so troubled the Istiqlal Party is not that it is held responsible for unpopular government policies. In Morocco's parliamentary monarchy, assigning blame for bad policies is extremely complicated: when problems arise, blame can land on the king, members of the makhzen, the government minister most closely connected to the issue, the political party to which that minister belongs, the prime minister, or the political party to which the prime minister belongs—not to mention multinational corporations, illegal Islamist groups, Sahrawi separatists, or sinister global conspiracies. In an environment in which responsibility is so fragmented and so widely shared, decisions about where to place blame often seem more like a reflection of preexisting opinions than a driver of them. Istiqlal is not regularly criticized for what the governments it participates in have *done*; the most common critique is about what they have promised and then *not* done. As one interlocutor put it, "they promise twenty things and they only do two, one of which turns out to be good."[53] The problem is not the one bad program; it is the eighteen promises that never materialized— the idea that Istiqlal cannot be trusted to do what it says.

In this section I focus on common interpretations of Istiqlal's behavior among two populations that might, in theory, serve as important allies:

citizens outside party politics and left-leaning activists and academics (who have been uneasy but recurrent allies of the Istiqlal, via the USFP, in the past). The gulf between Istiqlal and these key groups accounts for a great deal of its isolation and thus its neutralization. I suggest that what most insidiously and effectively discredits the co-opted is the disconnect between their stated commitments and their observable behaviors. While incorporated parties may have Romantic narratives that validate their contemporary compromises through a vision of future success, those narratives are—for systematic reasons—highly unpersuasive to outside actors. Because they so often choose to describe the present as a future past, co-opted groups emphatically trumpet their commitment to democracy (or socialism, or Islamism, etc.). Yet, when read without reference to such imagined futures, the incorporation of committed democrats in clearly undemocratic regimes makes little sense. To make sense of it, observers grasp for other explanations—foremost among them, that these groups are either cynical, manipulative hypocrites or corruptible sellouts. In what follows, I explore several such alternative accounts and close the section by investigating why these alternative interpretations have been more persuasive than the "democratic journey."

Perhaps the most explicit and sophisticated critiques of Istiqlali hypocrisy come from intellectuals associated with the political left. These critiques attack Istiqlal's lack of credibility, but not in the clichéd sense of noting that they often fail to deliver on their campaign promises. Instead, leftists point to specific instances in which the party has denounced an election, constitution, or other development as utterly unacceptable—and then proceeded to participate in it anyway. As Moroccan political scientist and activist 'Abd al-Latif Husni puts it, the problem with the "parties that sprang from the nationalist movement," Istiqlal first among them, is that

> their visions and their ideas differ from the positions and their behavior in national political life, such that we observe in many of them a gross schizophrenia between the ideas and visions they call for and what they do in reality. This schizophrenia is what has deepened their isolation and left them unable to influence the Moroccan masses; their discourse has lost its credibility and their organizations are generals without soldiers; their primary job is to serve the regime and depend on it and repeat its slogans.[54]

Husni cites several specific examples of this "schizophrenic" behavior, all of which he reads through a presentist lens: Istiqlal says this but it does that. The party claimed that the 1977 elections were fraudulent and unfair, he points out, but joined the resulting government anyway.[55] It then did the same thing in the early 1990s, when it rejected the king's proposed constitutional reforms (which passed anyway) but ultimately agreed to work within the institutions laid out by those reforms. This, to Husni, makes little sense: "If the constitution weren't democratic [and Istiqlal claimed it was not], how could Istiqlalis achieve democracy, and succeed in setting up credible democratic institutions, while they knew for sure that they had no powers and all authority was in the hands of the king?"[56] This snapshot portrayal of tension between rhetoric and practice is not incorrect or necessarily unfair—but it is contained in the present in a way that Istiqlal's own narrative of the same moment is not.

Istiqlal described its decision to continue to work within the system after the 1992 reforms in distinctly different temporal terms. Husni implies that the passage of the constitution, which Istiqlal opposed but could not block, should logically have entailed a rejection of the institutions that constitution put in place because the *present* state of the system rendered democratic change impossible. A lead editorial in *al-ʿAlam* in May 1993 argued, however, that "democracy, like independence, is a practice [*mumārisa*] more than an event that happens and then the matter is finished. The constitution passed. But passing a constitution is not everything. The constitution is a practice. . . . The stage of practice has just begun, and it is more important than the stage of election."[57] This analysis is forward-looking: it is about what must be done in the next stage to improve upon the previous one. Moreover, Istiqlal admits no contradiction between its democratic goals and accepting a disappointing constitution: any tension will be resolved by what comes next: the "stage of practice." As usual, the party reaches for the future to dissolve what might look like hypocrisy in the present.

Husni does not speculate about *why* Istiqlal behaves in such a hypocritical fashion. Another critic from the activist camp, Ali Ouasri, provides the most common answer: parties, and especially party leaders, are pursuing their own personal interests under the guise of calling for political reform. Writing about the process of cabinet formation under Istiqlal president Abbas El Fassi in 2007, Ouasri argues that "the reactions of the majority parties [among them Istiqlal] were hostage to narrow interests structured by personal aims, which meant that the parties' stated positions, whether opposing a certain appointment or defending another one ... could be traced back to personal reasons that were not necessarily connected to party, political, or national interests."[58] In a common pattern, Ouasri implicates all parties—the members of parliament and the USFP are not spared—but in the case of the 2007 cabinet, it is Abbas El Fassi and the Istiqlal who come in for particular criticism. El Fassi "took dictation" from the regime as far as ministers were concerned, and orchestrated a cabinet formation process in which party leaders "gave up trying to defend their programs and threw their entire weight into a feverish struggle to grab the largest number of comfortable ministerial seats."[59]

In a more quotidian register, ordinary Moroccans are also likely to speculate about perks, individual ambition, backroom deals, and personal connections. Cabinet and parliamentary seats are widely seen as rent-seeking positions, opportunities to pursue individual enrichment at the expense and under the guise of a political program. Explaining why she and her friends do not bother to vote (their first response to my questions about Istiqlal), a young woman told me, "What they do is not what they say. We now say we just want someone who won't steal, because we know they won't do the things they promise."[60] Another interlocutor brought up a recent scandal involving prominent Istiqlal member of Parliament and former health minister Yasmina Baddou. In 2014 Baddou was discovered to have bought two upscale apartments in Paris's 8th Arrondisement worth more than a million dollars. She was called before parliament by her peers and asked to account for where she got the money; she eventually agreed to sell the properties and invest the money in Moroccan assets. In the media, this was largely covered as a nationalist issue: why would Istiqlal, of all parties, be condoning capital flight?[61] Yet another interlocutor traced it back to a broader pattern of corruption in Baddou's past, citing an incident during her tenure as health minister in which she was responsible for purchasing a vast quantity of flu vaccines that ended up being useless and had to be thrown out.[62] Whenever a corruption scandal or matter of incompetence surfaces, it becomes fodder for preexisting narratives about ministerial greed.

To some extent, this is a reputational problem that plagues all Moroccan parties.[63] A National Democratic Institute study of young Moroccans' political attitudes in the summer of 2011 found that "parties clearly face a collective crisis of credibility, with participants consistently complaining that parties disappear after elections and rarely keep their promises to citizens."[64] One citizen the NDI interviewed stated succinctly: "The first thing that comes to my mind when I hear 'political parties' is a set of nouns: hypocrisy, deceit, lies, double standards, and the list goes on."[65] While this opinion may sound normal to an American, Belgian, or Indian citizen, Morocco is an authoritarian regime. Real executive power lies with the king, and yet explanations for lack of political progress tend toward "the parties are corrupt" rather than "the parties lack the power to implement their own programs."

Istiqlal, however, is vulnerable to a particularly virulent strain of the general complaint about party corruption. After explaining that he did not like the Istiqlal because they had been in "power" (2007–2011) and failed to improve the country, one Moroccan told me, "the Istiqlalis and the socialists [the USFP], their origins are in Fez. And people in Fez, they like to take care of their own."[66] "They're out for themselves and each other," another told me. When asked why, he replied, "They're all Fassis."[67] Of course, much of Morocco's political elite traces its origins to Fez, and not all prominent (or corrupt) Istiqlalis are Fassis. Deviations from the norm, however, do little to disrupt the narrative. Indeed, one man told me that the party's turn toward conciliation with the regime in the 1970s was primarily due to Boucetta's origins in Marrakesh, the historical seat of the *makhzen* elite.[68] Again, personal connections are perceived to take priority over programmatic commitments.

Why have some interpretations—corruption, Fassi identity—have won much wider appeal than Istiqlal's claim that it is a heroic party sacrificing in the long struggle for democracy? Answering this question requires us to attend to the logical and evidentiary demands of competing interpretations. At the risk of using a politically unsavory metaphor, different interpretations of opposition behavior exist in something like a discursive marketplace. Opposition groups must make difficult choices, and their behavior will be open to multiple interpretations. We can understand something about a group's credibility by paying attention to the logic of the readings it advances and the logic of alternative accounts. This is not to say that the discursive playing field is level (it never is in markets either): more effective arguments draw on historically entrenched suspicions and prejudices, including some promoted by authoritarian rulers themselves. It is simply to suggest that the logic of arguments seems to matter and that attentiveness to logic gives scholars a way to analyze credibility beyond simple measures of popular support.

The Romantic "democratic journey" narrative is an extremely demanding one: it requires that the listener suspend judgment of Istiqlal's actions until an unspecified time in the future when something vindicatory—democratization—may or may not occur. From a social science perspective, the democratic journey narrative is unfalsifiable, which may explain why scholars so quickly dismiss it as spin. From a non–scholarly perspective, more importantly, it is unverifiable. The only development that could be cast as evidence of the narrative's accuracy would be unambiguous progress toward democracy—and very little of Morocco's halting, two-steps-forward-one-step-back progress toward popular sovereignty could be described as unambiguous.

The transactional and Fassi narratives, by contrast, require comparatively little of the listener. To be sure, the claim that benefits-for-quiescence exchanges taking place does require that one believe in the existence of secret, unobserved transactions. This should be more of a problem for scholars than it seems to be, but it is not a problem at all for citizens in authoritarian polities, where all manner of political processes happen in secret and reliable information is chronically unavailable.[69] In such contexts, few political outcomes can be made sense of *without* imagining secret interactions. Moreover, when corruption scandals do inevitably surface, they can serve as metonymic confirmation of transactional accounts. The Fassi narrative (like, unfortunately, many racist and otherwise bigoted interpretations of political behavior) does not require any additional verification. Indeed, it is self-verifying: Istiqlal's leaders participate in the regime because they are Fassis, and we can observe that they are both cooperating and Fassis. One does have to hold certain preexisting ideas about Fassis, however, and it is important to note that such ideas are historically constructed as publicly available scripts on time scales much longer than those under consideration here.

Thus, on balance, the transactional and Fassi counterinterpretations require little supporting evidence and allow an observer to pass judgment—as humans are wont to do—in the present. The "democratic journey," by contrast, requires an indefinite suspension of judgment and

offers essentially no evidence to support its conclusions. It is little surprise, therefore, that Istiqlal's own narrative has found fewer adherents
beyond the party.

Romantic Struggle and Negative Feedback

Readers may justifiably wonder why the Istiqlal Party remained co-opted for
so long. As the 1970s gave way to the 1980s and 1990s, Istiqlal's electoral
results and popular credibility were declining. Hoped-for democratic reforms
were slow to arrive, and at times progress gave way entirely to authoritarian retrenchment. To be sure, Istiqlal took some critical stances, opposing
the king's constitutional reforms in 1992 and declining repeated invitations
to join the cabinet in 1993 and 1994. Yet the party never boycotted a legislative election or withdrew from an incorporated position in protest over
regime policies.[70] Istiqlal would denounce electoral manipulation but then
insist that the democratic journey was still ongoing and exhort citizens to
have hope in the future when the next election came. In retrospect, this pattern of behavior may look like a baffling strategic error. Why did Istiqlal
persist in its generally participatory policy even as democratic progress
largely failed to materialize and its popularity declined? At the very least,
why not adjust the party's structuring metaphor to one less amenable to
uncharitable reinterpretation?

Attention to the specifically Romantic structure of the democratic journey, however, sheds some light on the metaphor's persistence—and on the
stickiness of co-optation itself. Romantic narratives are particularly adept
at normalizing setbacks because the existence of crushing obstacles and
moments at which victory seems impossible are integral parts of the Romantic story arc itself. In a Romantic narrative there are "encounters with
antagonists or enemies" and "heightened moments when Darkness seems
poised to vanquish Light"—but, in the end, "the victorious deliverance"
reveals the Romantic hero's perseverance to have been wise.[71]

Istiqlal's mistakes (if we decide to view them that way) evoke two broader
questions in comparative politics. First, why do opposition groups make
decisions that do not, to social scientists, appear strategically optimal?[72]
Second, why do patterns of organizational behavior—especially seemingly
dysfunctional ones—persist? Theorists of path dependence and historical

institutionalism have long argued that path-dependent outcomes involve positive feedback that helps "lock in" patterns of behavior over time. According to Paul Pierson, "in path-dependent processes the *relative* benefits of the current activity compared with other possible options increase over time."[73] Although path dependence can lead to suboptimal outcomes in the long run, at each step of the way continuing with a particular pattern of behavior is perceived as having an advantage over available alternatives. But Istiqlal's participatory stance produced a great deal of negative feedback. How are we to understand the persistence of costly practices over time?

In this section I draw our attention to metaphor as a "mechanism of inheritance" that reproduces organizational practices over time—even when those practices seem to be in error.[74] The notion of error seems to assume, in its more moralizing instances, the existence of a course of action that was *not* a mistake, an assumption that I plan to problematize in the book's conclusion. I do not, therefore, wish to explain why opposition groups make wrong choices as opposed to "right" ones, but I will explain why they persist in courses of action (here, continued incorporation) despite signs that the chosen course of action is not producing desired results. I begin by emphasizing metaphor's relationship to action, conventionally understood. I then turn to the "democratic journey" metaphor to emphasize how its Romantic qualities worked to normalize what might otherwise have been processed as negative feedback, using Istiqlal's response to the fraudulent 1984 elections as an illustration.

Metaphor as Structuring Action in the World

Metaphor is not restricted to explicit invitations to think about one thing in terms of another. Metaphorical language, and language that would not make sense without a metaphor operating implicitly in the background, suffuse the way people make sense of experiences. This is especially true when it comes to abstract phenomena—love, thinking, political change—that can be difficult to grasp without relating them to something more concrete (metaphorically speaking).[75] Following J. L. Austin and others, I am not invested in a hard distinction between speech and action. Indeed, a speech/action distinction is a key facilitating condition for co-optative neutralization: without distinguishing speech (cheap) from action (real), critics could hardly diagnose hypocrisy. What I suggest here is that figures of speech, including metaphors, have deep consequences for the kinds of practices that social scientists conventionally understand as "actions"—electoral boycotts, cabinet participation, joining protests, and so on. As conceptual metaphor theorists (most famously, George Lakoff and Mark Johnson) argue, metaphors not only help us make sense of ambiguous information or events but also "structure the actions we perform" as we engage in metaphorically conceived activities (argument-as-war, for example, or political-change-as-journey).[76]

The guidance provided by metaphor can be particularly essential in circumstances of pervasive uncertainty, where details about events' causes, meanings, and consequences are unknown and the burden falls more heavily on structuring metaphors to make sense out of what is happening. Authoritarian politics constitute just one such environment, heightening the salience of metaphor as a structure that guides thought, speech, and other forms of action. Moreover, as Hannah Pitkin has argued, metaphors are intimately connected to the project of actively changing how people relate to the world they inhabit—the project of political theory but also of political reform.[77] The political theorist—and, I might add, the activist—"invites us to a new organizing schema for making sense of our concrete reality," she argues. "If we accept the invitation, our familiar world will seem changed, and as a result we shall live differently in it."[78]

Organizational ethnographers have documented the power of discourse—and the fundamental assumptions that constitute it—to affect organizational decision-making for the worse. In her stunning historical ethnography of the *Challenger* space shuttle disaster, Diane Vaughan argues that NASA engineers did not ignore or fail to see warning signs that a cold-weather launch might be dangerous.[79] On the contrary, they were well aware of such indications; the problem was not that dissenting voices had been silenced or key information concealed. Instead, NASA engineers had coped with the dangerous and experimental nature of human spaceflight by coming to think differently about risk. "NASA," she explains, "had made a decision that certain risks were not eliminable; so the phrase 'acceptable risk' which horrified many after the fact was in fact a totally normal part of NASA thought."[80] Engineers came to operate along "a pattern in which signals of potential danger—information that booster joints were not operating as predicted—were repeatedly normalized in engineering risk assessments."[81] The concept of "acceptable risk" could accommodate negative feedback without necessitating a change in behavior—with catastrophic results. I want to suggest that the democratic journey metaphor is doing similar work in Istiqlal's case. Rather than encouraging readers to ignore or look away from obvious setbacks, the metaphor makes them an expected—indeed, a necessary—part of the overall narrative. Challenges will arise, but continued forward motion—not rethinking or a change of approach—is what is incumbent upon the Romantic hero. I illustrate this argument through Istiqlal's response to the disappointing 1984 parliamentary elections.

I cannot prove that each member of the Istiqlal sincerely *thought* in terms of the metaphor, only that they collectively *acted* in a way consistent with the logical implications of the way the metaphor ordered political life. One might object that it is therefore impossible to know whether the metaphor "caused" Istiqlal's course of action or was epiphenomenal to it. I suggest only that these two categories, direct causation and epiphenomenality, do not exhaust the possible relationships of ideology to political life. Returning to the quasi-Havelian conceptualization offered earlier, ideology's role is not uniquely causal—people always have other reasons for undertaking a given action—but the story of how they become enmeshed in a system or committed to a certain action is never only the story of those other reasons.

The 1984 Elections

In the 1977 elections, the first major test of the post–Green March return to parliamentary life, Istiqlal outperformed all other political parties. With a 21.7 percent plurality of votes, Istiqlal claimed 51 of 264 seats in parliament. Although independent candidates (many of them regime loyalists) formed a majority, Istiqlal did substantially better than its opposition-party peers. Five prominent Istiqlalis were named to the subsequent cabinet, and the party retained five cabinet positions through reshuffles in March 1979, November 1981, and November 1983. It seemed as though Istiqlal was to be a regular component of the government in the post–Green March era.[82]

The 1984 elections, however, soon put an end to this promising start for Istiqlal's career as co-opted opposition. The vote, originally planned for September 1983, had been postponed to avoid holding a contest during sensitive international negotiations over the Sahara. Two newly formed umbrella parties for regime loyalists, the Constitutional Union and the National Rally of Independents, dominated the election, taking more than 40 percent of the total votes and 142 of 301 seats. Other opposition parties did well: the Popular Movement and the USFP gained more than 30 seats each. Istiqlal, however, lost 11 seats, reducing its total seats to just 40. No Istiqlalis were named to the cabinet—as the fourth-place finisher, it would have made little sense even if monarchical appointments reflected vote totals—and while the party decried what it claimed was widespread electoral fraud, it did not publicly demand cabinet positions.

Thus, the 1984 elections were the first major test of the "democratic journey" in dire circumstances. Would the metaphor be able to absorb signs that democratic reform was not actually progressing and that the country might, in fact, be moving backward? The scale of defeat initially seemed unreadable in the metaphor's terms. The day the election results were announced, the front page of al-ʿAlam declared, paraphrasing party head Boucetta's comments to a London magazine, "there are pressuring forces moving to abort [l-ijhāḍ] any democratic trend."[83] Boucetta's comments were from before the September 14 election; al-ʿAlam was reprinting them afterward, signaling that Istiqlal did not only cry foul after poor results had come in. The temporal lag between statement and publication, though, left the meaning of the abortion metaphor unclear. The reader might think that the process of political reform had in fact been aborted on September 14, a situation from which there is no return other than to begin again from scratch. Or one might conclude that Boucetta's statement still held in its anticipatory form: forces "were moving to abort" democratization, but the embryonic new system could still be saved.

Within a day, however, the "democratic journey" had returned to Istiqlal's statements in full force. Al-ʿAlam signaled that the party recognized the scale of the setback, denouncing not just the 1984 vote but the June 1983 local and municipal elections, which had also been marked by fraud. In this reading, the situation at hand was not an anomaly but part of a broader pattern of retrenchment—logically, all the more reason to reconsider whether the country was actually on a democratic journey. Yet the newspaper's main above-the-fold headline continued to place the danger in the future, still perhaps avoidable:[84] "the goal [of electoral fraud] is the elimination of democracy and the establishment of institutions without credibility."[85] And yet there is no turning back, so to speak; the headline concludes: "The Istiqlal Party chose democracy as its struggle and it will not retreat."[86]

To be sure, the spatial metaphor of not retreating from the struggle for democracy could be compatible with a rejectionist position, one that would advocate a withdrawal in protest from regime institutions or attempts to destabilize them from the outside. The same editorial, however, makes a specific argument about the harm done by electoral fraud: it "makes the people feel that there is no point in participating, and spreads frustration with the possibility of setting up institutions that represent the people's free choice, to remove their hands from the democratic game."[87] The response to this threat cannot be to give antidemocratic forces what they want by refusing to participate; people must be encouraged to maintain hope in the ultimate value of participating in politics. Istiqlal here advocates the continued participation, despite disastrous election results, because eventually the outcome will be different: "The bet," the article concludes, "is always on the future."[88] While the notion of a "bet" (al-rihān) may initially seem to suggest that some uncertainty has crept into the narrative, "rihān" can be used in Arabic even when an outcome is certain. The eventual outcome will show that the bet was a good one; a rihān is a present conceived of as future past.

That one would respond to a pattern of unexpected negative feedback—here, electoral fraud—with a dogged commitment to continue one's previous strategy as if nothing had changed makes sense in light of the overarching Romantic structure of the democratic journey. Metaphors that summon up Romantic emplotments are particularly adept at normalizing setbacks because the existence of crushing obstacles and moments at which victory seems impossible are integral parts of Romantic narratives themselves. The hero in such a narrative, in order to be ultimately vindicated, must persevere in the face of these trials. As Scott describes the typical Romance,

> it has the shape of "a quest": the protagonists (invariably associated with the new, with Light, with order) undertake a perilous journey; there are encounters with antagonists or enemies (invariably associated with the old, with Darkness, with disorder); the inevitable conflict ensues between these irreconcilable principles; there are heightened moments when Darkness seems poised to vanquish Light; and finally the victorious deliverance or overcome from bondage, from evil, comes.[89]

The expectation not only of conflict, peril, and obstacles but of obstacles so great that "Darkness seems poised to vanquish Light" can work powerfully to normalize negative feedback. Rather than serving as evidence that the narrative of future progress is inaccurate, setbacks can be seamlessly integrated into that narrative itself. To abandon the mission in response to such setbacks would be to fail at the fundamental responsibility of the Romantic hero: to persevere despite challenges, always believing that vindication will come.

It is precisely by returning to previous experiences of struggle, sacrifice, and vindication—that is, by working the connections metaphor draws between concrete experiences and those still new and unfamiliar—that Istiqlali texts summed up the 1984 election. Two days after the vote, the regular front-page editorial argued that "democracy has confirmed again and again through its historic progress across the globe that it is not an easy choice, and that the way to it is a hard one."[90] Reaching back to the concrete successes of the 1940s and 1950s, when mass protests (and armed rebellion) won Morocco's independence, the article continued: "just as the journey of independence [masīrat al-istiqlāl] had thousands of victims, so too does the journey of democracy [masīrat al-dimuqraṭiyya]."[91] The parallel here is striking because thousands of Moroccans were killed or imprisoned during the struggle for independence; who the victims of that struggle were is clear. It is less obvious, however, who the victims of the struggle for democracy might be. To be sure, thousands of political dissidents had been rounded up, detained, disappeared, and tortured between 1965 and 1984. But even implicitly denouncing the desert prisons and the persecution of Islamists has never been part of Istiqlal's repertoire. In the wake of such a stunning electoral defeat, it is difficult not to read Istiqlal as the "victim" of the democratic journey. But what is incumbent upon the victim—who is also the heroine—is that she perseveres; she may be teetering on the edge of total defeat, but she will win in the end.

Lessons for Scholars

Co-optation works through discourse. Neutralization is not achieved through buyoffs; it is achieved through the *notion* of buyoffs. Skeptical readers may still suspect that transactions are doing the work and that Istiqlal's

Romantic rhetoric is nothing more than cynically deployed spin. One of the central arguments of this chapter, however, is that reading co-optation in the present, doubts about sincerity and the contention that "there must be something else going on" are precisely what neutralizes co-opted opposition. Scholars must be wary of repeating these claims as though they were unmediated facts—as though repeating them were just a description of co-optation rather than the enactment of it. My goal here is not to suggest that Istiqlal's future-oriented reading of Moroccan history is more or less factually accurate than the critical, presentist one advanced by scholars and other observers. Both are ways of interpreting political life that accord with some evidence and have much to commend them. I suggest, however, that scholars have tended to treat the presentist interpretation as fact and the future-oriented one (when it is acknowledged at all) as misguided fantasy or pure spin. I propose instead that we step back and consider the ways in which these two temporal orientations are different and explore the consequences of the friction between them rather than elevating one or the other to the status of truth.

FOUR

Co-optation as Interpretive Dilemma

The Wafd at War

ISTIQLAL'S JOURNEY METAPHOR was born of an exceptional circumstance: the conjunction of a changed sense of political possibility and a literal march. While generic journey metaphors are common, they often lack a tangible referent: for every Green March, there are many more journeys not rooted in a transformative historical experience. Readers of the previous chapter might rightly wonder, then, how specifically Romantic narratives have emerged in other co-opted parties. This chapter answers that question by turning to the Wafd's co-optation metaphor: the war for political change. While Istiqlalis spoke of steps, burdens, and uphill climbs, Wafdists opted for battles, casualties, and long campaigns. Although they differed in content, these two metaphors shared similar Romantic structures. Both emphasized gradual progress, expected setbacks, and pinned their hopes on future vindication. And both worked to facilitate co-optation while also inviting its most damaging consequences. In their origins, however, the two metaphors diverge. The Wafd's war was not rooted in a literal armed conflict; it did not refer to an inspiring event prior to co-optation. Instead, it arose from the experience of co-optation itself. Unlike Istiqlal, the Wafd was never invited into formal politics; the party had to fight its way in, primarily through legal channels. Wafdists read their successful co-optation as proof that the system could indeed be changed from within. The party's struggle for legal status became the first successful battle in a long war for democracy.

The Wafd's experience therefore demonstrates that the theoretical frame-work developed in chapter 3 travels beyond a single case. But it also reveals something Istiqlal's story does not: co-optation can serve as proof of its own efficacy. Conventional theories assume co-optation always works as it did in Morocco: the regime, seeking increased stability, offered a co-optative arrangement that Istiqlal decided to accept. The Wafd reminds us that co-optation does not always work that way. Egyptian president Anwar Sadat tried to keep the Wafd out of formal politics at every turn, so the party's leaders turned to a newly empowered judiciary to force their way in. When incorporation is wrested rather than bestowed, it can serve as powerful evidence that *more* change from within is possible; co-optation can, in a way both sinister and seductive, actually facilitate itself.

This chapter proceeds in three parts. In the first I argue that the Wafd was co-opted in a way existing theories do not expect. While cursory accounts often assume that Sadat wanted to lure opposition parties into the system, I demonstrate that the Wafd faced persistent executive-branch opposition from its (re)founding in 1977 onward: it took the party eight years to win its legal status—and it only did so by turning to Egypt's quix-otic courts. In the second part I turn to the martial metaphor born out of the long battle for legal status. With the democratic journey in mind, I high-light the metaphor's Romantic features and show how the Wafd used war to make sense of setbacks. In the final part I take up the Wafd's more recent history, drawing on examples from the 2010 election campaign to demon-strate how Romantic argumentation fails to protect party credibility.

The Wafd Refuses to Take No for an Answer, 1976–1984

Models of co-optation usually assume that regimes want to co-opt their opponents. After all, if co-optation contributes to authoritarian durability, why would rulers not pursue it? In transactional accounts, the regime is usu-ally "selling" co-optation and opposition is "buying" it, paying with their oppositionality for the perks of inclusion. As Michael Willis puts it, political parties "clearly provide some sort of service to these [executive] elites, oth-erwise their presence in the system would not be tolerated."[1] The Wafd's experience reminds us, however, that co-optation can also be a prize extracted despite regime reticence. When co-optation is wrested from unwilling hands rather than bestowed by manipulative ones, the logic of transaction is upended: co-optation is its own reward—and, as we will see, its own justification. In this section, I recover the tale of the Wafd's co-optation in greater complexity. I make several key claims: first, that the Wafd was not welcomed into formal politics by Sadat or Mubarak; second, that the party won its status only because of its successful resort to the judiciary, which was at the time undergoing significant change; and third, that Wafdists (reasonably) read their party's co-optation as a sign that the system could be further reformed from within.

A Party of Lawyers Confronts Bounded Multipartyism, 1976–1978

Sadat deliberately opened the Egyptian political system to a form of limited pluralism, but his steps in that direction were much more limited than they were pluralist. The change began modestly in early 1976, when he directed the Arab Socialist Union to divide itself into three "platforms" (manābīr): one "right," one "left," and one "center," the latter identified with the government. All these platforms were expected to espouse basic regime commitments; their left–right variation was envisioned entirely within the universe of Egyptian nationalism and 1976 socialism.[2] In March 1976 the manābīr were permitted to become independent organizations; in November, they gained the status of "parties" (aḥzāb). The right minbar became the Liberal Party; the center took the name Egypt Party, with a Sadat loyalist as president;[3] and the left became the party we now know as Tagammuʿ. Law 40 of 1977 codified this new system, laying out a series of demanding requirements for the formation of new parties beyond the initial triumvirate. Any applicant organization had to submit an exhaustive application to the new Party Affairs Committee (PAC), proving that its ideology conformed to the 1952 and 1970 revolutions but did not duplicate that of any other party. Both the PAC and the People's Council—where any party application needed the support of twenty sitting members—were packed with regime loyalists. This was not a system designed to facilitate entry.

The Wafd's leaders, however, were undeterred. On January 5, 1978, Ibrahim Farag delivered to the PAC 10 copies of the New Wafd's platform and bylaws and 120 briefcases containing the personal information of 591 founding members.[4] The application was complete and correct. None of the founding members came from professions banned from political activity (the armed forces, judges, or police); the party was clearly marked as separate from the "old" Wafd since no pre-1952 party was allowed to reconstitute itself; and its positions were carefully phrased to conform with regime guidelines.[5] Although 66 members had once been banned from politics, the Wafd used Sadat's "corrective revolution" against him: the president's 1970 reforms had lifted most political isolation sentences, leaving New Wafdists in the clear.[6] Moreover, and to the great surprise of Egypt's political class, months of lobbying had won over 22 members of the People's Council.[7] This accomplishment was, metaphorically speaking, a coup: the Wafd had not only met but surpassed the law's most demanding condition for party legalization.

The Wafd's careful attention to the letter of the law—no matter how biased that law was—makes sense in light of the party's historical association with lawyers. The old Wafd drew support from the urban sons of middling landowners, many of whom worked in Egypt's then-burgeoning legal profession.[8] Early leaders Saad Zaghloul and Mustafa Nahhas were both lawyers by training; indeed, the Wafd has only had one president who was *not* a lawyer in its entire history.[9] Ibrahim Farag and Fu'ad Sirag al-Din were both lawyers, and the New Wafd attracted younger legal processionals as well.[10] Sirag al-Din announced his intention to refound the party in a three-hour speech at the Lawyers' Syndicate in August 1977. If ever there were an opposition party equipped to test the limits of a new legal structure, it was the Wafd.

Surprisingly, the party's initial bid at legal status was successful. In February 1978, after six sessions devoted to considering the party's application, the PAC announced that there was no reason to keep the New Wafd from forming. Declaring it the "rightmost" of all existing parties (which was not saying much since all existing parties were legally required to be socialist), the PAC cleared the Wafd to take its place within the system.

In keeping with legal requirements, the Wafd's formation was formally announced in the People's Council. Member of Parliament (MP) Hilmy Murad gave a speech to mark the occasion. Murad, a member of the interwar Misr al Fata party (and thus a onetime rival of the old Wafd), had joined the New Wafd as soon as it emerged.[11] In his speech he argued that the Wafd's victory at the PAC—its very co-optation—meant that Egyptian politics had fundamentally changed. "We must at this time," he told the assembly, "commend the role of President Anwar Sadat in providing a measure of democracy and an atmosphere of freedom that that paved the way for the establishment of the Wafd Party."[12] There was applause in the chamber at the mention of the president's name—this was an authoritarian parliament, after all—but Murad's comments were not empty praise for the president. "Earnestness and sincerity," he continued,

> urge us to demand more democracy and the completion of the atmosphere of freedom through the cancellation of the remaining restrictions on public and personal freedoms, first among them the restrictions that limit the freedom of the press and the confidence of journalists; the realization of full jurisdiction for the normal judiciary, setting aside the military courts; and the repeal of the restrictions set out in the Law 40/1977 in the shadow of which we formed our party.[13]

There is no fully formed metaphor here yet, but the idea that an initial victory bodes well for future progress is clear. The Wafd's co-optation proved that there was some openness in the system, some "measure of democracy." Murad marked the party's initial success by demanding more.

Sadat Strikes Back, 1978–1981

The supposed regime loyalists of the Party Affairs Committee had signed off on a legal Wafd, but the president himself remained unwilling to do so. The legal barriers of Law 40/1977 having proved insufficient, Sadat immediately sought other ways to keep the Wafd out of politics. He began with a presidential decree reimposing political isolation on Sirag al-Din and several other party figures. Sadat then put the matter to a popular vote, introducing a referendum that would ban the Wafd's leadership from politics under the guise of "protect[ing] . . . unity and social peace." The Wafd called for a boycott, but the referendum passed easily, with 98.3 percent of voters in favor (as the party has occasionally noted, no referendum in Egypt's independent history has ever failed[14]). The vote replaced Sadat's decree with a new law, 23/1978, titled The Protection of the Home Front and Social Peace.

The Home Front law gave Sadat the power to dissolve any political party, and it seemed as though the Wafd was living on borrowed time. But the party's lawerly instincts apparently kicked in. On June 2, 1978, the Wafd's High

Executive Committee (HEC) announced a freeze (*tajmīd*) on party activities. The exact circumstances surrounding the freeze, however, are unclear— quite possibly by design. Some accounts suggest that the Wafd's General Assembly (GA) voted to dissolve the party entirely, but was then overruled by the HEC, which preferred a freeze; in other accounts, "freeze" and "dissolution" (*ḥall*) are used interchangeably even though they are legally distinct. One particularly intriguing version suggests that the HEC decided to dissolve the party, but Sirag al-Din, acting alone, never submitted the necessary paperwork to the government. Hassanayn Karam reports that Sirag al-Din told him, "After the decision to dissolve was taken, Dr. Mustafa Khalil called me and asked me to send a copy of the decision, so I said tomorrow, *in shā' allāh*, it will get to you, but I never sent it. So he called back a few days later and asked me to send it, and I said, tomorrow, *in shā'allāh*, and I never sent it, until he forgot about it."[15] When asked for his reasoning, Sirag al-Din replied that "he could not give that kind of a document to them so that they could use it against us if circumstances changed and we decided to return to our [political] activities."[16] The decision was apparently never recorded in the Wafd's own files to prevent leaks—although, in a statement whose accuracy will be recognized by any Wafd researcher, Sirag al-Din also mentions that the party lacked the administration to store records anyway.[17] Whatever the specific details, the Wafd managed to signal that it had disbanded without actually doing so, thus avoiding a presidential dissolution order and leaving open the possibility of another return. That feat would prove crucial in the legal struggle to come.

Egypt's Revived Judiciary

That the judiciary could be used against the executive would be unthinkable in many authoritarian regimes—including the Egypt of just a decade earlier. The coup-makers of 1952 deliberately sidelined courts and lawyers in their attempts to abolish the ancien régime.[18] Abdel Nasser's authoritarian reforms stripped the judiciary of its autonomy and introduced new "revolutionary" courts, while nationalization starved the legal profession of the profitable commercial cases that funded firms and offices.[19] Law went from being a prestigious major to the "university garage," fit only for low-performing students.[20] A concomitant decline in social prestige eroded the political and cultural deference once accorded to men of law.

Initially, these changes seemed to buoy the emerging authoritarian regime. Over time, however, the lack of independent courts became a liability. By the early 1970s the regime faced both economic and administrative challenges it could not handle without a more robust judiciary. As Tamir Moustafa argues in his landmark study of Egyptian constitutional politics, local and international investors shied away from a country with no checks on expropriation.[21] And, perhaps more importantly, the ballooning state bureaucracy could not be monitored for corruption or malfeasance.

To keep *infitāḥ* afloat and the state under control, Sadat introduced a series of changes that remade the Egyptian judiciary. The 1971 constitution created a Supreme Constitutional Court (SCC) with real powers of judicial review. When the SCC heard its first case in 1980, it was a "self-contained and self-renewing institution in a way that few other courts in the world operate."[22] The administrative courts were also revitalized, opening up new ways for citizens to challenge the state. According to Moustafa, the "regime restored the strength of the administrative courts in 1972 and further in 1984, by returning to them substantial control over appointments, promotions, and internal discipline, which were stripped from them by presidential decree in 1959."[23] To be sure, the judiciary was still subject to authoritarian restrictions and still paralleled by secretive military and security tribunals. But Sadat's changes afforded it an unusual degree of autonomy from presidential control. That autonomy is best understood not as judicial independence but as the freedom to be arbitrary. Judges and courts ruled in ways that sometimes frustrated the regime, sometimes citizen plaintiffs, and sometimes everyone involved. The sliver of daylight between the regime and the judiciary, however, was a weakness that opposition parties could exploit.

The Wafd's Legal Campaign, 1981–1984

As of September 1981 the Wafd's prospects seemed dim. Its public activities were on hold, it was not running candidates in elections, and its top leaders were banned from political life. Sirag al-Din was in prison, having been rounded up with hundreds of other dissidents in a far-reaching crackdown. But Sadat's death in October 1981 brought a shift in the party's fortunes. New president Hosni Mubarak released many of Sadat's detainees, including Sirag al-Din. The latter was invited to a press event on the steps of one of Mubarak's palaces—but instead of expressing gratitude, he emphasized his party's long-standing demands. "The isolation law issued by Sadat," he told the media, "prevents me from giving any comment, and when that law is repealed, I will talk to you."[24]

On August 23, 1982, the Wafd's GA met at Sirag al-Din's Garden City mansion.[25] When their discussions finally ended at 1:30 the next morning, the GA announced that the party would resume its political activities.[26] The PAC responded two days later that the Wafd could do no such thing since it had dissolved itself in 1978. But of course the Wafd had not actually dissolved itself—and thus the party's legal campaign began in earnest. Led by a team of lawyers (including Sirag al-Din, party vice-president Wahid Ra'fat, and future party president Noman Goumaa), the Wafd now aimed to "get a birth certificate from the judiciary."[27]

To get to the judiciary, however, the Wafd needed to use elections. Even under authoritarian conditions, theories of party politics often focus on elections as the ultimate sites of political contestation. But in the early 1980s the Wafd approached elections not on their own terms but as a way to gain standing where it really counted: the courts. Local elections were scheduled for 1983; the party put forward candidate lists in two Northern Cairo constituencies (El Sahel and Rod al-Farag) to force a confrontation over its legal status. As usual, the Wafd followed procedural rules meticulously, submitting the necessary paperwork to a low-level state employee on September 27, 1983.[28] That employee predictably refused to accept the lists, arguing that the Wafd had no legal right to run candidates. The party then appealed this rejection to the Northern Cairo committee overseeing candidate lists, where they were again rejected. Only after pursuing the correct set of administrative appeals did the Wafd file suit in the courts, demanding that their candidate lists be accepted—and, therefore, their legal status recognized.

The strategy worked: on October 29, 1983, the first-instance Court of the Administrative Judiciary ruled in the Wafd's favor. The government, still unwilling to accept a co-opted Wafd, appealed the decision to the Supreme Administrative Court (SAC). In the end, however, the original ruling held. On January 4, 1984, the SAC confirmed that the Wafd was legal and cleared it to run in the March 1984 parliamentary elections. Another victory soon followed: the Court of the Administrative Judiciary lifted Farag and Sirag al-Din's isolation sentences on February 12.[29] Technically, Mubarak could have appealed all these decisions to the SCC, but—perhaps already wary of the SCC's potential to rule against him—he did not. Seven years after its refounding and still with no explicit approval from the executive branch, the Wafd was at last a legal participant in Egyptian politics.

The Martial Metaphor

In the remainder of this chapter, I turn from the sequence of historical events to the Wafd's narration of those events. Out of the struggle for legal status came a martial metaphor, which took hold in the mid-1980s, the golden era of Wafdist rhetoric, under *al-Wafd's* editor-in-chief, MP Mustafa Sherdy. As the party experienced setbacks and disappointments, Sherdy led a chorus of Wafdists who cast political reform as a long war in which some battles would inevitably be lost and some comrades would inevitably fall. They argued that redemption would come one day, at the hands of God if not in the worldly realm. In what follows, I trace the origins and the Romantic features of the Wafd's martial metaphor before turning to a specific historical moment—the 1987 elections—to show how a war narrative could work to normalize setbacks and facilitate further co-optation.

The Battle That Started It All: Origins of the Martial Metaphor

With legal party status came the right to publish a newspaper. Fu'ad Sirag al-Din entrusted this task to Mustafa Sherdy, who shepherded the first issue of *al-Wafd* to press in the spring of 1984. Sherdy, whose vibrant prose appears often in this chapter, was both a respected journalist and a Wafd luminary. Born in the canal city of Port Said in 1935, he began working for a local paper when he was just a teenager. At the age of twenty, Sherdy found himself on the front lines of the 1956 Suez Crisis; he took shocking photographs of civilian casualties that were eventually introduced as evidence at the United Nations.[30] The incident catapulted Sherdy into the spotlight, but his career as a war correspondent had only just begun: he went on to cover the June and October Wars, the latter at the front.[31] For him—unlike many other Wafdist authors—war was a firsthand experience, not "just" a metaphor.

Sherdy's party credentials were no less impressive. He served as an MP for his Port Said district in the 1984 and 1987 parliaments and held enough sway within the party that he could disagree publicly with Sirag al-Din and still keep his job (as we shall see).

During his time at the helm, Sherdy set the tone for *al-Wafd*'s coverage with his daily signed editorial, which was printed on the front page, above the fold. Whereas *al-'Alam*'s daily *"al-iftitāḥiyya"* was collectively approved, Sherdy's editorials were his own work. He never represented a Wafdist consensus—something that has never really existed anyway—but he spoke to the perusing public as an exemplary (and loud) Wafdist voice. The paper he helmed took on greater significance in what was, at the time, a severely restricted media environment.

In *al-Wafd*'s first issues, writers cast the party's legal struggle as a battle. Doing so may have made strategic sense at the time: the tale was long and complicated, and readers might be bored or confused by its intricacies. Moreover, the 1952 coup had roundly discredited judges and the legal profession; would readers know how to make moral sense of a "birth certificate from the judiciary?"[32] Figuring the process as a battle made it more immediate and more comprehensible. Take, for example, Magdi Mehanna's April 5 feature article, "The Battle to Confirm Existence between the Wafd and the Government." The piece recounted the party's various challenges and successes as though they were the tale of an armed conflict: an organized series of violent encounters between two combatants. Adumbrating themes that would recur throughout party discourse, Mehanna argued that the war was forced upon the Wafd. "Since the moment it was announced on February 4, 1978," he wrote, "the Wafd faced a fierce campaign in which pens and noses were enlisted [*jannadat fīhā*]. . . . It was up to the Wafd to defend itself." Setbacks marked the beginning of new battles: when the party's candidate lists were rejected by the PAC in 1983, "it was up to the Wafd to . . . begin another decisive battle among its previous battles . . . a battle centered around establishing its legitimacy." The subsequent court cases were "the first round of the clash between the government and the Wafd before the judiciary, which ended with the Wafd's victory at the end of the round." Needing to accommodate the crucial role of the courts, Mehanna shifts between describing a battle and describing a boxing match, adopting the language of rounds and implying the presence of some kind of arbiter. The framing in this early articulation is superficial, but it would strengthen with time.

Meanwhile, other authors were articulating Romantic themes even without martial language. As the 1984 elections approached, Wafdists declared that the party's co-optation heralded a new era in Egyptian politics. Mehanna himself summed up this position: "Through the . . . integrity and courage of the Egyptian judiciary, the Wafd Party was confirmed, and this by itself is a win that the Wafd is proud of. . . . So it is not right to say that the Wafd Party has not offered anything from its establishment in 1978 to today . . . [It has] offered proof of the integrity of the judiciary and opened a new page in Egyptian judicial history."[33] Other authors explained that an empowered judiciary could support other moves toward democratization. Ahmed Aboul Foutouh, for example, argued that the Wafd's co-optation both heralded greater change and endowed it with a special responsibility. "For the first time," he explained, Egypt "has a party drawn from the ranks of the people and not by order of the ruler, that practices its right[s] thanks to the judicial branch, by a ruling in the name of all Egyptians. . . . Because the Wafd is the first step toward democracy, it is incumbent upon it to work to complete [istikmāl] all the principles of democracy."[34] Echoing Hilmy Murad's speech to parliament six years earlier, Aboul Foutouh framed the Wafd's legalization as the first phase of a much longer process. In doing so, he laid the groundwork for later articulations of successive battles as part of a greater, ongoing war.

The country's new president was another source of optimism. Although we now know that Mubarak was just as authoritarian as his predecessors, in the early years of his reign many political actors were unsure of his commitments. Wafd vice-president Wahid Ra'fat wrote a lengthy column in al-Wafd's inaugural issue offering several reasons why the upcoming parliamentary elections would be unprecedented. One was the presence of an opposition party not approved by the executive, of course. But another was Hosni Mubarak, who, Ra'fat argued, "despite his presidency of the National Democratic Party . . . is at the same time president of the Republic and therefore president of all Egyptians."[35] Moreover, Mubarak's decision not to appeal the Wafd's court victories to the SCC signaled—to Ra'fat, at least—some commitment to democratic principles. Mubarak, he explained,

> has proved more than once that when there is a conflict between the two roles that he prioritizes his public role over his private roles to remain a fair judge among the powers. . . . This was demonstrated by his neutral position on the

Umma Party and then the Wafd Party itself ... when the judiciary issued its rul-ing in the courts of first instance and then in the appeals court that the found-ing of the New Wafd was legitimate, President Mubarak initiated the recogni-tion of it and set that in motion completely and that is the greatest example of the duty to respect the rulings of the judiciary and not circumvent them.[36]

Yet again, the Wafd's legalization suggested that something about the sys-tem had changed. Mubarak could easily have directed government lawyers to appeal the SAC rulings to the SCC, keeping the Wafd in legal limbo. Or he could have issued a new presidential decree banning the Wafd and its lead-ers on some other grounds. Mubarak did neither: he let the court decisions stand and therefore allowed the Wafd to contest the 1984 elections. He may not have been able to keep the party out forever—the SCC might well have ruled against him—but he declined to exhaust his available options. That set him apart from his predecessors.

Despite an overall sense of optimism, Wafdists were no Pollyannas. Another vice-president, Ibrahim Dessouqi Abaza, acknowledged that the 1984 elections might be rigged. But he encouraged citizens to vote anyway. "Do not despair and do not fear," he urged them, "for the gates of the future are open before you, and our great judiciary, which saw that justice was done for the Wafd, will see that justice is done for you in your struggle against forgery and those who forge."[37] In this statement, Abaza confirms the party's vision of elections and court challenges as linked strategies for change. On a more thematic level, he emphasizes several Romantic tropes: the importance of hope, the potential of the future, and the promise of vin-dication. Although the war metaphor was still taking shape, the architec-ture of a Romance was already becoming visible. Party sources paired opti-mism about the future with a sense that many more battles lay ahead. Wafdists would build on those themes in the years to come as Egyptian poli-tics were thrown into turmoil by the developing rivalry between the judi-ciary and the executive.

The Era of Unconstitutional Parliaments, 1984–1990

Understanding the Wafd's martial metaphor requires some sense of its his-torical context. Over just six years in the 1980s, Egypt—a presidential system—held three parliamentary elections. As the newly empowered judiciary fought to establish and expand its jurisdiction, it ruled two successive electoral laws unconstitutional, invalidating the parliaments elected under them and throwing the country's politics into turmoil. The Wafd navigated this turmoil much as it had the "battle for legitimacy": by participating in elections (usually) but keeping one eye on the courts.

The decade's contest between judicial and executive hinged on the status of independent candidates. Sadat's multiparty experiment necessitated new electoral laws; statues passed in 1979 and 1983 created a party-list proportional representation (PR) system.[38] Throughout the 1980s oppositionists challenged the electoral system on the grounds that it discriminated against independent candidates. The 1971 constitution supposedly guaranteed equal political rights for all Egyptians, regardless of their party membership status. Forcing candidates to join a party in order to run in elections, activists argued, violated this principle of equal political rights.

Counterintuitively, the Wafd sided with the activists. That a political party would reject party-list PR and advocate for independent candidates might seem odd—especially in Egypt, where we now know that independent-friendly elections would decimate opposition parties. Given their commitment to electoral reform in the 1980s and their outraged surprise in the 1990s (when an independent system returned huge wins for the NDP), it seems that Wafd leaders simply did not anticipate that the party might fare better with PR than without. Indeed, there were good reasons to think that the PR system decreased opposition representation. The 8 percent national threshold effectively blocked any single party except the Wafd from winning seats in parliament. Most opposition parties had no hope of ever reaching that threshold; even Sirag al-Din felt it was wise to join an electoral alliance in 1984 to ensure that the Wafd would. Moreover, the PAC continued to reject new party applications. If more opposition groups could not break their way into the party system, new dissident voices in parliament would *have* to be independents.

The Wafd's complaints about the electoral system went far beyond PR, touching on malapportionment, the lack of neutral oversight, and the regime's consistent resort to coercion. But it was objections to the party-list system that succeeded in the courts. Late in 1986 the SCC signaled that it would rule the 1984 electoral law unconstitutional, rendering the sitting parliament invalid. The regime moved to evade the ruling by (superficially) complying with it: before the SCC announced its decision, the NDP-dominated People's Council passed a new electoral law (188/1986). The new law created forty-eight independent seats, technically complying with the spirit of the SCC's imminent decision.[39] By preempting the court, however, parliament declined to acknowledge the SCC's jurisdiction over the matter. Mubarak then put the new law to a referendum in February 1987. Observers at the time seemed unsure of whether presidential decrees or popular referenda were subject to SCC scrutiny. In the pages of al-Wafd, authors often speculated that referenda were attempts to insulate controversial decisions from judicial review. The judicial system was changing, and opposition and regime alike were struggling to understand their new roles.

With a new electoral law in place, yet another election was scheduled for April 1987. The SCC, however, was hardly finished: while the new system made some room for independents, unaffiliated candidates were still disadvantaged vis-à-vis their party peers. The hammer fell in May 1990, when the SCC ruled Law 188/1986 unconstitutional and the 1987 parliament "invalid since its election."[40] The regime now had a real problem on its hands. President Mubarak was due to be renominated by parliament in 1990; if the People's Council was invalid, the constitutional basis for his own rule might crumble as well. Unwilling to either confront the court directly or recognize its jurisdiction, Mubarak dissolved parliament by decree. The 1971 constitution granted the president the power to dissolve parliament, but only under very specific conditions—and, as Wafdists argued, having parliament already dissolved by the judiciary was not one of them.[41] Perhaps to insulate his decision, the president called for a referendum on the matter and instituted a new electoral law by decree (since there was no longer a sitting parliament to pass legislation). In December of 1990, then, parliamentary elections were held under a system that created more space for independents but did nothing about malapportionment, coercion, or fraud. The Wafd, along with all other opposition groups except Tagammuʿ, chose to boycott. The electoral law of 1990 created the independent-friendly system that the NDP would exploit for the next two decades. Overall opposition representation in parliament dropped and stayed low for fifteen years.[42]

The irony, of course, is that the new electoral system was (partly) the product of concerted opposition activism. From 1984 to 1990, the Wafd consistently defended the judiciary, reflecting the party's continued interest in the law as a vector for political change. The Wafd boycotted all of Mubarak's referenda, arguing that the executive could not use plebiscites to circumvent judicial authority.[43] The party also called for the dissolution of both the 1984 and 1987 parliaments. From a transactional standpoint, it might seem odd that a party would want to dissolve parliaments in which it held seats. The Wafd had captured fifty-eight seats in 1984 and thirty-five in 1987—perhaps not stunning victories but certainly impressive showings. One could argue, of course, that the party leaders expected to increase their vote share in new parliaments and therefore were simply perk-seeking when they advocated dissolution. Such an explanation founders, however, when one considers that the first dissolution of parliament (in 1986) led to a decrease in total Wafd seats; why would more dissolutions not have similar effects? Moreover, in 1990 the party gave up entirely on parliamentary participation and chose to boycott. Short-term seat maximization does not seem to have been a key goal during this period.

Viewed in light of the Wafdist commitment to the judiciary, however, the party's behavior makes considerably more sense. It was the courts, not elections or parliament, that had wrought the most political change in the preceding decade. The Wafd repeatedly—and not unreasonably—looked to the judiciary as an avenue for democratic reform. If the courts had to dissolve a few parliaments along the way, so be it. As Sirag al-Din put it in April 1984, "the Wafd was the largest and strongest political party in the history of Egypt. That is how it always was, and that is how it shall return again, under the aegis of the fair judiciary."[44] In the Wafd's public imaginary, it was never just elections that would change politics. Elections did matter, but the real path to change lay elsewhere.

War as Metaphor

As it took shape in the mid-1980s, the Wafd's martial metaphor cast politics as a series of battles against despotic forces. But using violent imagery to describe political events is hardly unusual. What distinguishes the party's war metaphor from familiar, haphazard references to debates as "clashes" or campaigns as "fights"? First, the Wafd's metaphor was comprehensive and overarching, providing a structure into which various political developments could be plugged. Second, Wafdists adhered to a specific notion of war, which excluded many forms of unstructured violence. And third, the Wafd's war was a narrative (and, as I argue later in the chapter, a Romantic one at that). I elaborate upon each of these three points in turn.

The Wafd's war metaphor is not simply a trail of casual references; it is a structuring metaphor made up of many smaller components. The political scene is a battlefield or an arena for single combat. Periods of crisis or heightened activity become distinct battles in an ongoing conflict. Parties, citizens, and the regime have weapons; political actions are victories, advances, withdrawals, or retreats. Opposition activists are guards or martyrs in the service of the nation; regime actors are thugs and bullies who transgress the rules of fair combat. While the metaphor draws succor from the actual violence of Egyptian politics, it unfolds in distinctly historical terms.[45] Party sources speak of bows and arrows, swords and spears, and sticks hewn from fruit trees. Nowhere in this discourse does a reader find a tank or a pistol, nuclear weapons or a grenade. By consistently referencing older technologies of violence, Wafdists may have been avoiding charges of incitement. But they were also conjuring up a colorful, dramatic world. Far from just using terms (like *clash*, in English, for example) drained of their original violent content, Wafdist authors present a (more or less) coherent imaginary with a clear moral message.

That moral message is an emphasis on war as an organized, bounded form of conflict. As one reads through *al-Wafd*, one quickly realizes that not all violence counts as war. Wafd authors denounce unfair regime practices as "terrorism" or the work of "gangs" or "thugs" (rather than soldiers or armies). Indeed, sometimes the metaphor of choice shifts to single combat, a form of war even *more* structured by rules. Wafdists accuse the regime of resorting to illegitimate forms of violence to hide its own weakness. Consider the following example from *al-Wafd*'s editor-in-chief, Mustafa Sherdy, in the aftermath of the fraudulent 1984 elections:

> The test-tube baby [the NDP] lived in the ICU under an oxygen tent, and suddenly they brought it out into the field of competition and demanded that it confront a skilled fighter [*mulākim muḥtaraf*] . . . which led it to enter the ring with an arsenal of weapons in its hands: swords, sticks, and antelope-horn daggers, until the thugs [*balṭagiyya*], drug dealers, and gangsters allied with it to evade this dangerous test, even if by violence, killing, terrorism, and fraud.[46]

Sherdy contrasts structured hand-to-hand combat—no weapons allowed—with "violence, killing, terrorism, and fraud," which are unacceptable means of armed competition. The "swords, sticks, and antelope-horn daggers" ensure that the NDP will win the fight, even if it is the weaker party. The bounded rules of war, in Wafd accounts, parallel the bounded rules of elections: both demand competition but, ideally, also distinguish between acceptable tactics (campaign advertisements, infantry charges) and unacceptable ones (murdering your opponents, executing prisoners). The Wafd's metaphorical war is not an all-out contest in which all means are justified. Fair politics rely on fair rules—a position appropriate, after all, for a party whose slogan is "right over might."

Finally, the Wafd's war metaphor is a narrative: temporally situated, with beginning, middle, and end. The beginning is sometimes the "battle for legitimacy" but more often earlier struggles for human rights, self-determination, and democracy. The middle is the plodding work of democratic reform, while the end is the ultimate vindication of success (or, if worldly success is impossible, divine redemption). I explore this narrative structure in greater depth in the following section, which lays out the metaphor's Romantic features. In all, though, the Wafd's war metaphor is neither accidental nor ordinary: it offers a robust, consistent language with which to speak about politics and—as we shall see when we come to the 1987 elections—a richly imagined moral universe.

War as Romance

Although the Wafd's war metaphor differs from Istiqlal's democratic journey in its content, the two figurations are structurally similar. Like the democratic journey, the war for political reform includes a model of stepwise progress in which some advances have been made but many more remain, an acknowledgment that the process is costly and burdensome, and an orientation toward future vindication.

Each battle—whether electoral, judicial, or otherwise—forms one link in a longer chain of confrontations. The tale of the long war stretches both back and forward in time, in keeping with the Romantic tendency to "orient . . . sometime toward the past, sometime toward the future."[47] This *longue durée* perspective draws on actual historical wars, blurring the boundary between realities inside and outside the metaphor. Ibrahim Farag put it this way:

> Despite the fact that the concept of freedom has completely settled after crushing battles that humanity entered against its [freedom's] enemies in every time and place, which felled millions of victims and martyrs until the banners of freedom were raised high . . . after the decisive victory in the Second World War against the forces of fascism and Nazism . . . there are still those who live with the mindset of the jungle and permit themselves the right to understand freedom as though it is simply a slogan, or a gift that can be given and taken away.[48]

Here the Wafd's story is just a subset of a broader human one: the party is fighting against freedom's enemies in its own corner of the world. By situating Egypt's democratization in a global narrative, Farag provides reason for optimism—many battles have already been won—without denying that more struggles lie ahead.

Farag's reference to the "millions of victims and martyrs" evokes another of the metaphor's Romantic features: the expectation of hardship. War metaphors are particularly adept at showcasing sacrifice—while long roads may be wearying, long wars are always deadly. Wafdist authors are under no illusions about the costs of co-optation. In a moment of extraordinary clarity after the 1984 elections, Mustafa Sherdy acknowledged that competing in a fraudulent contest endangered the Wafd's credibility. "This is the question," he wrote, "the question of many people that I have heard in the streets, or in TV interviews, or in the mail. The question is: how did you trust those people? How were you convinced to enter the elections? Can people like you really be democrats? And can anyone among you imagine stepping away for a second from the sphere of rule, authority, and power? How did they trick you and how did you fall for it?"[49] The specter of transactionalism lurks among these questions. "How were you convinced?" implies that perhaps the Wafd received promises unknown to the public. "Can people like you really be democrats?" casts doubt on the party's sincerity. And the rhetorical question that follows—would you ever turn down a chance at power?—suggests that the party's real interest is in gaining status, not defending democracy. Sherdy's response, however, highlights the power of Romantic tropes to render loss as sacrifice. "I say to those questioners," he continued, "that our entering the elections met a national duty (*wājib waṭanī*) and was on the basis that the existence of a strong opposition on the scene could combat the hypocrites who rule Egypt. That confrontation could lead toward progress toward reform."[50] The Wafd had to take the risk, even if it eventually paid the steep price of defeat.

Sherdy and others often refer to duty and responsibility when discussing party strategy. In the aftermath of the 1984 elections, Gamal Bedawy noted that parliamentary opposition was now "a responsibility carried by the Wafd alone" since no other party had crossed the 8 percent threshold.[51] Sherdy elaborated on this theme elsewhere in the same day's paper: "The Wafd, in the eyes of the masses now, is the party responsible, under the dome of parliament, for building correct democracy and protecting it. It is the party entrusted by the people of Egypt to enter a pitched war [*ḥarb ḍāriyya*] against corruption."[52] Such responsibility prevents the Wafd from, say, withdrawing from parliament in protest; it is what keeps the party in the authoritarian political game. Metaphorically, the costs of participation are obstacles for the Romantic hero to overcome. A heroic party must be prepared to enter elections "no matter the circumstances," as Sherdy once put it, even if the consequences are fraud, defeat, and damaged credibility.[53] Such consequences are an integral part of the Romantic story: they prove the hero's commitment to the cause.

And although the costs may be steep, the heroic party will eventually be vindicated. For the Wafd, ultimate redemption takes on a divine cast common to Romances.[54] It is God who most often emerges as the giver of victory and defeat, of justice and punishment, in the end. After all, in a war one runs the risk of dying before the end of the story, before one's side can experience victory. God's redemption may be all a soldier can hope for. After the rigged 1987 elections, Gamil Hana Masiha surveyed the scene in a column titled, "Wa wadaʿt al-ḥarb awzārihā," a phrase that literally means "the war has laid down its burdens" (the phrase is Qur'anic, although Masiha was Christian). He acknowledged that an electoral war was waged and that his party has lost: "the war has laid down its burdens and the government has achieved its aims and received an overwhelming majority." The greater struggle, however, was not over. Masiha closed with the following warning:

> I have one small word directed to their excellencies the MPs from the ruling party in the new council as they celebrate their victory. . . . You know that the

theft of the people's voices and the conscience of the nation are crimes whose punishment is death. You will not be punished now, but death is coming, inevitably, and there is accountability and there are punishments. Do you not realize the nature of these punishments, according to all the heavenly religions?[55]

In Masiha's prose, the Romantic orientation toward the future becomes an orientation toward the inevitability of death and divine judgment. Although more likely in times of war, death is always an absolute certainty—and it is with absolute certainty that Wafdists imagined the eventual victory of justice (if, perhaps, not democracy). There *will* be an eventual accounting, they argued, and that accounting will vindicate the Wafd and doom its enemies.

In all, the Wafd's war metaphor shared the democratic journey's Romantic structure. It could therefore work to facilitate participation, suspend judgment, and normalize setbacks—all crucial tasks for co-opted parties whose controversial, costly choices rarely bear fruit in the short term. In the following section, I illustrate how Wafdists turned to the war metaphor—and the work it could do—when the interpretive dilemmas of co-optation became particularly stark.

The Metaphor at Work: The 1987 People's Council Elections

The 1987 parliamentary elections posed a classic interpretive dilemma for the Wafd. By that point it was difficult to argue that the vote would be free and fair: local and national contests since 1984 had been consistently marred by fraud, malapportionment, and coercion. The NDP would certainly win, and whatever opposition squeaked through into the People's Council would have little leeway or influence. Thus, the Wafd could no longer argue, as it had in 1984, that the vote might mark a real shift toward democracy or even yield a sizable opposition bloc in parliament. Why, then, compete at all? The Wafd had to justify their participation *and* encourage citizens to vote despite indisputable evidence that the election would be rigged. The martial metaphor gave Wafdists a vocabulary for this colossal task, one that emphasized that participation was a duty, sacrifice was inevitable, and redemption was nevertheless guaranteed.

Mustafa Sherdy's election-day editorial, "Your Vote Is a Sword in the Hand of the Nation," masterfully demonstrates the metaphor's potential. Sherdy himself had initially supported a boycott, making his case against Sirag al-Din's participatory stance on the front page of *al-Wafd*. Ever the good party soldier, however, Sherdy complied with the ultimate decision to run and defended it in similarly public fashion. He did not change his assessment of the election's integrity though: not only would there be manipulation, Sherdy pointed out, but the entire electoral law was invalid to begin with. The NDP legislators who had passed Law 188/1986 had done so specifically to circumvent the courts, and any elections under that law were therefore unconstitutional.[56]

"This fact," Sherdy nevertheless argued, "must not bring us backward or permit our despair to be victorious over our will. Instead, we must overcome the feelings of despair within us and go to the ballot boxes and all cast our votes."[57] By associating despair (that is, lack of hope) with nonparticipation, Sherdy cements the affinity between hope and co-optative participation that runs throughout Istiqlal and Wafd discourse. He reminds readers that the future will bring redemption, relying heavily on the war metaphor in the process:

> If they held elections every month, eventually they will tire of the fraud game and realize that Egypt has woken and will never sleep again. We must increase our pressure every time, until we grab the spear [*ḥarba*] of despair out of our chests and sink it in their hearts, until the party of janissaries realizes that the people may have been conquered to some extent, but they are not defeated. Victory is theirs [the people's] in the end, because God promises that falsehood will lose and God always keeps promises and makes the people victorious over their oppressors.

The election may be lost before it begins, but that is no excuse to relax. Democrats must keep up their pressure on the regime; one day, that pressure will force real change. As long as there is a just God—and that, in Egyptian politics, is rarely questioned—eventual victory is absolutely certain.

Later in the editorial, Sherdy expands upon the idea that the upcoming election is just one stage in a much longer conflict. The war for political change will not be won or lost by one election alone: "The elections being held today are invalid, but they are like a war that is forced upon us and compels us. We must enter into it no matter the circumstances, because we will not win the war against tyranny in Egypt in one round, or even a number of rounds. Rather, we must firm ourselves for a long war, for numerous and pitched battles. The other side wants us to do nothing but feel despair and turn our backs on the arena so it can . . . run wild as it wishes."

For the third time in a short text, Sherdy reaffirms the connection between hope and participation. He also evokes themes of hardship and responsibility. "A war that is forced upon us and compels us" is a Qur'anic reference. During a discussion of war in Surat al-Baqara, the following verse appears: "Fighting has been enjoined upon you, though it is hateful to you. But perhaps you hate something and it is good for you, and perhaps you love something and it is bad for you. And God knows, while you know not."[58] Sherdy is the consummate party warrior: although he himself opposed participating, he defends his party's choice to do so with a line of argumentation that acknowledges his own objections ("perhaps you hate something and it is good for you") but nevertheless enjoins participation. He invites readers to suspend judgment, to cast doubt on their own initial assessments, and to trust that the same God who promises justice may know something they do not.

Going even further, Sherdy argues that the costly path is the right one. The put-upon hero must suffer en route to redemption, so abandoning his duty is unthinkable; it would disrupt the entire narrative structure. "There is no path before us in the struggle for national freedom except this path," Sherdy wrote. "There is no option but combat [qitāl] and no option but struggle. . . . No option but being wounded in the midst of battle. No option but that martyrs fall in the arenas of jihād, and no option to save Egypt from its catastrophe other than to carry her above our shoulders as long as we survive, and to lay down our bodies for her to walk over when we are martyred."

The costs are clear. Warriors will fall, wounded or dead, but the forward motion must continue. Sherdy pulls no punches, so to speak: not only should voters expect a loss, they should expect a damaging one, with many casualties. The grim, short-term outlook, however, is no excuse for sitting at home. He closes with the following passage: "Every citizen can, today, transform their vote into a contribution, into an arrow shot against the enemies of the people. . . . Every citizen is asked today to heed the call of the prisoner of war [ʿasīr] that is the nation, which cannot bear any more of prison's oppressions or more wounds, tortures, or humiliation."

The image of a captive nation suffering in an enemy prison certainly raises the stakes of the conversation. Sherdy walks a fine line between acknowledging that the struggle will be long and emphasizing that each battle is nevertheless urgent. If he is correct about the country's political situation, the prisoner of war will not be rescued the next day, when votes are tallied, nor for many years. No matter what citizens do, the nation will have to bear more of "prison's oppressions." A Romantic narrative may not, in the end, be the most rousing get-out-the-vote effort: promising people a hard, long road may not motivate them if opponents are offering quick fixes. But here the Wafd's specific martial content shines: it drapes what might be an unappealing analysis in the language of nationalism, martyrdom, and glory. It enchants a confusing, seemingly pointless process of gradual change, transforming defeats into opportunities for heroism.

In the end, the election went much as Sherdy predicted. The day after the vote, *al-Wafd*'s banner headline read, "Worst Parliamentary Elections in the History of Egypt." Above the fold, another headline introduced "The Victims of the National Party." Below it were three images of injured men: one with a swollen face and balancing on a crutch; another with bandaged arms laying in a hospital bed; and a third laying listlessly, the caption indicating that he was beaten into unconsciousness. A smaller headline reported that NDP henchmen in one district "gave a polling place manager a concussion and punctured one of his eyes."[59] The visual implication is that the country has just witnessed a violent conflict, not an election. As though surveying the battlefield, Sherdy titled his daily editorial, "Bury Your Dead, May God Have Mercy on Your Dead." Flipping the visual script but remaining within the metaphor, he argued that the NDP was the battle's true casualty. Despite the regime's resort to fraud, the "ruling party was like a corpse carried by some mourners . . . around and around the polling places."[60] Sherdy, meanwhile, wrote from the "historical fortress of the Wafd," in Port Said, with celebratory crowds—he had been reelected—chanting outside his window.[61] A battle had clearly been joined, and there were casualties on both sides.

Meanwhile, other authors pivoted, as always, toward the future. In a column titled "We Have Not Lost Hope . . . Yet," Ibrahim Dessouqi Abaza promised disappointed Wafdists and voters that victory would still come.[62] "The battle, first and last, is for the sake of Egypt and the future of Egypt," he reminded them, "and even though the rays of life have not emerged yet, we have not lost hope even as the hour of deliverance has been delayed, but it is certainly coming. . . . Despite all that has been lost—despite the crushing weight of all that has been lost—hope remains. The future is near, and history will record the names of the heroes who protected the nation's honor just as it will dump the corpses of the counterfeiters, forgotten, in the dark."[63] If the last sentence sounds familiar, it may be because Istiqlali Abdelkrim Ghellab used almost the same words in his 2017 remembrance of M'hamed Boucetta: "History will record the periods of success and ascribe them to those responsible, and will record the periods of failure and ascribe them to those who maneuvered . . . in favor of their own self-interest, not carrying the burden of the national interest."[64] The present is only history when viewed from the future; Abaza, like Ghellab, is encouraging readers to suspend judgment. This particular battle is not the end of the story, and its true heroes will not be recognized until much later. "No, we have not yet lost hope," Abaza continues, "what is happening is nothing but a single battle in a long war against one party's robberies, and against the error of its followers." Egypt, this time, is the ultimate redeemer: "No, we have not yet lost hope . . . for the government knows . . . that the people will not forgive those who put them in graves and killed the hopes of their youth. The accounting will be terrible." "Egypt," Abaza promises, "will not forgive. She has waited a long time, but the punishment will be harsh."[65]

By leaning on a martial Romance, Wafd writers made two key moves in spring 1987. First, they encouraged electoral participation even though defeat was an absolute certainty. And second, they made sense of that defeat as a reason to continue rather than reconsider their strategy. A metaphor that can do this work is immensely valuable to a co-opted party, especially one whose co-optation does not seem to be producing much change. It elides any tension between participating in a rigged system and calling for democracy, rendering the two consistent and complementary. It is impossible to know whether the authors quoted here were aware of what the metaphor was doing. Did they deploy it cynically? Were they themselves thinking with it and in its terms? Were they able to think *outside* it? Such questions intrigue, to be sure, but they may not be so consequential as they seem. Metaphor can structure thought and speech even if we do not actively choose to invest in it. Whether they meant to or not, Wafdists put a narrative out into the world. Once out, that narrative was on its own, examined and evaluated by a much wider audience.

A Participatory Metaphor in Rejectionist Times, 1990

In 1987 Sherdy and his team of contributors seemed ready to justify electoral participation under any circumstances. Readers familiar with Egyptian politics, however, know that the Wafd boycotted a national parliamentary election just three years later.[66] My claims are not deterministic: it is not the case that a party adhering to a Romantic narrative will *never* back out of co-optation. But if, as I argue, Romantic metaphors have an elective affinity with participation, then what becomes of them when co-opted parties choose to boycott elections? Istiqlal's experience is little help here; it has not boycotted a parliamentary vote since adopting the "democratic journey" narrative. The Wafd has. In this section, I briefly discuss what we can and cannot say about the party's decision-making in 1990 and examine how the war metaphor was adapted to suit a boycott.

Overall, the Wafd's behavior in 1990 casts doubt on transactional models of co-optation. The party openly advocated the dissolution of a parliament in which it was the largest single opposition group and then boycotted the elections for that parliament's replacement. If Wafdists were angling for more seats (or perks, influence, benefits, etc.), they were running a long game indeed. Yet the party was hardly shifting into open rebellion either. What the Wafd claimed to want was judicial review and constitutional sovereignty, not the collapse of the entire system. It neither allied with illegal groups nor participated in illegal demonstrations. The 1990 boycott illustrates the sizable gray areas inhabited by co-opted parties—areas poorly captured by formal theoretic dichotomies between compliance and rebellion.

The 1990 confrontation revolved, yet again, around judicial review. Wafdists had claimed since 1986 that electoral Law 188/1986 was unconstitutional and the 1987 parliament therefore invalid. Appropriating the Brotherhood's famous slogan, they argued that "dissolution is the solution" (the wordplay is even better in Arabic because the two words are the same: *al-ḥall huwa al-ḥall*).[67] In early 1990 the SCC agreed, ruling the law unconstitutional—a move that should, according to the Wafd, have dissolved parliament automatically. President Mubarak, however, refused to acknowledge the court's authority in the matter. Instead, he dissolved parliament himself, by presidential decree. Such decrees are normally considered outside the purview of the SCC, but the Wafd argued that the president could not dissolve a parliament that had already ceased to exist.[68]

Following his predecessor's script, Mubarak put his decree to a national referendum, which—of course—passed easily. For the Wafd, which looked to the judiciary as the engine of democratic change, such behavior was unacceptable.

It was not, however, new. Mubarak had sidestepped judicial authority before; it was his attempt to avoid judicial review that created law 188/1986 in the first place. As is so often true, it is not entirely clear why the Wafd boycotted in 1990 but not in, say, 1987. The party's complaints in 1990 do not differ qualitatively from those put forward three years earlier. As I argue in chapter 2, external conditions are poor predictors of party behavior. Co-opted parties usually have good reasons to participate in elections *and* good reasons to abstain. What changes when a party decides to boycott is not the objective oppressiveness of the regime but the party's internal balance of power or even a single leader's preferences. Such changes are not impossible to observe contemporaneously—I will do something of the sort in part 3—but recreating them historically is a challenge. We do know that the decision was not unanimous (Wafd decisions rarely are): forty-three members of the High Executive Council voted to boycott while two voted to participate.[69] Given Sirag al-Din's exceptional stature and his prior record of making major decisions unilaterally, the roots of the 1990 boycott probably lie in his own preferences and coalition-building, which are difficult to access reliably three decades later. The sorry state of Wafd record-keeping, itself a consequence of Egypt's restrictive associational environment, further exacerbates the problem.

Explaining the boycott, however, is not my task here. I want to consider instead what became of the martial metaphor when its Romantic features were not needed, when the party did not need to justify participation or normalize defeat. The Wafd did not abandon the metaphor entirely; as we will see, party sources retain martial language and attempt to connect the boycott to an ongoing narrative. But the interpretive dilemma had lessened: the party was no longer participating in elections it also denounced, so the contradictions of co-optation were less apparent. In such a context, the metaphor's considerable powers were superfluous. The language of war persisted, but its work was less essential.

Wafdists made two key rhetorical moves during the boycott. First, they argued that the elections no longer counted as war. The rules guaranteeing just combat had evaporated; the regime would not abide by even the most basic standards of fairness. New editor-in-chief Gamal Bedawy—Sherdy had died in 1989—explained this line of thinking three days after the boycott was announced:

> The government that prepared this law in the absence of the opposition parties has offered no guarantees for the process of holding free and fair elections; instead, they issued official comments confirming that the opposition would not receive the seats it held in the dissolved Council. And who told them about that result before it was announced? Indeed, before it was even possible to declare a candidacy?! Does that not show that the electoral battle has been decided before it was held, and that elections will just be theater to deceive the masses, and after them the government party will come out and will have received the lion's share of the booty!! And if the government was confident in the popularity of its party, then why force this secrecy on the electoral law and why did it alter the electoral districts? And why did it not show these two laws—which are the basis for the electoral process—to its fellow participants in battle?[70]

The language of war has not disappeared, but its relationship to elections has changed. If the contest at hand failed to qualify as war, the Wafd could boycott it without reneging on its national duty. Bedawy argues that the battle's outcome—not just an NDP victory but the exact number of opposition seats—had been decided in advance, violating the idea of battle as a space of uncertainty, in which ground can be won or lost according to the skill, luck, or courage of combatants. He criticizes the electoral law (here standing in for the laws of war) because it was drawn up without input from the regime's "*shurakā*." The term is striking: it can be translated as "fellow participants" but also as "partners," implying an essential unity between combatants. The sense that rules should be agreed upon together confirms that the war Wafd texts imagine is not an all-out struggle for survival but a controlled contest between two sides that share basic commitments. The NDP's refusal to participate in the ritual of consultation denies this unity and renders the election something other than war. By denying the elections battle status, Bedawy dodges the party's promise to enter electoral battles "no matter the circumstances."[71]

Meanwhile, other party authors cast extrainstitutional politics as yet another "front" in the larger war. In doing so, they emphasized continuity:

the arenas of battle may have shifted, but the overall struggle continued. The party had already spoken of judicial and electoral battles; in 1990 it added a new category to the list: the "battle for democracy," which would be fought among the masses. The "battle for democracy" was a common refrain at party events that fall. Coverage of an October rally in Daqhiliyya proclaimed, "The Wafd boycotts the elections in order to enter the battle for democracy."[72] About a week later, at an event in Port Said, Fuad Badrawi elaborated on the idea. "Our decision," he explained, "is to boycott the elections—and enter into the democratic battle for the sake of the people."[73] The Wafd would "move . . . its activities from underneath the dome [of parliament] to the wider masses through its [local] branches," adopting a more grassroots organizing style.[74] The details, however, remained scant: it was not clear what the branches would do, or what (metaphorically or otherwise) the "battle for democracy" entailed. Weren't the earlier electoral and judicial battles also battles for democracy? The language of war is similarly scarce; these sources contain no martial imagery beyond the term *battle*.

All this suggests that while the war metaphor could survive a boycott, it had very little to do. Since many Egyptians already "boycotted" elections by never bothering to vote, and since the Wafd had spent six years complaining about electoral irregularities, there was not much to explain. The party did need to dispense with its prior argument that electoral participation was a national duty, which Bedawy did. But beyond that, the powerful Romance of war sat idle.

Romance Versus Transactionalism

As we saw in chapter 3, Istiqlal's commitment to the democratic journey sapped the party's credibility over time. Potential allies diagnosed a schizophrenia, a disconnect between Istiqlal's words and its other actions. In the space created by that disconnect, transactional interpretations thrived. The Wafd has suffered through a similar experience. In this final section I explore how Romances and transactional accounts interact. Romantic metaphors are powerful, but their power depends on the future. Only by reaching for the future can they dissolve the tension between democratic commitments and co-optation. Viewed strictly in the present, Romances lose much of their power. Indeed, they may actually become a liability, inviting the transactional rumors that saturate both local conversation and transnational scholarship.

To illustrate these dynamics, I turn to the late Mubarak era. The Wafd's behavior presented a classic interpretive dilemma: after loudly demanding major electoral reform throughout the year, the party chose to run in elections that, according to its own analysis, could never be free of fair. In contrast to the more restrictive 1980s, the rise of a quasi-independent private press and the proliferation of digital media beginning in the 2000s give us a thicker understanding of the discursive environment surrounding the Wafd as it made the controversial decision to run in the 2010 parliamentary elections. Although the party eventually withdrew from the elections after the first round (see chapter 2), its decision to run disappointed allies and fueled persistent rumors that the Wafd had made a "deal" (ṣafqa) with the regime. Although Wafdists had abandoned the war metaphor—a casualty of an overall decline in messaging coherence—they continued to rely on Romantic lines of argumentation. Their invocations of gradual progress, necessary sacrifice, and future victory, however, did little to combat transactional counterinterpretations.

Egypt and the Wafd in 2010

No water, no electricity, no bread . . . but we still have a president.

—CAIRO NEWSPAPER HEADLINE, SUMMER 2010[75]

Something was afoot in Egypt in 2010, even if many observers—myself included—could not quite figure out what it was. Social movement groups, including the April 6th Youth Movement and the remnants of Kefaya, were challenging the regime and established political parties. Respected diplomat Mohamed ElBaradei returned to Egypt after decades abroad to found his own movement, the National Association for Change (NAC). With rumors swirling about a possible presidential bid in 2012, ElBaradei promoted a set of seven demands for political reform and sent young people into the streets to promote them. A man named Khaled Said was murdered by the police outside an internet café in Alexandria, sparking summertime protests. Incidents of sectarian violence put communities across the country on edge. Above all this loomed the prospect of a leadership transition: President Mubarak was in his eighties, and his son Gamal seemed to be waiting in the wings. Would the regime that had overthrown a monarch in 1952 permit a father-to-son succession? How would the military respond to a president with no experience in the armed forces? If the aging Mubarak were replaced by his much younger son, would political change be delayed for another generation? Few people truly imagined that a mass protest movement would soon topple Mubarak, but decisive events were clearly on the horizon.

The Wafd approached these events as a pale shadow of its former self. The party had never recovered, electorally, from the 1990 boycott—or, ironically, from the new, independent-friendly electoral system that it had long demanded. In 1995, 2000, and 2005, the Wafd won only a handful of seats in parliament. A 2008 wave of the World Values Survey reported that, in a hypothetical election, just 3.8 percent of those surveyed said they would choose the Wafd.[76] In the 2005 elections, the party's five-seat haul was dwarfed by the eighty-eight seats taken by the Muslim Brotherhood: the Wafd was not even close to being the largest opposition bloc in parliament. There were internal struggles as well. Sirag al-Din died in 2000, and his successor, Noman Goumaa, was an unmitigated disaster who nearly split the party in two. An emergency replacement, Mahmud Abaza, had stabilized the situation, but he too proved divisive. In 2010 Abaza was challenged for party leadership by El Sayyid el-Badawy, a wealthy pharmaceutical executive and media magnate. The Wafd touted its internal elections as an example of what democracy could look like in Egypt. The two faced off in a televised debate; voter turnout was high; and when Abaza lost, he conceded and allowed el-Badawy to take over.[77]

But democracy did not seem to be taking root in Egypt. After three decades of multiparty competition, the Emergency Law (reimagined as an antiterrorism law) was still in effect, the NDP and the president still dictated policy, and elections were still unfree and unfair. The future to which the Wafd aspired was not materializing. Thus, in 2010 the interpretive dilemma of co-optation—why keep participating when nothing is changing?—was as pressing as ever.

In April of that year the major opposition parties announced a joint initiative for systemic reform. The so-called Coalition of Egyptian Opposition Parties (CEOP) included the Wafd, Tagammu, the Nasserists, and the new Democratic Front Party (DFP).[78] The Wafd joined the CEOP under Abaza and continued to participate actively under el-Badawy. The coalition launched a campaign against Egypt's Emergency Law, which severely restricts civil liberties and political organizing.[79] Unsurprisingly, the Emergency Law was renewed anyway on May 11, 2010, prompting a wave of condemnation from the CEOP, which was explicitly concerned that elections under emergency could never meet basic standards of integrity.[80] The Wafd signed on to these initiatives and also pursued its own: in early August, the party released a draft law to strengthen electoral protections. In characteristic Wafd style, the proposal offered detailed technical fixes and promoted a stronger role for the judiciary in election oversight.[81]

As these proposals were successively ignored or dismissed by the regime, talk of an electoral boycott was—as usual—in the air. On August 30 ElBaradei called for a unified boycott, noting that his seven demands for change had not been met. Advocates argued that a full boycott, honored by all political parties and the Muslim Brotherhood, would send a strong signal to the regime and the international community. With the 2012 presidential vote approaching, they argued that the opposition needed to take a stand on electoral integrity. Yet, despite the Wafd's yearlong insistence that the coming elections could not be free or fair, the party eventually voted to participate in them anyway. Wafdists were divided, as usual: when the GA took up the issue in September, 57 percent of its members voted to participate while 43 percent supported a boycott.[82] Majority ruled, however, and the HEC confirmed the GA's position in October, with twenty-five of thirty members present voting for participation.[83]

Disappointed Allies

The Wafd's decision to run candidates disappointed its (potential) allies within the CEOP and among nonparty movements. Without either the Wafd or the Brotherhood boycotting, the entire enterprise fell apart: Tagammu and the Nasserists ended up running too, leaving the DFP and al-Ghad alone in their boycott. These latter two parties had the support of the NAC and other nonparty movements, but boycotting is an easy decision when one is not actually a political party. The situation thus ended up reinforcing the preexisting split between the "established parties" and "new political forces," sowing frustration and distrust at a moment of potential cooperation.

Criticism from potential allies was swift and clear. As the GA vote was held in September, a small group of protesters (some apparently from ElBaradei's NAC) gathered outside the Wafd's Dokki headquarters to encourage a boycott.[84] Their demands followed a straightforward logic: one was quoted as saying, "Since the government did not approve the [NAC's] seven demands of change, we must boycott the elections." Another proclaimed, "I call on al-Wafd to follow the other opposition groups and parties and boycott the elections. We all know that the poll is nothing but a mess."[85] Such statements are, if nothing else, internally consistent: they recognize that the election will not meet stated demands and therefore must be boycotted. The Wafd had publicly agreed with the first half of the equation—the election would not be free or fair—and now needed to sign on to the second.

When it did not, disappointment prevailed. Osama al-Ghazali Harb was the head of the DFP, which had been left in the lurch by the Wafd's decision to participate. In early October he published a column in the independent *Al-Masry Al-Youm* titled, "Yes, the Wafd Disappointed the Nation." Unlike many outside observers, Harb took the Wafd's potential clout seriously. "Like it or not," he wrote, "the Wafd is the first, most prominent, and oldest embodiment of Egyptian nationalism and Egyptian identity."[86] It "was the most active force in drafting many . . . documents, both as part of the Coalition and on its own." Despite its weakened status, the Wafd still mattered. "What increases the Wafd's responsibility," Harb argued, "is the effect it has on the positions of other political forces." The Brotherhood, for example, had long argued that it would only boycott if all the opposition parties did so as well;[87] as soon as the Wafd broke ranks, the Brotherhood was free to participate. Harb argued that the Wafd's boycott had influenced the Nasserists and Tagammuʿ as well—but, "luckily, the electoral weight of these two parties—just like the electoral weight of the Democratic Front Party— remains limited in comparison to that of the Wafd and the Muslim Brotherhood."[88] Taken only in the present, this statement makes no sense: the Wafd's five parliamentary seats were much closer to Tagammuʿ's two than to the Brotherhood's eighty-eight. But Harb is talking about history here: the Wafd's legacy matters in way that few other parties can replicate, and that is precisely what made its behavior so disappointing. He relates the moment when he learned the Wafd would participate: he was in Washington, DC, at a conference of the Egyptian-American Alliance on political reform. When the news reached the attendees, he recalls, "a surprising state of frustration and disappointment took hold of the room." In deciding not to boycott, the Wafd had "not only denied itself and its history but in fact disappointed the entire Egyptian nation."[89]

An Interpretive Dilemma

Harb describes the Wafd's interpretive dilemma in unsparing terms. The party had been a leader in the CEOP all summer, hosting important conferences and drafting demands for electoral integrity. Indeed, the invitations sent out for the Wafd's August 4 conference on its reform proposal bore the slogan "No elections without guarantees!" And yet, just over a month later, the Wafd had decided to run in elections without guarantees. "We never heard from the NDP or any part of the government," Harb explained, "offering a serious response to the numerous demands put forward by the Egyptian opposition—with the Wafd at its head." He then identifies the disconnect, demanding an explanation: if "the Wafd . . . did not get an honest, serious response from the NDP as to its conditions and guarantees for electoral integrity, then on what basis did its change its position and decide to enter the elections without guarantees?!!"[90]

Harb does not answer his own question, but others were ready to do so. The Wafd's apparent volte-face revived longstanding rumors about secret deals with the NDP. These rumors usually involved the Wafd and the ruling party collaborating at the expense of some other opposition actor (usually the Wafd's longtime frenemy, the Muslim Brotherhood). Early in the year political analyst and regime critic ʿAmmar ʿAli Hassan penned a bombshell report alleging a secret deal to undermine ElBaradei's reform proposal and take seats from the Brotherhood.[91] Hassan's evidence was thin: a supposed phone call from an anonymous Wafdist and several (unpublished) pages of notes from party deliberations.[92] But evidence was beside the point: a secret deal would, by definition, not leave many crumbs in its wake. As is so often true of transactional interpretations, the ṣafqa account was powerful not because it was well supported but because of the work it did. If the Wafd had not received the guarantees it demanded but ran candidates anyway, the party—logically—must have received something else. The ṣafqa rumors persuaded by making sense of the otherwise baffling inconsistency in the Wafd's behavior.

El-Badawy was repeatedly asked about these rumors in news interviews, and he repeatedly denied that any deal had taken place. But rather than offering another interpretation of the Wafd's apparent hypocrisy, he simply refused to see it (at least publicly). In a late September interview, el-Badawy maintained that electoral fairness required major reforms even as he admitted that such reforms would not materialize before the upcoming vote. "There will be no political reform without legal and constitutional reform," he argued but then noted that he "did not expect any constitutional changes, at least, to happen before the People's Council Elections." He claimed that the Wafd had pivoted to focus on "demanding guarantees that will realize the integrity of the elections," but some of these new foci—like the adoption of a PR voting system—would still have required constitutional amendments or major legal changes.[93] Unwilling to recognize these contradictions, the party was in no position to explain them.

A Resort to Romance

By 2010 the Wafd's messaging was in disarray. No subsequent *al-Wafd* editor-in-chief had paired the journalistic chops and party status that made Mustafa Sherdy so influential. Private media had proliferated, damaging party papers' role as alternatives to the government line. There had been rapid turnover at the editorial level, and the paper's web portal had an editorial team separate from that of the physical edition. Adding to the confusion, el-Badawy owned a satellite channel and, briefly, a private newspaper; observers were not sure who was speaking for the Wafd and its president.[94] Indeed, an adviser to el-Badawy told me in 2013 that the party did not have any editorial relationship with the newspaper, whose staff began electing their own editor-in-chief in 2011.[95] It may take a certain level of organizational coherence to maintain a metaphor: Istiqlal managed to do it for more than three decades, but Istiqlal is far better institutionalized than the Wafd. In Wafd sources from the 2010s, there is no sign of an overarching metaphor of any kind.

The trappings of Romance, however, had not faded: Wafd sources returned to the familiar ideas of gradual progress, inevitable hardship, and future vindication. As in the 1980s, the Wafd invoked successes to explain and encourage participation. Although none of the party's summer demands had been met, el-Badawy touted smaller concessions extracted from the regime. When the HEC met in October to take the final vote on participation, he opened the meeting with a list of demands to which NDP *had* acquiesced: voting by national identification card, a promise that the Wafd could broadcast campaign ads on national television, and technical changes to the rules regarding candidate representatives in polling places. One source present at the meeting said that these small victories helped persuade the HEC to vote, twenty-five to five, in favor of participation.[96] When he announced the decision on October 31, el-Badawy took a similar approach, citing the regime's concessions as meaningful advancements achieved by the Wafd on behalf of the people. The party, he claimed, "was able to cancel the certificates of nationality [requirement], which was a hurdle for all candidates. Every candidate now [under the prior system] has to get a certificate confirming that his father and grandfather and so on [were Egyptian]—the matter was really complicated, as though the candidate were going to enroll in a military college or the police academy!"[97] El-Badawy also highlighted the new ID card rule, stressing the NDP's initial reluctance to adopt it. Like the certificate of nationality, the voting card requirement disadvantaged voters and candidates across the political spectrum. Apart from the right to broadcast TV ads, the Wafd's wins were not particularistic: they made the entire process fairer, however slightly.

This behavior complicates the moral criticism inherent in transactional accounts. *Safqa* rumors usually imply that the co-opted party will be guaranteed a certain number of seats in exchange for its participation. Those negotiations, in theory, take place behind closed doors. What, then, are we to make of the fact that the Wafd—by its own public admission—negotiated with the NDP over issues like voter identification and nationality certificates? When concessions won in these negotiations are invoked to justify participation, the whole situation starts to sound like a deal—but a different deal, with different implications. Transactional accounts do sometimes acknowledge that a party might win policy influence (which is not what is happening here), but they overwhelmingly focus on material perks and patronage opportunities. These accounts confirm that, in the end, politics is just self-interested actors exchanging material goods. That is precisely what makes them repulsive to activists and appealing to a certain subset of scholars. Yet for all their focus on secret deals, transactional accounts often fail to see the deals taking place in broad daylight: deals that always fall short of opposition demands, deals made between the essentially powerless and the extremely powerful, deals that involve no solid quid pro quo. Perhaps these are not deals at all but some other category of interaction—and perhaps they are not so central as they seem. The Wafd certainly used its small victories in 2010 as grist for its Romantic discursive mill, but it had other options too. As we saw in 1987, the party could easily fall back on arguments about national duty when no small victories could be found.

Indeed, the Wafd's 2010 political advertisements evoke the same acceptance of defeat that prevailed twenty-three years earlier. In four brief clips, a voice actor intones sing-song, sometimes rhyming lines in Egyptian colloquial Arabic as clip-art-style graphics and keywords move across the screen. In one ad the narrator scolds the viewer for giving up on party politics: "You complain about economic problems, the level of education, health serves, social justice, the unemployment rate, traffic, and the housing crisis, and you never think once about joining a political party and participating in a positive way to change or solve these problems!"[98] Oddly for an election advertisement, the emphasis here is on *joining* a party, not voting for one. "The beginning of the solution," the ad continues, "starts with strengthening other parties so they can really serve you. Want change? Join the Wafd!"[99] The work of change imagined here is slow: what Egypt needs is not a Wafd victory tomorrow (which was impossible anyway) but a stronger party system with more active members. Joining a party is important, but it is also only the "start" of the "beginning" of a longer process. The ad links positivity and participation, echoing Wafdists' warnings against despair and surrender from decades earlier.

Another ad presents political reform as a long, difficult task that will eventually end in victory. It is worth quoting its text in full:

A very simple story
Called belonging
White or black
Win or lose
Either we rule and make change

Or we'll keep trying
And we'll get there [*masirnā hanawṣal*]
If you participate and decide between us
Blue or green?
Or . . .
Or the Wafd!

There may be no war metaphor here, but the imagery of struggle is very much present. When the narrator says, "or we'll keep trying," the image of a stick figure rolling a large ball up a steep hill appears on-screen. Logically, this is probably not a deliberate invocation of Sisyphus since Sisyphus never "gets there"; rather, it seems to be a symbol of effort in pursuit of a goal (see figure 4.1). The Arabic I translate as "we'll get there" is *masirnā hanawṣal*, a colloquial phrase that combines the future aspiration of *in shāʾallāh* with greater certainty and determination.[100] Here, in just a few words, is a summation of Romantic co-optation that could have come from the Wafd or the Istiqlal: "win or lose . . . we'll keep trying and we'll get there."

Such a summation, however, does not make for a particularly persuasive political advertisement. The voter is offered a choice—"decide between us"—but the Wafd sounds almost indifferent to the outcome. The party will continue its work whether it wins or loses; indeed, it implies that it will either win now (unlikely) or win later (certain). The ad does not explain what makes the Wafd superior to its competitors, or even exactly who those competitors are. The "green" could be the Wafd (the party's flag is green); the "blue" may not be a party reference at all, since the color is commonly used to mean "disastrous" or "bad" in Egyptian colloquial. The ad emphasizes Romantic themes of struggle, persistence, and eventual victory, but it does not explain how voters matter to the story—especially if those voters do not share the party's vision of the future. Nor does the ad do much to counter "secret deal" rumors; it acknowledges no contradiction between democratic commitments and electoral participation.

In 2010 the Wafd interpreted its co-optation much as it had for decades. The party focused on a future that was, to many observers, far from guaranteed. Rather than acknowledging and addressing the tension that fueled *ṣafqa* rumors, Wafd leaders simply refused to see it: from their future-oriented perspective, there was no contradiction. Viewed in the present

FIGURE 4.1 "Or we'll keep trying," Wafd campaign ad, 2010.
Source: "'ilanat al-wafd al-intikhabiyya," November 6, 2010, https://www.youtube.com
/watch?v=Tij8gVnH3Ls.

by voters, potential allies, and scholars, however, the Wafd's hypocrisy
demanded explanation—and transactional accounts were, as always, read-
ily available.

*   *   *

Over the last two chapters, I have explored how co-optation damages the co-
opted. I have argued that co-optation lays a sinister discursive trap: the
same narratives that facilitate participation also cause serious credibility
problems for co-opted parties. As parties' credibility disintegrates, they
become unappealing allies and, eventually, political afterthoughts. Part 2
therefore answers half of my original question—how does co-optation damage the co-opted?—but the other half still remains: how do co-opted parties survive? Many organizations would collapse entirely under the reputational, electoral, and organizational losses that Istiqlal and the Wafd have
suffered. Yet, decades after co-optation, both parties still exist; the Wafd has

even outlived the regime that initially co-opted it. Both recruit new members, run electoral campaigns, and hold party conferences. On occasion, both reassert a surprising relevance to national politics, intervening decisively in moments of political crisis. How can we make sense of their resilience— and their latent potential for confrontational action?

In part 3 I answer these questions by delving into the complex relationship between parties and families. While some of my conclusions are rooted in "actual" family connections among party members, my true focus is again on the power of metaphor: the idea of party *as* family. The Wafd and the Istiqlal used Romantic metaphors to narrate their co-optation to everyone, both inside and outside the party. Familial metaphors, by contrast, are more often invoked in internal discussions and conflicts. In both cases, as we shall see, metaphor structures behavior, facilitating some courses of action while making others difficult to imagine, let alone pursue.

PART THREE

Life Goes On

How Co-opted Opposition Survives

FIVE

Party-as-Family

ISOLATED FROM ALLIES and dismissed as hypocritical has-beens, the Wafd and the Istiqlal have been severely weakened by co-optation. They will never win power in ways that would allow them to implement their platforms or become robust patronage machines. Authoritarianism creates recruitment problems: without the chance of implementing policy, handing out benefits, or upturning the system, these parties have little to offer potential members. And yet, in cities and towns across both countries, Istiqlalis and Wafdists make sure that party pamphlets go to print, banners are hung in public spaces, and historical milestones are commemorated. They participate in internal elections, organize the party's candidate lists, and draft platforms. The work of members is critical to party survival, especially in electoral lean times. To ask how the Wafd and the Istiqlal have managed to survive co-optation is thus to ask not how they win votes but how they recruit and keep members.

It is surprising, then, that we do not have many theories to explain why people join nonruling parties in authoritarian regimes. We could extrapolate from theories of voting that material inducements or *wasta* motivate membership, but while party leaders may enjoy some perks, I found little evidence of those benefits trickling down to ordinary cadres—even if votes are being bought.[1] As one high-ranking Istiqlal official put it, "elections in Morocco are about money. But politics isn't just about elections."[2] Moreover, voting and membership are distinct activities: membership is more time-consuming, more public, and therefore easier to punish. Opposition party membership is thankless at best, but it can be dangerous at worst. Even if transactional models can explain voting, the decision to join parties remains a puzzling choice.

The theories of membership we do have suggest that extreme programmatic commitments are a key motivating factor. Drawing on Institutional Revolutionary Party–era Mexico, Kenneth Greene argues that people are opportunists: they join political parties to access power, perks, or patronage opportunities. In authoritarian regimes, citizens' opportunism is best served by a ruling or palace party, which can offer more benefits more credibly than its out-of-power opponents.[3] Thus, the only people willing to forgo these benefits are those who hold ideological commitments sufficiently extreme that the loss of benefits is outweighed by the expressive payoffs of opposition party activism.[4]

Although Greene's account is commendable for its attentiveness to party membership, it provides little insight into the Wafd or the Istiqlal. Politics in the Middle East—perhaps more so than in other world regions—are not at all unidimensional, and opposition parties are not always less "centrist" (even on economic issues) than regimes or palace parties. Indeed, the Arab Barometer, unlike the Latinobarómetro upon which Greene bases this part of his argument, does not even ask questions about left–right political orientation.[5] In Egypt and Morocco, the premise that nonruling parties will be more ideologically extreme than their ruling counterparts is almost nonsensical. Moreover, the Wafd and the Istiqlal are explicitly *nationalist* parties— that is, subscribers to widely shared ideologies of sovereignty and nationhood. Indeed, these parties—more so than the regimes they oppose—played a key role in inventing the nationalist tropes they now express. Nationalism is the shared bedrock of nearly all political groupings in both countries (with the possible exception of some Islamists); it is not at all a niche ideology. How, then, can we explain why these co-opted parties continue to attract members?

In this chapter, I trace member recruitment and retention—and therefore organizational survival—back to the idea of the party as a fictive family. This ideological phenomenon has literal roots: both parties are shot through with real ties of blood and marriage (themselves, of course, socio-ideological constructions more than biological realities). Party-as-family goes further, however. Even members who are not related to one another discursively figure party interactions as familial—and act accordingly. As I will show, overlap between family and party supports opposition survival in several ways. When repression intensifies or party popularity wanes, organizational politics can retreat into the space of the family, borrowing its events and spaces and adopting its norms, expectations, and practices. These ideologies of family then suffuse into party life, facilitating recruitment and impeding fragmentation.

In making this argument, I aim to complicate standard critiques of patrimonialism. While few observers would dispute my claim that family connections are a key feature of the Wafd and the Istiqlal, most read that fact as an unmitigated negative: "patrimonialism" is a source of dysfunctionality and a cause of opposition failure (not to mention unjust, unequal, and undemocratic). These critiques are especially common—and, given histories of Orientalism, perhaps especially pernicious—in Southwest Asia and North Africa (SWANA), where patrimonial culture is theorized to lie behind all manner of political ills. What these critiques miss, I argue, is the range of political work that patrimonial arrangements can do. If we cannot resist some moralism on the topic, we should at least recognize that patrimonialism may promote "desirable" outcomes (like opposition survival) as well.

The chapter proceeds in five parts. First, I trace how scholars have cast patrimonialism as a negative feature of SWANA political life. Second, I outline the "literal" family connections that underlie fictive kinship in the Wafd and the Istiqlal. In the third section, I turn to my main argument, offering three ways in which party-as-family helps the co-opted survive. I draw on the Wafd's quarter-century ban (1952–1984) to show how party politics can take refuge in family spaces during periods of repression. Fourth, I then turn to the Istiqlal to illustrate how generational transmission of membership supports recruitment even when a party's programmatic offerings are unappealing and its chances of victory slim. In the fifth and final section, I use examples from both parties to demonstrate how "familial connectivity" deters fragmentation by encouraging dissatisfied members to prioritize voice and ultimately loyalty over exit.[6]

Throughout this chapter and the next, attentive readers will recognize clear differences between the Wafd and the Istiqlal. Whereas Istiqlal has been almost completely immune to splits and defections since 1959, the Wafd has been a frequent victim of both. Each party has survived, but Istiqlal has unquestionably fared better. I suggest that the ideology of party-as-family less thoroughly saturates Wafdist life, for identifiable reasons.[7] The Wafd lacks the infrastructure of affiliate organizations that bring Istiqlalis in as children and support party-as-family. Even if Wafd leaders had tried to build such infrastructure, Egypt's more restrictive organizational laws would have made it impossible. The Wafd should thus be seen as a weaker version of party-as-family. Nevertheless, as the examples of internal contestation at the end of the chapter illustrate, Wafdists still act in ways that suggest party-as-family is at work.

Conventional Critiques of Patrimonialism

The critique of family-based forms of political organization has distinguished social-scientific roots. Max Weber made the original distinction between "patrimonial" and "rational-legal" administrative forms, which he considered to be two of a number of "structures of domination," or modes of exercising control that rested on subjects' compliance with norms.[8] For Weber, rational-legal domination is indicated by the presence of "fixed and official jurisdictional areas, which are generally ordered by rules."[9] A separation between official duties and private life ensures that "public monies and equipment are divorced from private property."[10]

In patrimonial organizations, by contrast, the rule of rules gives way to the "regulation of all relationships through individual privileges and bestowals of favor," constrained only by traditional precedents—including norms prescribing the roles and responsibilities of various family members.[11] Members, selected for their dependence on or loyalty to an individual leader, are often awarded duties in a haphazard rather than meritocratic way;[12] leaders retain the ability to intervene at will in organizational functions; and the solid distinction between public and private essentially disappears.[13]

Contemporary scholars have adapted Weber's hypotheses to explain the effectiveness of all sorts of organizations, from patrimonial state apparatuses to family businesses.[14] While some have suggested several ways in which patrimonial structures might be salutary, patrimonialism is still overwhelmingly associated with poor performance and dysfunctionality.[15] In

the SWANA region, patrimonialism is an oft-cited cause of opposition failure. Ellen Lust, for example, argues that "the political parties that do exist
[in the region] are more frequently known by their leader than by their party
name or platform," and thus have no policies to offer voters, who end up voting based on candidates' ability to access state patronage.[16] Since ruling or
palace parties will always outperform opposition in that department, patrimonialism locks opposition parties in a losing game. Willis, for his part,
cites patrimonial organization as a key cause of opposition party splits: "The
failure to establish formalized mechanisms of succession has inevitably led
to the build-up of tensions within parties. . . . It has been these frustrations
that have been regularly exploited by the regimes to weaken and control
parties. They are a major factor in explaining the splits and formal scissions
that regularly occur in parties."[17] Patrimonial organization also limits opposition parties' choices when it comes to nominating candidates. Patrimonialism is patriarchal, based on rule by an elder male, and that is precisely
what such parties' leaders tend to be. "If they were really serious about using
elections to connect with people," one prominent Egyptian activist lamented
in 2005 after yet another opposition party nominated its aging male leader
for president, "why not choose a woman, or a Copt, or someone young?"[18]
Local observers also criticize patrimonial parties for acting on family interests rather than national ones. When Istiqlal head Abbas El Fassi formed a
cabinet in 2013, Morocco's lively independent press argued that he "exploited
the mandate he was given by the party's National Council to nominate for
the cabinet a veritable family tree of the families of Fez." El Fassi, the article
continues, "was ultimately loyal to a family council, which serves as the fundamental decision-making body in the party."[19]

Critiques of patrimonialism in the region go beyond claims about opposition failure. For decades scholars argued that that all organizations, from
political parties to businesses to universities, shared a cultural format that
predisposes them to arbitrary rule by an elder male. Hisham Sharabi argues
that "whatever the outward ('modern') forms—material, legal, aesthetic—of
the contemporary neopatriarchal family and society, their internal structures remain rooted in patriarchal values and social relationships of kinship,
clan, and religious and ethnic groups."[20] Although Sharabi's near-essentialism
may have fallen out of favor, more contemporary scholars of "Arab authoritarianism" still use patrimonialism to explain the region's political woes,

from failed uprisings to lost wars.[21] Local norms of kinship, some argue, actually work to stabilize non-democratic rule. As Raymond Hinnebusch puts it, "a kinship culture is especially compatible with the use of clientelism by authoritarian elites as a form of political linkage with the masses."[22] Thus, patrimonialism is widely theorized to lie behind not only opposition party failure but also the entire architecture of authoritarianism in the region.

In what follows, I show that this perspective, while not entirely incorrect, is certainly incomplete. It captures a great deal of the normatively negative work that patrimonialism does but ignores the ways in which family spaces, practices, and norms can counteract authoritarianism's atomizing drive.[23]

Family Connections in the Wafd and the Istiqlal

The Wafd and the Istiqlal began their lives as broad-based movements. Neither was fully comprehensive, of course, but both developed metonymic relationships with anticolonial nationalism that allowed them to recruit members across social, age, and ideological categories. As these broad coalitions have decayed, both parties have come to exhibit striking overlap between party connections and family ones. Party leaders, midlevel functionaries, and ordinary members can routinely recite a family history with the party or list other members to whom they are related. These ties are recursively related to the ideological construction of party-as-family. They inspire it, serving as an initial vehicle for familial norms to enter party life. Yet, as time goes on, expectations that party and family will overlap become self-fulfilling.

Family Ties in the Wafd

Fu'ad Sirag al-Din had to break with his father to join the old Wafd in 1935.[24] Six decades later, firmly entrenched as the party patriarch, with two brothers in prominent roles and his grandson an up-and-coming party heavyweight, it was clear that the Wafd had changed (see figure 5.1 for a family tree of Sirag al-Dins and Badrawis in Wafd leadership). The party had a familial imprint from the moment it was refounded. Its leading organizers, Sirag al-Din and Ibrahim Farag, had been prominent members of the pre-coup

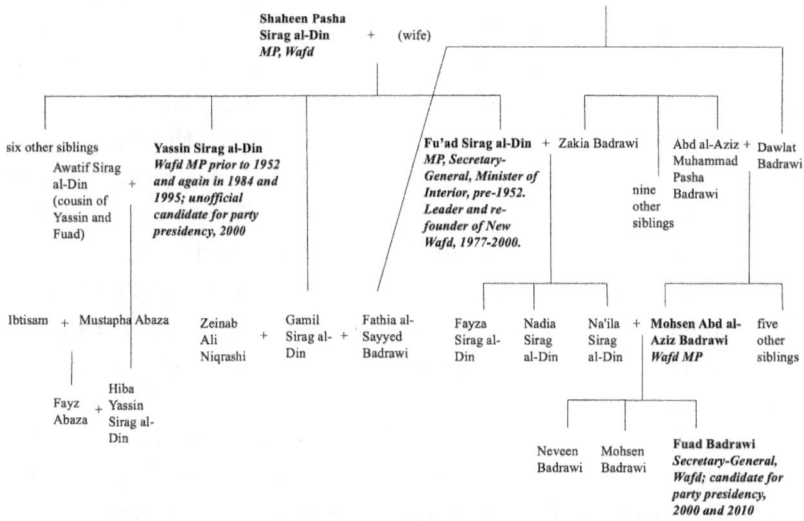

FIGURE 5.1 Family tree of prominent Wafd members.

party, and other old Wafdists—or their descendants, since many old Wafdists were no longer living—were a natural source of support. Thus, the New Wafd came to look like a generational update of the old party. Eric Trager describes the party's high-level cadres in the early 2010s:

> Mounir Fakhry Abdelnour, who served as [one of] the Wafd's secretary-general[s] until February 2011, is the grandson of Fikry Abdelnour, who served as a Wafdist parliamentarian from 1924–1942, and both his uncles were Wafdist leaders during the 1940s; spokesman Mohamed Sherdy's grandfather was on the Port Said governorate's Wafdist High Committee, and his father was a Wafdist MP from 1984 until his death in 1989; honorary chairman Mustafa al-Tawil's father was the Justice Minister in the 1950–1952 Wafdist government; assistant secretary-general Hussein Mansour's grandfather was an associate of Wafdist founder Saad Zaghloul, and served as MP from 1926–1937; High Committee member Mona Korashy's father was Wafdist Senator Ahmed Pasha Korashy, and so on.[25]

The list could go on, and the echoes sometimes have the air of history repeating itself: one of the old Wafd's most prominent Coptic members, Makram Ebeid, was a close associate of Saad Zaghloul but ultimately soured on

Mustafa Nahhas. He left the Wafd in 1942 and published a tell-all account of party corruption, the *Black Book*. His daughter, Mona Makram-Ebeid, has inherited her father's tumultuous relationship with the party: she has joined and left the Wafd no fewer than three times (to date).[26]

The Wafd presidency has not been passed down from father to son (in part because Fu'ad Sirag al-Din had no sons), but successive party heads have had either genealogical connections to the party or extensive clan connections within it. Fuad Badrawi, Sirag al-Din's grandson and the son of Wafd MP Muhsin 'Abd al-Aziz Badrawi, lost the questionably fair 2000 party election to his grandfather's lieutenant, Noman Gomaa, himself the son of a Wafdist and a member of the old Wafd's youth wing, which Gomaa joined in 1948 at the age of fourteen.[27]

Gomaa, of course, proved unpopular; he was replaced in 2005 when Mahmud Abaza, the scion of a powerful Wafd family from Sharqiyya, took up the central party leadership. A massive family popularly considered the largest in Egypt, the Abazas play a major role in political and economic life in Sharqiyya and beyond. While most Abazas are not Wafdists (in fact, they can be found in positions of power and prominence throughout the country), family connections gave Mahmud Abaza control over a formidable bloc of members within the party, according to both supporters and critics.[28] The Wafd has long been critiqued for this exact pattern of behavior: depending on clan loyalty and connections instead of forging programmatic links with the masses. Yunan Labib Rizq, for example, identifies an anti-democratic faction within the Wafd, which he calls the "barons": those Wafdists who had been involved in politics before 1953 and who therefore carried a deep grudge against the July regime that had removed them from power, confiscated their property, and banned them from politics.[29] The barons' "feudal thinking" led them to do their electoral work "through families," more interested in "arousing local *'aṣabiyya*" than in communicating with the masses.[30] Although Rizq is interested primarily in elections, much the same could be said for party membership.

Even family support, however, could not guarantee Abaza a second term as party president. He was defeated by the wealthy pharmaceutical and media magnate El-Sayyid el-Badawy Shehata, the rare Wafd president who either has no family links to the party or chooses not to emphasize them. Throughout his two terms in office, el-Badawy repeatedly faced challenges from Fuad Badrawi or Wafdists claiming to act on his behalf: the Sirag al-Din / Badrawis might have been out of power, but they were never far from the party spotlight. But Badrawi never succeeded in ousting el-Badawy (indeed, Badrawi ended up removed first from his position and later from the party, as I discuss below).

Term-limited, el-Badawy was succeeded by aging lawyer Bahaa Eldin Abu Shoka in 2018. Abu Shoka's selection is widely understood as a sign of increasing loyalty to the al-Sisi regime (al-Sisi nominated Abu Shoka to the 2015 parliament and Abu Shoka's son Mohammed was the president's campaign spokesman in 2017). Abu Shoka's connections to the regime are undeniable, but he has not parachuted into the Wafd: he comes from a family of lawyers in Asyut with party connections dating back to the colonial era. As Abu Shoka points out, his Wafd member number is 112—meaning that he was one of the first people recruited by Sirag al-Din when the party reemerged in the 1970s.[31]

Here we begin to see how actual kinship transforms into fictive kinship: clearly, Abu Shoka has an interest in playing up his Wafd credentials, especially as he steers the party ever closer to the regime. He takes material that is literally true—he does come from a Wafd-affiliated family, called upon by Sirag al-Din to participate in the party's refounding—and emphasizes it, perhaps as a defense against criticism that he is a regime puppet. In my interviews I often found ordinary members did the same when their positions or circumstances put them at odds with the rest of the party. One aging party activist, frustrated that he has never been placed on an electoral list or been able to leverage his party connections to secure jobs for his children, nevertheless recalled his father and grandfather's loyalty to the Wafd to justify his continued allegiance despite disappointment.[32] Another, much younger activist, who disagreed sharply with el-Badawy's leadership, happily volunteered his young son to serve as the face of the future Wafd at a major party event.[33] As the later parts of the chapter show, the invocation of family in times of tension is no accident.

Family Ties in the Istiqlal

While the Sirag al-Dins and Badrawis will always have the aura of Wafd royalty, their hold on their party pales in comparison to the grip of the al-Fassi family on Istiqlal.[34] Much like the Abaza family in Egypt, the extended al-Fassi clan is widely distributed throughout prominent positions in government, the economy, and media. Some politically active al-Fassis are not part of the Istiqlal at all, although observers often assume that they are.[35] In no other party or body, however, are they more prominent.

Allal al-Fassi began the tradition. One of a handful of early Istiqlal leaders, he became the head of the party after the 1958 split and continued in that position until his death in 1974. In just one example of parallelism between the two parties, al-Fassi's role and replacement bear striking similarities to Fu'ad Sirag al-Din's: in both cases, these were de facto (although not de jure) presidents for life. In both cases, they were succeeded not by immediate family members but by close allies—Noman Gomaa and M'hamed Boucetta, respectively—who were seen as closely linked to authoritarian incumbents. Gomaa's connections to the Mubarak regime are a common topic of party gossip;[36] Boucetta's family is from Marrakesh and rumored to be close to the *makhzen*.[37] And in both cases family members pushed back: when Boucetta stepped down in the chaos surrounding the Alternance in 1998, he was replaced by Abbas El Fassi, Allal al-Fassi's son-in-law, as Istiqlal's new secretary-general (see figure 5.2 for a family tree of prominent al-Fassis in the Istiqlal).

Abbas El Fassi presided over the party during a period of active cabinet participation, and his cabinet picks highlighted the deep family ties within the party's upper echelon. In the 2007 cabinet, these included Yasmina Baddou, daughter of prominent early Istiqlal MP Abderrahmane Baddou; Karim Ghellab, the nephew of *al-'Alam* editor Abdelkrim Ghellab; and Ahmed Tawfik Hjira, brother of Istiqlal mayor Omar Hjira and son of independence activist and Istiqlal Executive Committee (EC) member Abderrahmane Hjira. When Abbas El Fassi negotiated Istiqlal's participation in the 2011 cabinet, the two most prominent portfolios he secured went to close relatives: national education to his brother-in-law, Mohammed Ouafa, and economics and finance to his son-in-law, Nizar Baraka. By virtue of endogamous marriage, Baraka is also Allal al-Fassi's grandson and Ouafa his son-in-law.

Damaged by criticism of these cabinet choices (among other issues), Abbas El Fassi resigned in 2011. Prominent potential replacements included Abdelouahed El Fassi (Allal al-Fassi's son); former tourism minister 'Adil Douiri (son of longtime Istiqlal second-in-command Mohamed Douiri); and even the

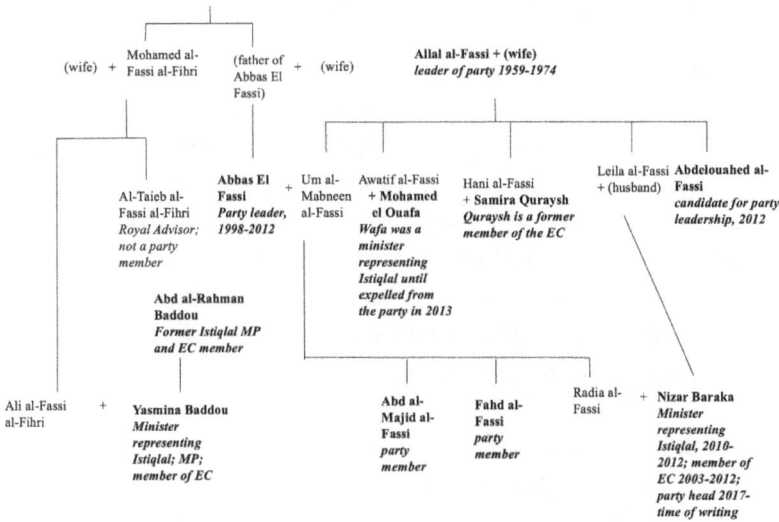

FIGURE 5.2 Family tree of prominent Istiqlal members.

widely disliked but extremely well-connected Nizar Baraka. In the end, however, the successful candidate was a family outsider although very much a
party insider: Hamid Chabat, the longtime Istiqlal mayor of Fez and the head
of the party's affiliated union, the UGTM. Chabat is not an al-Fassi and comes
from a decidedly non-aristocratic background: a welder by trade, he rose up
through the ranks to lead the UGTM. But his deep connections to the city of
Fez allow for a certain elision of "Fassi" (as in, a member of the family) and
"*fāsī*" (as in, from Fez) that permits observers to continue to dismiss Istiqlal
as a vehicle for Fassi/*fāsī* interests.

Chabat's one term in office, however, was only a temporary displace-
ment of al-Fassis from party leadership. He was soundly defeated in 2017
party elections by none other than Nizar Baraka. Baraka's campaign benefited from the support of one of Istiqlal's richest members, southern
"strongman"[38] Hamdi Ould Errachid, a latecomer to the Istiqlal. In an
amusing role reversal, *TelQuel* describes him as "being co-opted" by the
party, but he has lost no time in creating a new Istiqlal family.[39] One son is
a current EC member and another a National Committee member; two
nephews are on the party's intermediate-level Central Committee (one an

ex-MP); and one of his relations by marriage has taken Chabat's position at the head of the UGTM.[40]

Just as in the Wafd, family ties appear among ordinary members as well. The woman who manages the cavernous, overflowing library in the party's Rabat headquarters is the daughter of the previous librarian. Although she is active in Istiqlal's women's organization, she also continues her father's work in the library a few days a week.[41] And, as in the Wafd, children are an essential part of party activities. One key interlocutor in Rabat brought me to party events with his two young sons (their mother is also a party member) in the back seat; the couple who anchors the party's activities in one northern town proudly introduced me to two sons active in the party's youth wing.

Thus, in both parties, a "real" foundation of family ties underlies fictive party kinship. The specific proportion of members who are "actually" related to each other, or the prominence of those members, may fluctuate over time. As Hamid Chabat and El-Sayyid el-Badawy demonstrate, those without extensive family connections can rise to the highest levels of party life. And, in both cases, members could be exaggerating their actual connections to signal loyalty or status. It is not whether these parties are *literally* families that matters to their survival; it is the extent to which they can act as and through families.

Party-as-Family and Opposition Survival

The remainder of this chapter outlines three ways in which party-as-family protects opposition parties under authoritarian conditions. First, family can serve as a secondary party infrastructure: a network of spaces and events ever-so-slightly protected from state repression.[42] Second, parties that expect and facilitate the generational transmission of party membership will continue to attract cadres even when they are losing at the ballot box or advocating unpopular policies. Finally, the norm of familial connectivity, imparted to parties figured as families in specific cultural contexts, works to impede fragmentation and facilitate reconciliation by inducing members to prefer voice and ultimately loyalty to exit.[43]

Family Spaces for Party Politics

As regime restrictions tighten, family offers space into which party politics can retreat, lying dormant (at least from an outside perspective) until conditions improve. Istiqlal has never had to rely on this safety net, but the Wafd has. Banned for a quarter of a century, the Wafd nevertheless managed to maintain enough continuity to return in 1977 as recognizably the same party. Family was critical to this process: by retreating into family conversations, life-cycle events, and literal family homes, the Wafd kept its memory alive until it could reemerge into formal politics.

When Sadat moved to lift the ban on political parties in the mid-1970s, the Wafd was not the kind of loyal opposition he had in mind (as his rapid series of specifically anti-Wafd decrees and repressive actions show). As the last chapter illustrates, the Wafd faced significant challenges as it tried to break into the new system. In that struggle, however, it had allies: 591 founding members, including 20 sitting members of the supposedly loyal parliament, the People's Council. The party's ability to attract these MPs was a political bombshell, but it was not the first time that the banned Wafd had managed to produce an impressive display of support.

Mustafa Nahhas, the old Wafd's second president, died in 1965. Unexpectedly, thousands of Cairenes poured into the streets for the funeral. Nahhas had been under house arrest for more than a decade, banned from participating in politics. The regime had planned to stage-manage his funeral, with a government minister leading the procession. But according to foreign press reports, more than 10,000 Nahhas supporters descended upon the procession, seized the coffin, and conducted an impromptu march to Cairo's al-Hussein mosque before security forces were able to retake the body.[44] Although the moment might have had more to do with Nahhas's personal legacy or generalized dissatisfaction with the regime than with allegiance to the Wafd, it made visible the presence of a latent constituency for some kind of political alternative. The regime, at any rate, knew whom to blame—among those arrested in the aftermath was one of Fu'ad Sirag al-Din's brothers.[45]

When the Wafd began to hold public rallies in the late 1970s, its latent constituency became an active one. In May 1978 Fu'ad Sirag al-Din took the stage at a rally in Alexandria to support a Wafdist candidate in a by-election.

Party sources report a crowd numbering in the hundreds of thousands; although that specific number is probably an exaggeration, the sense of excitement the rally engendered within the party was real. As Farag Fouda, then a leading Wafd intellectual, wrote of the day, "I thought I was dreaming. The square was packed—you couldn't see anything but people!"[46] One scholarly source reports that several hundred thousand Egyptians joined the New Wafd in the 1980s.[47] And in each of its first two elections, the party captured more than 700,000 votes. Wafdists are justified in considering this comeback a "historical miracle."[48] But how was it possible?

Fu'ad Sirag al-Din offered one answer to this question on the evening of August 23, 1977. In a three-and-a-half-hour speech, delivered to a crowd gathered at the Lawyer's Syndicate in Cairo to mark the anniversary of Nahhas' death, Sirag al-Din spoke of his worried opponents:

> Do they imagine that the millions of Wafdists didn't have children? Even our late president [Abdel Nasser], I heard him with my own ears after we laid Nahhas to rest (God have mercy on his soul), he said, "What can we do? We teach them one thing at school and they go home and hear something else from their parents and grandparents." The Wafd is a national heritage, something that children inherit from their parents, and therefore all youth, sooner or later, will know about the Wafd. They will know Mustafa Nahhas, and Saad Zaghloul, and this phenomenon that I've explained to you is the only way to explain the secret that has confused so many people, the secret of the funeral of our eternally remembered leader, Mustafa Nahhas. These hundreds of thousands, maybe a million, most of them were youth. It was youth who were crying; youth who were chanting; youth who were shouting. How did they know Mustafa Nahhas? They hadn't heard him or seen him. They hadn't read his name in the papers. They knew him from what they had heard from their parents, their grandparents, and their relatives.[49]

Sirag al-Din's numbers for Nahhas's funeral are exaggerated. His fundamental point, however, remains sound. Banished from government, public spaces, and newspapers, the story of the Wafd and its principles had somehow made its way to a new generation. Not all the supporters of the New Wafd were, like Sirag al-Din, in their late sixties. As contemporary Wafdists explained to me, it was in family spaces that the party's message was conveyed.

Ahmed, who was a member of the Wafd until the early 2000s, shared his experience of learning about the party as a child in the 1970s.[50] His father, also a member, hosted political meetings in their home. He gave Ahmed a copy of Sirag al-Din's 1977 speech, quoted above, to help the young man better understand the party's cause. Despite no longer belonging to the Wafd, Ahmed described his own parenting as a continuation of his father's. "Wafd families," he told me, "have to teach two things. I teach my son that Gamal Abdel Nasser was bad, but I also teach him what he needs to say in school"— that is, that Abdel Nasser was a revolutionary hero.[51] As Fuad Badrawi put it, in the 1970s, "the Wafd was in every Egyptian home. Even if someone wasn't himself a Wafdist, his grandfather had been."[52] To be sure, not every family connection produced a reliable Wafd member. But its presence in families meant that the Wafd did not need to rely on a newspaper (which, until the mid-1980s, it was forbidden from printing) or on public speeches and rallies (which, until the late 1970s, it was forbidden from holding) to communicate its principles and historical achievements to Egyptians. The party existed within families as a personal, familial memory.

As in a family, the latent connections among Wafdists became visible on the occasion of life-cycle events like weddings, funerals, and birth or death anniversaries. Nahhas's funeral in 1965 was the most dramatic instance of this phenomenon, but it was hardly the only one. Fu'ad Sirag al-Din later explained that during his years of political exile, "the first thing I would do after breakfast is look through *al-Ahram* [Egypt's leading newspaper] to see who has died from the Wafdist families, so I can send condolences, and which of their children have married, so I can send congratulations—all to maintain links between these families."[53] Prominent Wafdists convened around graves as death claimed more and more of their comrades. Writer and party intellectual Farag Fouda recalled one such gathering:

On the anniversary of the leader Mustafa Nahhas' death in 1972, we met at his grave in the morning. It was Mr. Ahmed al-Saqa, Nahhas' former secretary, who was the first one I saw. . . . He repeated the same sentence that I heard every time we met, even if we were meeting daily: "What's going on, professor, have you forgotten us or what?" And my response was the same response as always: "Could I forget you, Mr. Ahmed?" That day he sat next to me, and I found myself saying: "today we are meeting without Lutfi al-Mahersawy, he fell from our ranks this year. And God only knows who here will fall before we meet on the same anniversary next year." The faces of those sitting with us became sad and regretful in remembering Mr. Lutfi, and Mr. Ahmed and I repeated together, "God bless him." Only a month later, one of my friends called to tell me that Mr. Ahmed al-Saqa had died.[54]

The regime could attempt to keep such events orderly, small, and quiet (as they tried to do with Nahhas's funeral). They could detain key members of major Wafdist families, including Fu'ad Sirag al-Din. But banning family gatherings, weddings, funerals, graveyard visits, and social calls would have been a tremendous undertaking, far beyond the capacity or apparent aspiration of the Egyptian state.

Sometimes, family provided literal space for party activities. The party has a long history of relying on family homes as centers of party activity. During the movement's early years, Saad Zaghloul and his wife, Safiyya (nicknamed *umm al-misriyīn*, "the mother of Egyptians"), kept a political home, opening their mansion in the central Cairo neighborhood of Mounira to meetings as well as to citizens in need of help. The house became known as the "home of the nation" (*bayt al-umma*), a name subsequently applied to the museum commemorating Zaghloul's life, to the current Wafd party headquarters, and metonymically to the party itself.

In the postcolonial period, Egyptian political parties and social organizations have always struggled to secure appropriate spaces for their activities. Under the Emergency Law of 1981, public gatherings of more than five people were illegal without a permit, forcing parties to find private spaces for basic organizational functions. But private spaces held their own dangers: rented apartments might be bugged or otherwise surveilled; unsympathetic landlords might make trouble on the regime's orders. One Wafd activist who had worked in the Delta governorate of Mounira, for example, recalled that the Ministry of the Interior had interfered with the party's attempts to rent a flat for its local offices.[55] While the ruling NDP enjoyed the use of a Nile-view building on Tahrir Square and a network of local branches, opposition parties had to scramble to find properties. As one Wafdist in a *shaʿbī* neighborhood lamented to me as we sipped orange soda in his home, "the NDP has 45 regional offices, and I have to meet citizens in coffeeshops!"[56] Indeed, our first meeting had been in the back room of a lobster restaurant.

The Wafd, however, had no need to hold its most important meetings in seafood restaurants. Nasser's land reforms had eroded the agricultural basis of wealthy Wafdists' power: the Sirag al-Dins and Badrawis lost most of their agricultural holdings and many of their financial assets through both generalized land reform and specific sequestration decrees targeting "capitalist reactionaries."[57] Yet Fu'ad Sirag al-Din was able to keep his mansion in Cairo's Garden City neighborhood as a personal residence. When the Wafd was revived in 1977, it had no legal status under which it could rent or purchase space. Press conferences, meetings, and other activities were all run out of the Garden City villa, which was large enough to accommodate big gatherings and impressive enough to lend an imprimatur of seriousness befitting Egypt's former governing party.[58] As Sirag al-Din's niece, Samia Seragaddin, describes in her thinly novelized memoir, "the Cairo house, so long dormant, shook off its cobwebs and came back to life: the great doors were flung open, the ponderous wooden window shades were drawn up on their creaky chains, the chandeliers blazed; the halls and salons teemed with people; the phones rang off the hooks."[59]

The party later moved to a nearby space in Mounira, and then to another glamorous villa in the upscale Dokki neighborhood, where it remains to this day. This "home of the nation" has massive stained-glass windows, thick carpets laid over wooden floors, soaring ceilings, and warrens of offices and meeting rooms. The villa had originally belonged to a Badrawi, and while offhand comments around headquarters implied that it had remained within the family until it was bequeathed to Fu'ad Sirag al-Din, the actual story is more complicated. It was in fact sequestered from the Badrawis after the 1952 coup, becoming state property. In the throes of *infitāh*, it was sold to the Arab Contractors group but soon returned to state control as the offices of the Socialist General Prosecutor. After the massive 1992 earthquake damaged the Wafd's Mounira headquarters, the party rented and then, within two years, purchased the villa.[60] When the Mubarak regime tightened restrictions on public gatherings in the late 1980s, ostensibly to curb Islamist mobilization, "we were lucky," a high-ranking Wafd official told me, "because we had such a large headquarters—the other parties were in apartments!"[61] The fact that the building's story—which is not particularly familial—was colloquially presented as such is yet another illustration of how party-as-family spreads beyond technical realities, becoming a key element of the stories that party members tell about themselves.[62]

Generational Recruitment

The Wafd demonstrates how party can retreat into family when normal political activities become impossible. This can happen suddenly (when a party is banned) or gradually (as co-optative isolation takes hold). When parties find that normal avenues of recruitment are closed, familial pathways to membership assume greater importance. As Istiqlal's electoral star has faded, it is increasingly difficult to explain why young people choose to invest their time and energy in a party popularly associated with corruption, hypocrisy, failure, and irrelevance.

Take the example of Yasmina Baddou. When she joined the cabinet as the Istiqlali minister of health in 2007, Baddou was young (forty at the time), stylish, and charismatic. When I saw her speak in her home constituency of Casablanca in 2015, she easily commanded the auditorium, taking selfies with the audience while other panelists were speaking and attracting louder applause than her higher-status male peers. Baddou had the skill set to excel in another party or affiliate with the *makhzen*; why would a privileged young person hitch her future to the underwhelming Istiqlal?

The story of how Yasmina Baddou came to the party turns out to be an illustrative one. She is the daughter of Abderrahmane Baddou, who was an anticolonial activist and eventually an MP and the head of Istiqlal's

قبلة الوفد القديم على خد الوفد الجديد

FIGURE 5.3 "A Kiss from the Old Wafd on the Cheek of the New Wafd." Party president Fu'ad Sirag al-Din and his grandson, future longtime party second-in-command Fuad Badrawi.
Source: Reprinted from Zuhair Mardini, *Al-ladudan: Al-wafd wal-ikhwan*. Cairo: Dar Iqra,' 1984.

parliamentary delegation in the 1960s. When a reporter asked her how she got into politics, the younger Baddou responded: "I grew up in a political family. My father, Abderrahmane Baddou, was an activist in the Istiqlal, and he was among the first who fought against the colonial regime. He tasted the bitterness of prison for the sake of the country. I lived through that, inside the home and within the party. I was raised within the party's structure and organizations, starting from when I became aware of political action."[63] More than a generation later, young people are still interpellated into the party through familial connections. In an interview with the Moroccan outlet *Hespress*, Hamid Chabat's wife, Fatima Tariq, explained the connection between her early marriage (she was sixteen) and party life:

> We wanted to make an investment in our early marriage to have kids, so that we could free up the future for political, union, and local government work. We wanted the kids to grow up alongside us as friends and participants, because we were aware of the battles waiting for us. Especially Fez—at the time, it was experiencing deliberate marginalization (dating back to the colonial era) and every indicator, from the late 1970s to the late 1980s, suggested that the city was on the verge of an explosion; this atmosphere, especially in the mid-1980s, is what led us to choose the name Nidal ["struggle"] for our youngest boy, because political and union work, and struggle more broadly were and are part of the air we breathe.[64]

Party-as-family is embedded in and encourages the transmission of party identity from parents to children. Members often come to the party through family and are raised within it, supported by in-home socialization, party children's organizations, or both. Successive generations expect party membership to be passed down from parents to children, and party structures emerge to facilitate that transmission—summer camps, children's classes, and scouting organizations, for example. Yet these structures, once built, can attract and socialize children whose parents are not in the party, perhaps especially those from single-parent, marginalized, or disadvantaged households who need the help the party can offer. Far from joining parties because of ideological fit, members who come as children enter the party before their own political preferences are even formed.

Moreover, they often stay despite significant conflicts between their own ideas and the party line.

I asked nearly every party member I spoke to in Morocco and Egypt how they came to join the party. The only person who refused to answer this question was Fuad Badrawi, who made it eminently clear that he did not want to discuss his grandfather, Fu'ad Sirag al-Din, or his family connections to the party—all too aware, perhaps, that this line of questioning usually ends in critique. The others told stories that, more often than not, involved family members (or stand-ins for absent family members) and processes of socialization that sounded nothing like adults with clear programmatic preferences joining the party that best matched those preferences.[65] In what follows, I present a series of oral histories from the Istiqlal Party that illustrate these processes.

When I spoke with him, Omar was a member of Istiqlal's ruling EC and had been a longtime leader within the Shabiba (he only resigned from the latter on account of his advancing age). Omar's father had joined an armed resistance cell linked to Istiqlal before independence and had transitioned into the new Moroccan military after 1956. As a member of the armed forces, he was legally prohibited from political activity and therefore never joined the Istiqlal himself. He did, however, send his children to summer camps and youth activities organized by the party. When I asked Omar how he began his career with the party, I initially thought I had phrased the question poorly. Instead of discussing his Istiqlal origin story, he started to explain the party's own birth in the 1930s. "When Istiqlal emerged," he told me, "it didn't emerge as a political party. It was defending Islam, Morocco, and a set of national values. The Berber *zahir* tried to divide us—I myself happen to be Amazigh, you know—and that was the beginning of the nationalist movement."[66] Before I could clarify what I meant to ask, he continued:

> So Istiqlal was always linked in the beginning to identity and was always about that identity before it was about political work. Its first projects included the free schools, which was a way to get people out of the French educational system. Now there are lots of committees within the Youth League—the Women of the Renaissance [for young female Istiqlalis], the Education and Child-Rearing Committee [which manages summer camps], the School Youth League [for primary and secondary students], the General Union of Students [for university students]. There

are summer camps, all sorts of things. So when we came to the Istiqlal, we came as children.

Omar was describing a sense of identity, not a clientelist calculation or a rational comparison of programmatic commitments. He had come to the Istiqlal as a child, with his siblings, much as one might come to any other hereditary identity community. He noted, however, that his childhood experiences "did not translate automatically into belonging (intimā') to the party." As he got older, read more, and developed his own ideas, Omar explained, he increasingly differed from the Istiqlal party line. As he put it, "my tendencies at the time were to the left—and not just the left, the radical left."[67] Being socialized into an Istiqlal community in his youth did not prevent him from developing opinions that might put him at odds with party leadership.

Nevertheless, he never lost touch with the party's traditions. "The writings of Allal al-Fassi," he told me, "kept me tied to the Istiqlal." Drawing inspiration from the centrist (indeed, supposedly bourgeois) party's foundational texts was, for him, not incompatible with a leftist zeal for change. He joined the General Union of Students, Istiqlal's student syndicate, and took a leadership position in the Shabiba in 1998, the year of the Alternance. He was eventually elected to the EC and became a public face of the party. Istiqlal was an identity to which he returned and which he endeavored to transform, not a fixed platform against which he compared his own fixed positions.

The youth-focused institutions Omar described reached beyond established Istiqlal families. Larbi, an EC member whose parents were not involved with the party, first learned about Istiqlal as a child at summer camp. Growing up in a marginalized sha'bi neighborhood, Larbi had illiterate parents who were not involved in politics. In Istiqlal's camps, he found role models among the party's historical leaders as well as older children who could help him with his homework.[68] Another high-ranking official, Abderrahmane, entered Istiqlal's camps around the age of nine with his elder brother, whom he describes as "essentially the one who raised me."[69] Abderrahmane described how the camps helped him develop better hygiene habits and good nutrition. At thirteen, he joined the national conference of the party's youth wing. As soon as he turned eighteen, he became an official, adult member of his local Istiqlal branch. He has since become a leader in the youth wing, a member of Parliament, and a member of the EC. Abderrahmane—much like his political ally, Hamid Chabat—takes pride in having reached these positions *without* being the son of an Istiqlali. But even he does not describe his interpellation as a rational decision: "The factors that lead to belonging to the party aren't necessarily intellectual [*fikriyya*]. I found myself in the Istiqlal [*laqayt nafsi fil-istiqlal*]; I didn't have the opportunity to choose between Istiqlal and another party. Of course, my daughter is eleven, and she tells me that she wants to join the PAM [a palace-affiliated party]. I told her that when she's eighteen, it's up to her."[70] This may initially sound like a rejection of nepotism and party-as-family coming from a man who rose to the EC without the advantage of an Istiqlal lineage. But, as Abderrahmane knows, by age eighteen many young people have already formed a deep and highly resilient affiliation with the party. Even if his daughter does eventually join the PAM, she may one day find herself returning to her Istiqlali roots.

Familial Connectivity and Resistance to Fragmentation

There is no me, there is just us, my friend!

—HANDMADE POSTER, LOCAL WAFD BRANCH,
QASR AL-SAYYID [PSEUD.], CAIRO

In this final section I argue that a familial norm—connectivity—has come to characterize party life in the Wafd and the Istiqlal. Familial connectivity means that members are committed to changing the party rather than abandoning it and thus prioritize voice and loyalty over exit when they disagree with party leadership. Intraparty fronts, movements, and factions form to push for programmatic change or oust unpopular leaders, but these conflicts only rarely lead to major splits. When members do leave, it is usually because they have been expelled—and even then, reconciliations are common.

Two scenes related to the Wafd Committee in the *sha'bī* Cairo neighborhood of Qasr al-Sayyid illustrate how dissatisfied Wafdists often bind themselves more closely to the party rather than deserting it. Run out of a multiroom flat in a busy working-class neighborhood, the Qasr al-Sayyid branch was founded by a group of younger activists in 2010. Frustrated with the existing committee's lack of outreach or engagement, these activists launched their own Wafd branch. As one Qasr al-Sayyid activist told me, "They were only on paper, and we were in the streets."[71] Another told me that she was actually from Giza, but had come to work in Qasr al-Sayyid because there were no on-the-ground activities in Giza (ironically, the home of the party's national headquarters).[72] When I spoke with several of them in the branch office, their dissatisfaction with then-party president El-Sayyid el-Badawy was palpable.

And yet, that very same month, I watched as one Qasr al-Sayyid Wafdist, Ashraf, brought his young son to a high-ceilinged hall in the once-upscale neighborhood of Mohandiseen. Several Wafd leaders had gathered to speak in support of the new proposed constitution, due to be put to a referendum several days later. After all five speakers railed against international meddling in Egypt's affairs (how meddling related to the constitution was unclear), Ashraf ushered his son up to the podium. The boy, with his father standing supportively behind him, read out a simple statement about the rights accorded to children in the new constitution. Upon finishing, he crossed the podium and kissed the party's second-in-command, Fuad Badrawi, on the cheek. Ashraf's son was acting out his father's party loyalties.

Parties steeped in familial norms are internally diverse. Generational transmission creates parties defined not by programmatic agreement but by the accident of birth. Members of both parties commonly reference (indeed, idealize) this diversity. Fuad Badrawi recalls attending a meeting of the Wafd's High Committee in the 1980s at which the socialist Muhammad Anis was seated next to Salah Abu Ismail, a committed Islamist. "This," Badrawi recalls thinking, "is the Wafd!"[73] One young female Istiqlali explained that she was drawn to the party's diversity and its live-and-let-live attitude. Although her father had been an Istiqlal member, Rabia had joined the socialist USFP in her teens. "I wore a veil from the time I was very young," she told me, "and in the USFP they always used to make fun of me, to call me *ikhwanjiyya* [a derogatory term for a follower of the Muslim Brotherhood]. But when I came to the Istiqlal, I found it was a microcosm of society. When there's a break at a party meeting, some people go to the mosque to pray, and some people step out for a cigarette. There is freedom and diversity—it's like a miniature Morocco."[74]

And yet the manifest dissatisfaction of Qasr al-Sayyid activists did not lead them to abandon the party or start a new one. Instead they deliberately chose to out-Wafd the Wafd, so to speak, by launching a new party branch office in their neighborhood. Rather than withdrawing because he disagreed with el-Badawy, Ashraf leaned in, asserting his and his family's centrality to the party's future.

A resistance to division is a real asset for opposition parties under authoritarianism. Egyptian and Moroccan regimes have a track record of deliberately inducing schisms to paralyze threatening opposition parties. In Morocco, the king's interest in splintering the nationalist coalition after independence has been noted by scholars from John Waterbury onward.[75] Lust and Amaney Jamal, for example, argue that monarchical regimes tend to encourage party proliferation, cementing the monarch's image as a neutral arbiter.[76] Although they suggest that dominant-party regimes will, by contrast, endeavor to limit the number of political parties, Lust argues elsewhere that regimes may legalize new parties if they are similar in platform or social constituency to existing ones—an attempt to divide voters' allegiances.[77] Numerous observers have pointed to party splits and leadership disputes as phenomena that regimes encourage (if not create out of whole cloth) to sideline, discredit, or weaken opposition.[78]

Istiqlal in particular has resisted this trend. There was, of course, the major schism of 1959, which gave birth to the UNFP (later the USFP). But in the sixty years since, Istiqlal has seen no mass defections and no new spinoffs, despite the fact that barriers to party formation in Morocco are low by authoritarian standards. The Wafd has not been so lucky. It witnessed a wave of defections in 1984–1985, prompted by Sirag al-Din's ill-fated electoral alliance with the Muslim Brotherhood, and was stricken by internal disputes during Noman Gomaa's disastrous party presidency, which ended in violent clashes at the Dokki mansion in late 2005. Before he himself was thrown out of the party, Gomaa managed to alienate and then expel the Wafd's most prominent youth leader, Ayman Nour. Nour went on to found a new party, al-Ghad, and to finish ahead of Gomaa in the country's first (and deeply unfair) multicandidate presidential election.

At first glance, therefore, it may seem improbable to suggest that the same processes lie behind party unity in the schism-proof Istiqlal and the fracture-prone Wafd. The argument I make here primarily accounts for Istiqlal's unusual cohesion, but it also explains specific patterns of contestation, loyalty, expulsion, and reconciliation that characterize internal politics in both parties. The phenomenon to be explained here is thus not so much a single outcome as a process:[79] the process by which disputes emerge and are managed. I argue that familial connectivity facilitates an understanding of party and self that discourages splits and supports unity. When the party is analogized to the family, and the family constructed as an inalienable extension of self, abandoning the party becomes nearly unthinkable—as strange a proposition as abandoning oneself.

The term *familial connectivity* comes from anthropological studies of the SWANA region. In her study of family relationships in Beirut's urban quarters, the anthropologist Suad Joseph describes a phenomenon that she calls, following Catherine Keller, "connectivity": "relationships in which a person's boundaries are relatively fluid so that persons feel a part of significant others."[80] Connectivity is indicated and reinforced by simple practices like referring to parents as "father of" or "mother of" their eldest child, or by parents addressing their children as "mother" or "father."[81] It also manifests as extensive engagement with family members' life choices and a strong sense that the choices of close relatives impact one's own status and well-being. "Connectivity," Joseph writes, means "that persons expected intimate others to read each others' minds, answer for each other, anticipate each others' needs, [and] shape their likes and dislikes in accordance with each other. They saw intimate others as extensions of each other."[82]

Joseph argues that these dynamics are not unique to Beirut or Lebanon but are widespread throughout the Arab world and, as Marcia Inhorn puts it, "in most cultures in which individuation, autonomy, and separation are not valued or supported."[83] Many of the daily practices Joseph describes are common in Moroccan and Egyptian families, suggesting that similar norms of connectivity may be at work. In Egyptian Arabic, for example, when furious or disappointed parents sever their connection with a child, they might declare, "I am innocent of you!" (*anā mutabariʿ minak*)—the implication being that until family ties are severed, family members are presumed to be morally accountable for one another.

Familial connectivity, however, does not mean that relationships are free of conflict or disagreement. "Connective relationships," Joseph observes, "could be loving or hostile, compatible or competitive, fragile or firm, or simultaneously each of the above."[84] In combination, connectivity and hierarchical patriarchy (including, crucially, the rule of elder over younger generations) "underwrote the crafting of relationally oriented selves," which explains "why families had such a powerful hold on their members."[85] Although she does not explicitly say so—perhaps because the possibility is made so remote by precisely the conditions she describes—Joseph's argument implies that leaving one's family is an almost unthinkable proposition. One may disagree with one's family or have a hostile relationship with siblings, parents, or children, but the family remains an extension of oneself: if other members are doing something objectionable, they should be steered in another direction rather than abandoned (if abandonment were even imaginable). It is this dynamic, the impulse to reform rather than to leave, to exercise voice (and, in the end, loyalty) rather than exit, that is imparted to party life in the Wafd and the Istiqlal.

Interviews with Istiqlal members suggest a strong disinclination to leave the party, or even to work outside it—a disinclination that is repeatedly framed in familial terms (whether metaphorical or actual). When asked what explained the party's unusual unity, one member of Parliament—herself the daughter of one Istiqlali and the wife of another—said that "the first thing we learn in the party is that differences are acceptable but discipline is a duty. . . . We don't have political relations within the party, we have family relations."[86] Even youth leaders, who have historically been critical of main party leadership, echoed this sentiment: "In the youth wing," one told me, "we took many positions counter to that of the leadership, but always with a ceiling: the unity of the party."[87] This meant conforming to a clearly age-based patriarchal structure: the youth wing, although growing in strength and influence, was always ultimately subject to the will of the EC, which was made up of older members. Although they may have been deeply frustrated with major party decisions in the late 1990s and early 2000s, many of these youth activists remained committed to reforming the Istiqlal.

Sometimes the merging of family and party is literal. Hamid Chabat, for example, comes from a family of Istiqlal activists dating back to the colonial era. In 1959 Chabat's uncle Hassan decided to leave with the splinter UNFP. He was confronted by Chabat's father, who asked him to change his family name if he insisted on abandoning the Istiqlal. Hassan did, becoming Hassan Tariq.[88] Thus, Hamid Chabat's wife, Fatima Tariq, is in fact his cousin and originally a Chabat, their different family names a reminder of Istiqlal's one major split. "We met as cousins in a family," Fatima Tariq explained, "but our larger family was always the party."[89]

Dissident currents within Istiqlal need not be housed in preexisting institutions like the Shabiba. Often, unhappy party members will launch intraparty movements to advance their positions. In the aftermath of Istiqlal's hotly contested 2012 leadership election, losing candidate Abdelouahed El Fassi organized his supporters under the slogan "No mercy in the defense of principles!" That slogan, shortened to "No mercy!" (*la hawāda*), was taken from a famous speech given by Abdelouahed El Fassi's father, Allal al-Fassi, in Casablanca in 1962. At that time, as hopes for a robust parliamentary system faded and a weakened Istiqlal faced a consolidating monarchy, Allal al-Fassi promised his supporters that the party would continue its fight to liberate the country from "foreign capitalists" and lingering colonial powers, rejecting the claims and actions of the "splittists" who had broken away to form the UNFP.[90] Fifty years later, Abdelouahed El Fassi similarly rejected splittism, launching a highly critical media and legal campaign against his opponent, Hamid Chabat, but refusing to leave the party or launch a new one. He and twenty-one of his followers were expelled from the National Council by Chabat, ostensibly on the grounds that they had violated an obscure procedural rule relating to meeting attendance, but they remained active members of the party.[91] Indeed, *la hawāda* remained a recognized faction in Istiqlal's internal politics even years later.[92]

Recently, Istiqlal's immunity to splits has faced a significant test. Already riven by the conflict between supporters of Chabat and those aligned with the al-Fassi old guard, the party was mired in debates over cabinet participation after the 2016 elections. When I asked whether these sharp divisions—which were ultimately about the party's position vis-à-vis the monarchy and therefore about the entire political system—might lead to a split, party members immediately dismissed the idea. Indeed, after explaining the rancor and stakes of the dispute in great detail, they often seemed surprised that I would think such a conflict could cause a schism. I asked Rabia, the young, veiled activist mentioned earlier in the chapter, why not. She relayed to me a version of the judgment of Solomon (in the Islamic tradition, the wise king is Daoud) that she had heard circulating among members of the EC:

> Do you know the story of the two women fighting over a baby? Each one says that it is her child, so they take their dispute to the king. And the king says, if you two cannot decide, we'll simply divide the baby in two. And then the mother of the baby says, "no, give it to the other woman." Because the real mother would

rather see someone else raise her child than allow the child to be harmed, right? That's how we feel about the Istiqlal.

In the unlikely event that splits do occur, party-as-family under conditions of patriarchal familial connectivity means that they tend to manifest as expulsions rather than resignations. These parties are not just spaces of familial connectivity; they are also patriarchal, meaning that older men often have disproportionate control over the lives of young people and women. That control can manifest as the right to disown, or to threaten to disown, wayward children. This pattern, visible in the expulsion of Abdel-ouahed El Fassi from Istiqlal's National Committee, can also be seen in the Wafd. Ayman Nour, the most famous recent Wafd defector, was in fact expelled (along with many others) by Noman Gomaa in 2001.[93] But there are other examples as well.

In 2014 Fuad Badrawi (grandson of Fu'ad Sirag al-Din) lost a bitterly con-tested election for the Wafd presidency to El-Sayyid el-Badawi. Badrawi stood on the grounds of his great-grandfather's Dokki mansion on the night of the election, announcing that he would resign from his post as party secretary but remain a member of the Wafd's High Committee, to cries of "Long live the Wafd!" and "One hand!" (a common chant for unity after 2011) from the crowd.[94] In the following weeks, however, he became increasingly critical, asking for an inquiry into voting procedures and publicly musing about the need for a "front for party reform."[95] On June 24, 2014, he was expelled from the party by the High Committee, which declared that he had "taken actions that threatened the very being [kayān] of the party."[96] In September 2014, however, the High Committee met to approve Badrawi's return to the Wafd. El-Badawy was reported to have told Badrawi during that meeting that "my weak spot when it comes to you is that you are Fu'ad Sirag al-Din's grandson"[97]—just one example of the way in which claims of kinship work to mediate conflictual relationships and provide a language for reconcilia-tion without costing (too much) face.

It is not only high-ranking Wafdists or direct descendants of party lead-ers who demonstrate a reluctance to abandon the party and a propensity to push for reform within it. Few recent events better demonstrate this pat-tern than the tale of the "Wafd Liberation Front" (jabhat taḥrīr al-wafd), which emerged in late 2014. Despite the Wafd's participation in the 2011 uprising, the party has since become—on the surface—a docile supporter of retrenching authoritarianism. The Wafd backed coup leader Abdel Fattah al-Sisi in his bid for president, joined the pro-Sisi "For the Love of Egypt" parliamentary list, and supported Sisi's 2014 constitutional reforms. More importantly for internal party politics, the Wafd has seen an influx of what longer-term members call "opportunists" (intihāziyīn): individuals who see in the Wafd an opportunity to get elected.[98] Some of these new members have unsettlingly close ties to the former regime, whether to the military/security apparatus or, more gallingly to many Wafdists, the former ruling NDP.[99]

In mid-December 2014, a thirty-one-year party veteran, Tariq Abu Rish, started a sit-in in the Wafd's branch office in Damanhour, the capital of the Delta governorate of Buhaira. Wrapped in heavy blankets against the winter chill, Abu Rish and several others slept on cots in the small office, protesting the presence of both former NDP members and what they called "members of Muslim Brotherhood sleeper cells" within the Wafd leadership in Buhaira. They demanded the appointment of an interim party committee for the governorate and the removal of all former NDP members from the Wafd's electoral lists.[100] The sit-in participants decorated the office walls with pictures and names of former NDP members now claiming to be Wafdists (one was an Abaza), prompting the Buhaira Wafd secretary-general to bring a legal case against them for slander.[101] The supposed "sleeper cell" members were not named—while hostility to and paranoia about the Brotherhood are common within the contemporary Wafd, the addition of the MB to their list of complaints seemed more like a preemptive defense against critics than a reflection of an actual problem within the party. Surrounded by handmade posters reading "The Wafd for Wafdists!," Abu Rish, asked if he would abandon the party, responded simply: "We will not allow the home of the nation [bayt al-umma] to become a hiding place for previous regimes."[102]

News of Abu Rish's action quickly spread beyond Buhaira. One Wafd member turned his two-thousand-member Facebook group, "The Wafd Party—Generation after Generation," into a forum for members to post incriminating information about former NDP members or updates on Abu Rish's fragile health, including his blood pressure and blood sugar levels. Sympathizers began to refer to themselves as the Wafd Liberation Front, writing press releases, speaking to the media, and organizing solidarity protests. Several prominent Wafdists, including former MP and current High Committee member Ashraf Abu al-'Aynayn, voiced their support for Abu Rish and the Wafd Liberation Front.[103] Fuad Badrawi was silent in public, although the

Wafd Liberation Front bore some resemblance to the "front for party reform" for which he had called earlier in the year.

Demonstrating the extent to which familial ideas suffuse internal Wafd politics, the discussion surrounding the Wafd Liberation Front quickly took on familial tones. One reporter asked Abu Rish about claims that he had actually approved an NDP entrant in his capacity as head of the Damanhour party committee. Abu Rish replied, "this is a slander designed to invalidate and cast doubt on the Wafdist credentials [wafdiat] of the sons [abna'] of Fu'ad Sirag al-Din and exclude them from the party. We see all the sons of Fu'ad Sirag al-Din expelled from the party, and we don't know why."[104] Several features of this statement are worth noting. First, Abu Rish clearly differed from Wafd leadership and was willing to risk his health to oppose them. Indeed, his primary concern is that he will be expelled from the party against his will. Instead of resigning in protest, he literally refused to leave the Wafd, camping out on its premises until his demands were recognized. Second, the use of kinship vocabulary here is metaphorical, not literal. Abu Rish is clearly referring to Fuad Badrawi's expulsion several months earlier, but he also seems to be indexing a wider category of "sons," both because "sons" is plural and because Fu'ad Sirag al-Din had no sons (only daughters). Abu Rish also seems to be identifying himself as one of these sons—alongside a recently expelled (from the High Committee) and slightly more literal (grand)son, Fuad Badrawi.

In keeping with patterns of familial connectivity, the central Wafd's response to the Wafd Liberation Front was indeed expulsions. The High Committee met on December 26, 2014, to consider the situation. They expelled Abu Rish and three other participants in the sit-in from the party and suspended the membership of two High Committee members who had supported them.[105] Abu Rish ended his sit-in, and the expected elections were postponed. But opposition to el-Badawy—and now to Abu Shoka—has not ceased.[106] The Wafd may be less thoroughly saturated with the ideology of party-as-family, but internal contestation still follows a connective, voice-first pattern.

*   *   *

As a microcosm of the dynamics explored in this chapter, consider the image of a young child holding a sign at a Wafd rally in al-Ghar (figure 5.4).

This is a child being socialized as a partisan in party disputes and as a member with a voice in the future direction of the Wafd, even though the adults who supplied him with the sign clearly disagree with the party leadership—indeed, disagree so starkly that they are willing to use the Arab Spring demand, *irḥal*, to articulate their dissatisfaction. Moreover, as the banner in the back illustrates, this act of simultaneous belonging and defiance takes place in a space marked—and potentially defended—by ʿaṣabiyya: it is the Raslan family welcoming the Wafd to their territory, not the other way around.

It is easy to dismiss party-as-family as rank patriarchy, just as it is easy to dismiss patrimonialism as an outdated, unequal, and ineffective mode of political organization that must disappear if the region is to move toward a less dismal political future. The blanket condemnation of all blurred

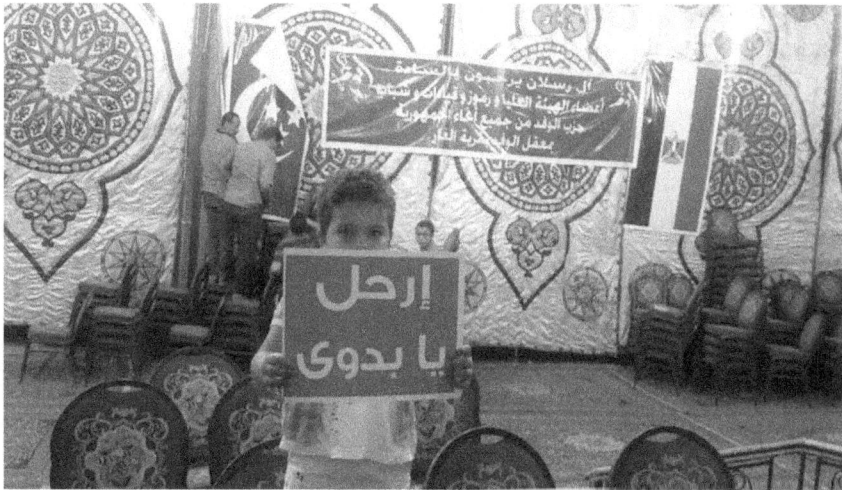

FIGURE 5.4 Child at a Wafd rally, 2015. A child holds a sign protesting Wafd leader al-Sayyid al-Bedawy Shehata before a Wafd rally. Echoing the claim "*irḥal!*" ("Get out!") used against Hosni Mubarak during the 2011 uprising, the child's sign reads, "Get out Bedawy!" The banner in the background reads, "The Raslan family welcomes the members of the High Committee and figures and leaders and youth of the Wafd Party from all parts of the Republic to the Wafd stronghold in the village of al-Ghar." Al-Ghar is in Sharqeyya Province, where two major Wafd families—the Raslans and the Abazas—are strong. May 1, 2015.
Photo credit: Hany Raslan.

boundaries between public and private, however, ignores how party-as-family—that is, the political use of familial norms, spaces, and practices—can act as a bulwark against the threat authoritarianism poses to pluralism and contestation. The Wafd and the Istiqlal are not analysts' ideal opposition parties; indeed, they are not many Wafdists' or Istiqlalis' ideal opposition parties. But they have survived decades of co-optation, and that is no small feat. Moreover, as the next chapter shows, they retain the capacity to shift into more direct opposition—precisely *because* of their familial nature.

SIX

Generation After Generation

Making Sense of Confrontational Turns

THE WAFD AND the Istiqlal are tenacious survivors, but they do more than simply persist. Co-opted parties vacillate between conciliation and confrontation; between obedience and defiance; between reformism and revolution. Their most surprising shifts are what I call confrontational turns: defiant actions that follow periods of relative docility. Defiance might take the form of an electoral boycott, an illegal protest, or a cabinet withdrawal—any refusal to continue formal politics as usual. When co-opted parties make such moves, they often leave significant benefits on the table: parliamentary seats not won, legal perks no longer enjoyed, rentier or influential opportunities not seized. Confrontational turns thus confound transactional theories of co-optation and require us to look beyond benefits for other drivers of party behavior.

Traditionally, scholars have sought to explain confrontational turns by focusing on external influences: perhaps the regime became more repressive (or less so); perhaps something changed in the country's political opportunity structure that rendered defiance less costly. Such approaches, however, pay insufficient attention to parties' internal dynamics. Co-opted parties may look stable from the outside, but—as demonstrated in the previous chapter—contestation simmers just below the surface. Generational recruitment and familial connectivity produce diverse parties bound together by norms that disincentivize exit, so unhappy factions press for change from the inside rather than leaving the party. This chapter explores one particular kind of intraparty contestation: the emergence of distinct generational cohorts. Brought into party life through familial recruitment but shaped by their political times, these cohorts can lean confrontational or conciliatory, depending on their histories. When a party's internal balance of power shifts (whether because of a sudden leadership vacuum, a coalitional realignment, or the simple passage of time), new cohorts can find themselves in positions of authority—and party policy can change rapidly.

By focusing on the role of generational cohorts, I complicate existing tendencies to associate confrontational politics with young activists. Both local and international observers often link confrontational turns to youth, pointing to the influence of youth wings and young militants in pressing for more defiant positions. Such analyses are consonant with broader social scientific arguments about young people's proclivity for defiance, disruption, and refusal. These accounts are not entirely incorrect: people in their teens and twenties were indeed associated with the confrontational turns I discuss here. They are incomplete, however. Party-as-family lays critical groundwork for youth militancy, for example: without generational recruitment or familial connectivity, these parties would not have young members at all—they would either never be recruited or would leave when party leaders disappointed them. Thus, the processes described in chapter 5 are essential conditions of possibility for defiant youth contingents.

In this chapter, however, I focus on another way in which youth-focused analyses fall short: the people most responsible for confrontational turns are often not youth at all. As I will show in the Istiqlal case, the "youth" in question are often employed parents in their thirties and forties, not students or recent graduates in their teens and twenties. Observers often paper over this reality, noting that in the Arab-majority world it is normal to consider people young until forty or forty-five, especially compared to political elites who routinely exercise power into their eighties or nineties. It is certainly the case that people in their early forties are often passed off (by regimes and by other organizations) as youth; whether they are accepted or perceived as such by others is another question. But regardless of the age range that counts as "young" in any particular cultural context, the activists I discuss here lack the sociological characteristics—leisure time, little to lose, few responsibilities, a predisposition toward fun—that supposedly make young people revolutionary in the first place.[1]

I therefore offer two amendments to the conventional wisdom on youth politics. The first is that what matters most to party behavior is not the power of young activists at any particular moment but the balance of power among distinct generational cohorts. Drawing on the work of Karl Mannheim, I argue that these cohorts are shaped by the political experiences of their formative years, which endow them with worldviews that persist long after they cease to be young. Confrontational cohorts prefer defiance not because they are currently young but because they were young at particular historical moments and interacted with those moments in particular ways.

Second, I suggest that youth must be understood not just as a literal descriptor but as a powerful metaphorical frame. All sorts of party actors, including both leaders and their critics, invoke youth and youthfulness when describing intraparty conflict, even when the people involved are not "actually" young. The language of youth invokes (deliberately or otherwise) familial and generational norms that work to naturalize dissent and protect pluralism. As such, youth talk is a critical part of the ideological infrastructure that allows internally diverse parties to survive.

This chapter's primary empirical focus is the Istiqlal Party and, in particular, one of its recent confrontational turns: a 2013 cabinet withdrawal in which the party openly defied the king's preference that they remain within the government. I trace the history of the generational cohort that advocated withdrawal: the "1990s generation," which came of age during one of Morocco's most turbulent political eras. In many ways, Istiqlal is an ideal case in which to study generational dynamics. Its youth wing, the Shabiba, is well organized and well documented; its members were open to ethnographic observation and oral history interviews. Regrettably, I cannot provide a similar account for the Wafd. The Wafd's "youth wing" is more a diffuse presence than a clearly delineated institution, making it much more difficult to trace the emergence and impact of distinct cohorts. More importantly, my research in Egypt became politically impossible before I had gathered the kind of data that inform my analysis of the Istiqlal.

That said, here as elsewhere the parallels between the two parties are striking. The Wafd's most recent confrontational turn (in 2010–2011) was also backed by activists who both presented themselves and were described by others as youth, in a context of persistent intraparty contestation. I therefore include a separate discussion of the Wafd toward the end of the chapter, focusing on its 2010 electoral boycott and 2011 protest participation. This discussion is limited in its detail; it aims to suggest the plausibility of my argument beyond the Istiqlal, not exhaustively document what occurred within the Wafd. My discussion of the metaphorical power of youth, however, is equally applicable to both parties.

A Surprising Turn: Istiqlal's Cabinet Withdrawal, 2013

Existing accounts predict that co-opted parties will become confrontational only when benefits lessen or cease. How, then, are we to make sense of situations in which co-opted parties leave benefits on the table, choosing a confrontational position over the apparent perks of incorporation? In this section I consider one such move in Istiqlal's recent past: the party's withdrawal from the cabinet in 2013. Istiqlal had been studiously nonconfrontational during Morocco's 2011 Arab Spring protests, disavowing demonstrations and agreeing to join the opposition unity cabinet that resulted from the hastily arranged 2011 parliamentary elections. By 2013, however, the party not only chose to leave the cabinet but did so in defiance of the king's clear preference that they stay. Cabinet seats are perhaps the clearest real-life equivalent to the benefits transactional theories imagine: ministerial positions bring with them not only a measure of influential authority but, presumably, at least some opportunities for rent-seeking. For a party to give up six of them is thus an a priori puzzling development.

Istiqlal's confrontational turn was preceded by a period of seeming docility vis-à-vis the regime. Indeed, in early 2011, many Moroccans saw no meaningful distinction between the party and the system itself. As protests swept across North Africa, Istiqlal found itself a central target of demonstrators' ire. Party leader Abbas El Fassi was prime minister, and his government came in for a great deal of criticism from what came to be called the February 20th Movement. El Fassi had made his share of errors and unpopular decisions, but he was also a softer target than the king himself, who cannot legally be criticized: calling for El Fassi to "go away" (irḥal) was a safe way to express dissatisfaction with the status quo. Despite the party's precarious position, some individual members did participate in the protests, including Muhammad al-Zahari, then president of Istiqlal's human rights affiliate. Others expressed solidarity with the movement's concerns. As

Istiqlal spokesman Adil Benhamza put it at a public event in 2014, "as far as diagnosing the problem is concerned, there's no controversy [between the February 20th Movement and Istiqlal's youth wing, the Shabiba]. But the issue of the political regime is not among our priorities."[2] Yet the party as a whole, trapped in part by El Fassi's premiership, refused to condone the protests, instead defending itself and El Fassi against demonstrators' critiques.

In response to the unrest, the king moved the scheduled 2012 parliamentary elections up to November 2011. The Islamist PJD—the only major opposition party that had not previously led a government—made its strongest showing ever, easily winning a plurality with 107 seats to Istiqlal's 60.[3] The new constitution required the king to choose a prime minister from the first-place party, so PJD head Abdelilah Benkirane was entrusted with forming a cabinet at a time of considerable upheaval. At 34 members—6 of them Istiqlalis—the expansive new cabinet announced in January 2012 echoed the Alternance government of fifteen years earlier. The king had brought the only major opposition party not marred by prior government experience (then the USFP, now the PJD) into "power," linking opposition to government as a way of guaranteeing the system's survival. The opposition parties, in 2011 as in 1998, fell in line, joining a cabinet too internally diverse and too powerless to achieve any significant policy results—and refusing to open up a divide between the parties and the regime that protesters could exploit.

Abbas El Fassi negotiated Istiqlal's cabinet position, but his term as party leader was up in 2012. As usual, a Fassi ran to replace him: in this case, Abdelouahed El Fassi, son of Allal and nephew of Abbas himself. But Abdelouahed El Fassi faced a surprising and formidable opponent: Hamid Chabat, a welder by trade who had come up through the ranks of Istiqlal's affiliate union, the UGTM. Chabat, long known for his combative style, won the election—and almost immediately found himself in conflict with the PJD's similarly feisty Benkirane. Chabat offered boilerplate critiques of Benkirane's administration and his relationship with the cabinet. By early 2013 Istiqlal was raising the possibility that it might withdraw as a protest against Benkirane's leadership.[4] Indeed, Istiqlal's withdrawal is often narrated as a conflict between two cantankerous party bosses: a clash of personalities, nothing more. What happened as soon as Chabat announced the withdrawal, however, highlights the moment's deeper implications.

Chabat released a statement on May 11, 2013, announcing that Istiqlal's six cabinet ministers would resign. That night the king reached out to Istiqlal leaders, requesting a dialogue about the matter. On May 12 the party sent a memo to the monarch detailing eighteen reasons for their withdrawal.[5] By May 13, however, the decision had been put on hold as discussions continued. As political analyst Ahmad al-Bouz pointed out, for the king to publicly involve himself in this kind of a situation was unprecedented: monarchs often mediated conflicts between government and opposition, but to openly play referee for two opposition parties in the same cabinet was unusual.[6] In its historical context, however, the king's involvement makes sense. Much was at stake: if Istiqlal left the ruling coalition, the PJD would lose its majority. If it could not cobble together a new coalition, new elections might be needed. And with no untarnished major opposition parties left to receive protest votes, the second Alternance could founder. As al-Bouz put it, when it came to withdrawal, "we are not talking about the matter of a majority. We're talking about the status of political stability in the country."[7] As processes of political change turned violent elsewhere in the region, the new government and constitution were critical to Morocco's self-proclaimed exceptionalism. When the machinery of formal politics most needed to be running smoothly, Chabat's withdrawal was, in the words of one Moroccan interlocutor, "a stick in the wheels" ('aṣā fī al-rawīda).[8]

Chabat, however, would not budge. On June 27, as continued maneuvering seemed to be taking place behind the scenes, he was characteristically blunt in his public statements: "the king does not decide our status."[9] Five of the six Istiqlal ministers finally resigned on June 30; the one who refused to do so, al-Fassi relative Mohammed Ouafa, was expelled from the party. Chabat's initial frustration may have been with Benkirane, but in the end the party also sent another message: by publicly rebuffing the king at a sensitive time, Istiqlal intimated that its support for the regime was not absolute. Thus, Istiqlal presents us with a classic case of the confrontational turn: a shift from a relatively docile stance vis-à-vis the regime to a more defiant one. How should we make sense of this change?

Youth and the Politics of Confrontation

The proximate cause of Istiqlal's withdrawal was Chabat's ascension to power. Chabat's rise, in turn, was supported and facilitated by the party's youth wing. He won the secretary-generalship by an extremely narrow margin: just twenty votes out of nearly one thousand. Shabiba leaders were his closest allies, figuring prominently among new members elected to the Executive Committee at the same conference, and Shabiba votes helped him edge out Abdelouahed El Fassi. Youth activists worked with Chabat to turn ideas that El Fassi might never have considered into party policy; according to Istiqlal's spokesman, "the first discussion of withdrawing from the cabinet took place in the Shabiba."[10] Without the youth wing, there would be no Chabat secretary-generalship—and no cabinet withdrawal.

Tracing militant or revolutionary behavior back to youth is, of course, a common move in recent studies of Southwest Asia and North Africa and the contentious politics literature more broadly. In media and scholarship from the early years of the Arab Spring, youth figured as a major force behind the uprisings.[11] Demographic arguments explained the timing of the uprisings by pointing to the region's "youth bulge."[12] Media scholars also focused on the role of the internet—enthusiastically adopted by young people—in facilitating mobilization.[13] And many activists, from the April 6 Youth Movement to teenage football "ultras," explicitly described themselves as young and as representatives of young people's grievances and aspirations. In (supposedly) leading the Arab uprisings, youth lived up to their social scientific reputation as disruptors. Asef Bayat, for example, argues that young people are predisposed to a disruptive "politics of fun" that reshapes seemingly apolitical spaces into political ones.[14] And Samuel Huntington famously argued that young people's sociological characteristics (free time, little to lose, a university education) make them "everywhere the protagonists of protests, instability, reform, and revolution."[15]

But in Istiqlal's case, the tidy narrative of young people pushing for change raises more questions than it answers. Why would co-opted and largely neutralized parties have youth members at all, let alone youth members so dedicated to the party that they will work to change its positions rather than join organizations that better fit their political preferences? Rates of party membership are abysmally low in Morocco and Egypt, and it is not clear why young people would want to affiliate themselves with stuffy, gerontocratic holdover parties. Party-as-family, however, serves as a safety net: generational transmission of party membership brings new people into co-opted parties even when traditional avenues of recruitment have closed. Moreover, familial connectivity makes exit difficult; dissatisfied young members work to change the party rather than abandoning it. Without these processes, it is unlikely that co-opted parties would have militant youth factions at all.

One important question remains, however: what are we to make of the fact that the "youth" cited as relevant to confrontational turns are often not actually young? As I show in subsequent sections, the label "youth" is often applied to parents in their forties with jobs—that is, people who share none of the sociological characteristics that supposedly predispose youth to confrontational politics. We cannot take the term *youth* at face value. Youth wings may include activists in their forties or even fifties, especially in leadership positions. Thus, those identified as youth because of their institutional affiliations are often not youth at all. I argue that it is not their current age that predisposes some activists to confrontational positions, but their own experiences when they were young, even if that was decades ago. The key actors in generational party dramas are not youth per se but specific generational cohorts. Youth still matters—following Karl Mannheim, I find that cohorts are shaped by the experiences of their formative years (especially their teens and twenties)—but not because young people are always politically defiant or organizationally influential. In the section that follows, I illustrate the analytical usefulness of this approach through the experiences of the people who brought Hamid Chabat to power. Although widely glossed as "youth" because of their membership in Istiqlal's youth organization, the Shabiba, these people had been in their teens and twenties during the 1990s—a particularly turbulent time in Moroccan politics.

Generational Cohorts

In his classic work on generations, Karl Mannheim explores how historical events interact with the "biological rhythm of human existence" to produce discrete "generational locations."[16] We are born, grow older, and die—and as we do, we experience historical moments in different ways. For the old, even dramatic changes can only be layered on top of prior experiences. But for the young, "formative forces are just coming into being, and basic attitudes in the process of development can take advantage of the molding process of new situations."[17] Although different young people may internalize new situations in different ways, the effects are lasting: "Even if the rest of one's life consisted in one long process of negation and destruction of the natural worldview acquired in youth, the determining influence of these early impressions would still be predominant." Mannheim is clear, however, that generational location is not deterministic. It "only contains potentialities, which may materialize or be suppressed";[18] and, of course, not every individual responds to formative pressures in the same way. Generational locations can produce multiple cohorts, or no cohorts at all. Mannheim suggests that it is under conditions of rapid change that distinct cohorts are likely to form precisely because their differences with other generational locations will be sharper.[19]

The question Mannheim leads us to ask about party members is not whether they are currently young, but when they were young and what was happening at that time. Authoritarian politics often alternate between moments of contestation and periods of repressed quiescence; knowing when a particular group of party members came of age helps us understand what kinds of politics will seem normal, natural, or acceptable to them. Will they be comfortable with more confrontational tactics? Will they be willing to discuss the nature of the political regime? Or will those practices and discussions seem like dangerous departures from the norm? To illustrate the lasting role of youthful experiences in co-opted party politics, I trace the trajectories of two individuals who helped bring Hamid Chabat to power. One, Abdelkader El Kihel, I will name (I am here drawing only on publicly available information about his life). The other I will call Brahim.

At the time of Chabat's election, neither of these men was a wild-eyed university student with extra time on his hands. El Kihel, born in 1971, was forty-one years old and a parent with a Ph.D. in criminology and a long history of work in both elected office and the state bureaucracy.[20] When he became head of the Shabiba in 2010, he had replaced Abdellah Bakkali, who was then fifty-three years old. The Shabiba now has a rule that members must leave the group at age forty, but historically age limits have been flexible. Brahim was only slightly younger, at thirty-seven, and was also married and a parent, having finished several graduate degrees. They were leaders in the Shabiba, but they were not themselves particularly young.

When Brahim and El Kihel *were* young in the conventional sense— teenagers and young adults—Moroccan politics looked quite different. Both men came of age in the 1990s, the most politically turbulent decade in Morocco's postcolonial history. King Hassan II was dying; the national economy, racked by austerity measures, was floundering. These simultaneous crises precipitated eight years of rough-and-tumble conflicts over the shape of the country's political system. The shocks began in late 1990, when a massive general strike kicked off riots that left an unknown number of people dead and hundreds more arrested. Many of the arrests, injuries, and deaths were among the labor community in Fez, leaving a lasting mark on the milieu from which Hamid Chabat emerged.[21] Over the next eight years, the country witnessed two parliamentary elections, two major constitutional reforms, two referenda on those reforms, and the historic Alternance government. Activism of all kinds spiked as intellectuals and ordinary people asked increasingly far-reaching questions about the overall shape of the political system. With a royal succession clearly on the horizon, the role of the monarchy—indeed, its very continuation—was no longer part of the political "taken-for-granted."[22]

El Kihel and Brahim had come into the party circle as children, incorporated by Istiqlal's youth organizations. Their Istiqlal socialization, however, did not prevent them from also being socialized as members of a broader generation of Moroccan youth. Across the country young people faced new choices and challenges: Hamid Chabat's three eldest sons, for example, had to flee to Casablanca, completing a year of school there—away from their mother and younger siblings—to escape the repressive aftermath of the December 14 strike in Fes.[23] Both El Kihel and Brahim were intimately involved in the upheaval. For the slightly older El Kihel, 1990 was a critical year. In support of the general strike, many students were boycotting classes and exams. At the time, El Kihel was the head of Istiqlal's school students' association in Salé. He chose to join the strikers, at significant personal cost: dropping out of school meant that he would not earn the *bac* certification he needed to enter a university. Barely twenty, El Kihel had already risked his future in the struggle for political change. His politics and the price he paid for them (he eventually had to seek a degree in Libya) did not affect his continued allegiance to the Istiqlal. In 1992 he became the head of the Shabiba in Salé and from there continued to move up the party ranks.

Brahim experienced some tension between his Istiqlal upbringing and the promise and potential of the 1990s. He explained that his time in children's and youth organizations "did not translate automatically into belonging (*intimā'*) to the party."[24] As he became a young man, read more, and saw what was going on around him, he told me, he increasingly differed from Istiqlal's official line (the party backed the 1990 strike and rejected the 1992 constitutional reforms, but it became more conciliatory as the decade wore on). As he put it, "my tendencies at the time were to the left—and not just the left, the radical left." The radical left, in the 1990s, were openly calling for a complete rethinking of the king's role. Although Brahim, who graduated from high school in 1995, drifted away from the party during this time, he never stopped thinking about it. "The writings of Allal al-Fassi," he told me, "kept me tied to the Istiqlal." Drawing inspiration from a committed monarchist who advocated taking the best from various systems of government was not, for Brahim, incompatible with a radical leftist politics.[25]

Thus El Kihel and Brahim were products of their time, influenced by ideas and styles of activism that became normal in the unusual historical crucible of the 1990s. Although both were involved with Istiqlal from childhood, that allegiance did not prevent them from taking to the streets and thinking past red lines with their generational peers. Moreover, because Istiqlal did not require programmatic conformity, they were never forced to choose between their activism and their party. As Hannah Arendt reminds us, the "human condition of natality"—in Mannheim's terms, the fact that new generations are forever being born—continually introduces the radically new into politics.[26] The generational transmission of party membership does not mean that children are carbon copies of their parents. They are new beings who, by interacting with the historical developments of their formative periods, introduce new ideas and practices into party life. That ever-changing but permanent influx of novelty is what makes Istiqlal and the Wafd prone to dramatic shifts: new constituencies for change are constantly emerging as generations emerge and senesce. And as changing circumstances interact with young members' formative years, new constellations of political commitments are continuously introduced into the parties.

The youth of the 1990s reshaped the Shabiba. Brahim told me that in earlier decades, the Shabiba had been little more than "a party accessory" (malḥaqa ḥizbiyya). It was a temporary warehouse for young people: the party relied on the Shabiba to "hand out fliers," set out chairs, and otherwise help at party events. As the 1990s generation rose to power within the Shabiba, the organization began to exercise a more independent political voice. Brahim, for example, saw the Shabiba as the "conscience of the party. It really doesn't have any outside pressures [i.e., to win elections or make deals with other parties], so it can be pure and maintain the ideas and the convictions of the party." Over the twenty-one years he was a part of the organization, it went from being "a youth wing that follows the party to a youth wing that makes decisions in the party." Under the influence of the 1990s generation, the Shabiba became a space in which radical ideas could be accommodated, regardless of their bearers' literal age. As 1990s teenagers transitioned into adulthood, they continued to use the Shabiba as an arena for some of the party's most far-reaching conversations.

In December 2014 I attended a Shabiba event in Salé that showcased the organization's role as a home for the edges of the Istiqlali political spectrum. The gathering's ostensible purpose was to elect delegates to the national Shabiba conference later that month, but the program also included a great deal of ceremony: renditions of national, party, youth, and scouting anthems; young women dressed in caftans modeled after the red-and-green Moroccan flag and the pink-and-white Istiqlal logo; Quran recitation; and honored guests. One of these guests was Muhammad al-Zahari, then the head of Istiqlal's human rights affiliate, al-ʿAṣba al-maghribiyya lil-difāʿ ʿan ḥuqūq al-insān (known by its French acronym, LMDDH).[27] Himself a product of the Shabiba and a member of the same generational cohort as El Kihel and Brahim, al-Zahari has long been out ahead of the party on rights issues. As one member of the EC told me, "he was among the people who went out with the February 20 Movement and called for the fall of the regime [isqāṭ al-niẓām]."[28] The language of bringing down the regime—with its implicit critique of monarchy—was in direct contradiction to Istiqlal's official policy.

The LMDDH had recently decided to boycott a major human rights conference taking place under the regime's aegis in Marrakesh. The conference was an international event—the Casablanca airport was decked out with signs welcoming participants to Morocco—and boycotts by domestic groups threatened to mar the regime's image. Shortly after the LMDDH announced the boycott, al-Zahari's son Yacine was arrested in a café by police, who claimed he had been carrying drugs. The arrest was widely interpreted as a shoddy attempt to discredit and threaten the young man's father in retribution for the boycott. This kind of targeting, especially of activists' children, is not a common experience for contemporary Istiqlal activists; indeed, it fed an emerging suspicion that King Mohammed VI was returning to the harsh security practices more commonly associated with his father.

Toward the end of the gathering, al-Zaharis père and fils ascended the dais. I was seated on the main floor of the stadium. The actual shabāb—that is, the teenagers—were largely relegated to the stands; those seated around me included much older members of the main party, older Shabiba activists, and observers. As al-Zahari was presented, some of the people around me stood to cheer him, making the three-fingered salute of Istiqlal's scouting association or otherwise voicing their solidarity. Others sat firmly in their seats. At the time, I did not yet know who al-Zahari was or what was at stake: all I noticed was clear disagreement. Some Istiqlalis were comfortable supporting a man who had taken to the streets with protesters targeting Istiqlal's own leader, then–prime minister Abbas El Fassi. Others were not, even if his son had been subjected to unfair treatment by police.

This incident highlights three important points. First, the Shabiba of the mid-2010s was not solely or primarily a space for people in their teens and twenties (like Yacine al-Zahari). Instead, it was led and shaped by activists in their forties—people old enough to have teenage children themselves. Second, in keeping with their own formative experiences, these activists accepted within the Shabiba a wider range of positions—especially regarding the nature of the regime—than could be easily accommodated or promoted by the main party. Third, as I argue next, in doing so they benefited from the ideological consequences of marking a space as youthful.

Youth as Metaphor

The invocation of youth as model, constituency, and identity permeates intraparty conflict; youth wings, whether organized or not, are discursively constructed as spaces in which contestation, zeal, and refusal live. Dissenters are described as youth (*shabāb*)—or, when that becomes completely untenable, their status as sons or daughters (*abna*ʾ) is used to invoke their generational position instead of their chronological age. Activists identify themselves as young or as acting on behalf of the young. And leaders use youth rhetoric to explain intraparty contestation to both internal and external audiences. More is going on here than literal description.

The language of youth evokes an entire familial imaginary that naturalizes pluralism and change without denying the tensions they cause. The cultural contexts in which the Wafd and the Istiqlal operate (along with many others) share the idea that young people are often hot-headed, impatient, rebellious, and inclined to chafe against the choices of their elders. These

commonsense ideas underlie Huntington's belief in youth as perpetual rev-
olutionaries and Bayat's connection between youth and the disruptive politics of fun. Youthful rebellion is a stage to be expected and survived, just
like teething or puberty. Questioning authority as one moves from childhood
to adulthood may not be socially encouraged, but it is socially understood.
Having a rebellious teenager at home does not make one a bad parent; it
evokes sympathy from other parents who have struggled with children in
the same phase.

The idea that youth rebellion is natural—and therefore less threatening
because it is experienced, grown out of, and then repeated by a subsequent
generation—is what gives it political power. Most families, after all, experience some tension among their constituent generations. Such tension does
not threaten the family so much as constitute it: family is the unity that
holds despite inequalities of power and differences in generational location.
By presenting dissent or demands for change in youthful terms, party members can render their complaints less threatening. Youthful calls for change
are to be expected; they are not a sign that party discipline is collapsing or
that time is out of joint. When a dissenter claims to be a young person, to be
acting on behalf of young people, or to be the "son" of a prior party leader,
they dissent within the bounds of party-as-family.

Indeed, party leaders often invoke youth when justifying confrontational
stances to outside audiences (namely, potentially repressive regimes). It is
no accident that both the Wafd and the Muslim Brotherhood initially
announced their participation in the January 25 uprising as happening
through or being motivated by their respective youth. By making these
(questionably accurate) claims, leaders toss up their hands, pleading for the
sympathy of a paternalistic regime: *What can we do with these hot-headed young
people? No matter what we give them, they are never grateful and always want more!
Perhaps one day they will realize their errors and thank us.*

Moreover, for someone to class a dissenting position as that of youth is to
suggest that it may be a good approach—just not at the present moment.
Youth are, of course, not permanently young; as the rise of the 1990s generation within Istiqlal has made clear, even the rowdiest and most radical
young people eventually become elders. In time, they will confront their
own dissident *shabāb*, imparting a sense of balance to internal conflicts. If
natality ensures that the new will always be introduced into party life, mor-
tality guarantees that the new will eventually become old—and die. Fu'ad

Sirag al-Din and Allal al-Fassi may have been party presidents for life, but even they could not be anything more than that. Death and generational progression provide a literal-metaphorical language for transition that naturalizes defeat as part of life, either because it is not yet one's turn or because all things come to an end. Hamid Chabat, knowing that he was about to lose the 2017 internal election, told the press, "it's natural that Chabat should die, but the Istiqlal Party will not."[29] Critics dismissed these comments as literal, wondering why Chabat was raving about imagined assassination attempts. He may have been. But he was also, intentionally or unintentionally, giving voice to the rhythm of change in parties-as-families: youthful upstarts become elder statesmen and then departed legends.

Youth rhetoric can thus assuage all manner of internal tensions. When winners in a party conflict depict their opponents as youth, they play the role of wise elders, tolerating youthful dissent but reining in its excesses. When losers claim youth, they remind the winners that they are the future, and that no control is permanent. And when the winners self-identify as youth, they minimize shame by reminding the losers that generational handovers are a natural, expected part of family life.

If they are to survive, parties like the Wafd and the Istiqlal need ideologies that can handle internal diversity, intense conflict, and rapid shifts of position without calling into question the existence or continuity of the party. Few ideologies of the explicitly programmatic kind (i.e., communism, Nasserism, Islamism) can do that. A commitment to procedural democracy might be one, and these parties have come in for their fair share of criticism for not adopting a more explicitly democratic internal structure. Such critics, however, have overlooked the fact that party-as-family can do some of the same ideological work. Familial norms can of course also work to repress, suppress, and coerce in all societies. But they are not one-way streets: they can be invoked to defend dissent, carve out space for pluralism, and advocate for change. Party-as-family has surprising pluralistic potential— potential that may yet be only partially realized in the Wafd and the Istiqlal.

Youth and Confrontation in the Wafd, 2010–2011

Having laid out my arguments with reference to the Istiqlal experience, I now consider their plausibility for the Wafd. Although available data are limited, the Wafd does exhibit similar patterns: confrontational turns reflect intraparty contestation and are steeped in youth rhetoric. Without better data, I can say little about whether generational dynamics are at work. The following discussion aims to identify how the Wafd's experience of a recent confrontational turn, poorly explained with reference to external influences, rhymes with that of the Istiqlal.

The Wafd and the Egyptian Revolution

Nearly every parliamentary election in the Wafd's postcolonial history has been preceded by an internal debate about a boycott. The boycott camp prevailed once, in 1990, but otherwise participation has always won out—despite the constant reality of electoral fraud, an uneven playing field, and voter intimidation. The party repeatedly complained about these violations but, when election time came around again, dutifully participated in yet another rigged game.

At first the fall 2010 parliamentary elections seemed like a continuation of this longtime pattern. Despite actively debating a potential boycott (and a series of alliances with other political forces, including the Muslim Brotherhood), the Wafd decided to participate on its own. When the first-round results came in, however, the party rapidly shifted position, pulling out of the election in protest over regime manipulation. As discussed in chapter 2, a purely transactional account cannot explain this behavior: in the first round alone, the Wafd had won six seats, one more than their previous overall total. While the Brotherhood was clearly being shut out of power, from a Wafd perspective little had changed. The election was not over: by withdrawing, the Wafd left potentially winnable seats on the table.[30]

Just as the Wafd's electoral boycott is puzzling from a transactional standpoint, so too is its subsequent participation in the January 2011 uprising. Lust's theory of co-optation suggests that in divided structures of contestation (such as late-Mubarak Egypt), incorporated opposition groups will not participate in contentious protest if they expect that illegal groups will join in. Afraid to risk the benefits they enjoy as legal opponents, parties like the Wafd will stay on the sidelines.[31] Yet in this case, the Wafd looked at a whole host of illegal and a-legal groups planning to protest—the April 6th Youth,

Kefaya, We Are All Khaled Said, the Muslim Brotherhood—and joined in anyway.

Just over a month after the belated boycott, the Wafd announced that it would participate in protests planned for January 25, 2011. Although the party was by no means an initiator of the movement, it did send representatives into the streets on the uprising's first day. By doing so, the Wafd preceded most of its incorporated party peers. The other two long-standing co-opted parties, Tagammuʿ (the leftist *minbar*) and the Nasserists (a socialist challenger party), declined to participate entirely. Tagammuʿ claimed that it could not participate out of respect for Police Day, the national holiday activists had deliberately chosen to call attention to police brutality. The Nasserists dodged the entire question, simply saying they were closed for the holiday.[32] The only legal party to precede the Wafd in announcing its participation was the tiny Democratic Front, a challenger vehicle for Mohamed ElBaradei that had been founded in 2007 and won no seats in the 2010 election.

The Wafd not only joined the protests—it also stayed with them. The party could not be lured to disavow the demonstrations or participate in regime-brokered elite unity schemes, despite multiple meetings with regime representatives. These meetings began as early as January 25, when, according to a former state television executive, two Wafd MPs were called into the office of the minister of information and scolded for their party's participation in the protests.[33] That the regime would respond to the overwhelmingly non-party protests by reaching out to the country's oldest political party highlights the extent to which authorities did not understand what was happening. That said, it is not impossible to imagine an Egyptian version of a pacted transition, with figures from the "legitimate" opposition joining elite soft-liners to oversee an election that did not include a Mubarak.

On January 30, El-Sayyid el-Badawy Shehata declared in a late-night press conference that Mubarak had "lost his legitimacy" and called on the president to respond to protesters' rapidly escalating demands and step down. One might, of course, speculate that el-Badawy hoped to win voters or supporters by associating the Wafd with the uprising. Just five days in, however, it was far too soon to know what the uprising would become or how it would be viewed. Moreover, on January 23, when the Wafd announced its participation, no one had any idea how many people (or, indeed, if any people) would show up. Although the Wafd was no leader of the protest movement, it did take risks. El-Badawy has said that intelligence chief Omar Suleiman called him on the night of the thirtieth asking him to cancel the press conference. He refused. "I said to the leaders of the Wafd after the call that I would hold the press conference, so get ready for prison."[34] His recollections may be self-serving, but they are also consistent with prior regime behavior and contemporaneous skepticism about the uprising's prospects.

As the protests progressed, the regime continued to communicate with Wafd elites. But only once, on February 3, did the party publicly suspend its participation in the protests (and then only for a matter of hours). At times the Wafd was criticized for participating in talks: on February 3, its representatives met with Omar Suleiman (newly anointed vice-president) in discussions that the MB, ElBaradei, and other groups had rejected, demanding that Mubarak leave first.[35] At others, as late as February 6, the Wafd was joined by representatives of the Brotherhood, Tagammu', ElBaradei, and some of the youth movements in Tahrir. But a deal with the regime never emerged from these discussions. Even the co-opted opposition could not be induced to participate in a regime-backed unity scheme, keeping one potential de-escalation tactic out of Mubarak's reach.

The Wafdist Youth

The role of youth in the Wafd is more diffuse, in part because the Wafdist Youth (shabāb al-wafd) are more a notional group than an organized one. On paper, there is a committee for youth with a president and a series of local branches. The actual organizational infrastructure, however, was in disrepair in the early 2000s. To take one example, in the summer of 2010 a group of enterprising youth in Gharbiyya Province attempted to launch a campaign to elect a new president for the local branch of the Wafdist Youth. The election had to be canceled, however, when it became clear that there were no membership lists and therefore no way of knowing who would be eligible to vote.[36]

Nevertheless, people describing themselves or described by others as youth pushed for both the boycott and the subsequent protests. In the runup to the election, media attributed pro-boycott demonstrations outside the party headquarters to young activists.[37] According to an adviser to el-Badawy, youth exerted "powerful pressure to participate" in the January 25 protests; the presence of a strong youth contingent, he argued, is what set the Wafd apart from its more hesitant party peers.[38] That pressure culminated in a meeting on the evening of January 23, 2011, inside the Dokki mansion. Seated around a square conference table with the party leadership, self-identified youth encouraged the party to bless their participation, intimating—like the stereotypical rebellious teenager—that while they would prefer to be supported by the party, they planned to participate no matter what. One speaker, who looked to be in his twenties, addressed el-Bedawy directly: "We will participate. What I want to say is, if the Wafd participates . . . the Wafd *must* participate!"[39] Some reports suggest that the meeting was heated, but el-Badawy's final message was clear: "go for it!" (*inzilū!*).

Immediately after the meeting, the "Wafdist youth" (here it is not clear whether the youth involved are the formal party wing or simply self-identified youth within the Wafd) released a statement titled "Why January 25" in which they explicitly referenced Police Day, which celebrates a stand made against British troops by policemen in Ismailia in 1952. Rather than hiding behind the holiday, as the Nasserists and Tagammu' had done, they connected it back to the Wafd's own history of struggle: "the commemoration of this day is linked to the leader of the Wafd, Fu'ad Sirag al-Din [Egypt's interior minister in 1952], who gave orders to the men of the police force that manifested national dignity [*al-karāma al-waṭaniyya*]."[40] The youth contacted peers in branches around the country (insofar as such branches existed, which is to say unevenly) to plan banners and make other arrangements.[41] The *shabāb* made a strong showing on the morning of the twenty-fifth, marching to Tahrir with Hussam al-Khawly, head of the Youth Committee.[42]

Al-Khawly had come up through a more organized branch of the Wafdist Youth, in Alexandria. He became the leader of that branch in 1988 before aging into full party leadership roles in the early 2000s[43]—a trajectory that puts him in his forties in 2011. He was a close associate of El-Sayyid el-Badawy Shehata, who himself had been elected as party president just months before the 2010 election. El-Badawy is no Hamid Chabat; a wealthy pharmaceutical magnate in a neoliberal authoritarian regime, el-Badawy had neither a confrontational history nor a combative personal style. But he did need to build support within the party; multiple factions, whether loyal to Mahmud

Abaza or longing for a return to Badrawi/Sirag al-Din family rule, were skeptical of him. Without more information, it is difficult to know whether his insecurity as new party head made him more likely to assent to youth-led initiatives—or, for that matter, what precisely it was about al-Khawly and other youths that predisposed them to back the uprising. As in the Istiqlal, however, in the Wafd we see a confrontational turn, pushed by people who were both formally (by committee membership) and informally (in intraparty discourse) glossed as youth, taking place shortly after the election of a new party leader.

Conclusion: The 2011 Generation

The politics of youth are shifting in both the Wafd and the Istiqlal. New Wafd president Bahaa Eldin Abu Shoka seems to be making youth organization a priority. This may be intended as a short-term electoral strategy but, should it simultaneously increase childhood socialization, will eventually bring novel ideas into the party. A recent national camp for young Wafdists featured speeches by both Abu Shoka—a noted regime ally—and Fuad Badrawi, a longtime internal Wafd dissident whose position vis-à-vis the regime is less clear.[44] In Istiqlal, most of the 1990s generation have now aged out of the Shabiba; a number now sit on the ruling EC. They are old enough now that they consider contemporary youth as a new generation and wonder about whether those youth will also militate for change and confrontation. In 2014 Brahim was not optimistic. Young people at the time, he said, were "feeling comfortable"; they were taking the political system for granted rather than interrogating it. Between the February 20th Movement and the Hirak Movement in the north, this has hardly been a docile decade. But it has also been a sobering one: from Syria to Libya, Moroccans have watched attempts to force political change deteriorate into war. Syrian refugees have made it to the streets of major Moroccan cities, living reminders of what can happen when a regime refuses to give up power (or, in a less democratic reading, when protesters ask for too much).

In both countries, then, one major question looms: what mark will people who were young in the 2010s leave on the party? The exhilaration and catastrophe of the past decade have left a complicated legacy: we may eventually see the emergence of what Mannheim calls "generational units":

members of the same generational cohort who have internalized their formative experiences in distinct ways.[45] Some, all too aware of the costs and perhaps futility of defiance, may tend toward careful and conciliatory positions; others, with memories of collective effervescence and the sense of possibility that gripped the region as uprisings spread, may lean defiant. The long shadow of 2011 has endowed both parties with young members whose political consciousness took shape in decidedly extraordinary times. If we choose—and are able—to follow their trajectories, we will be much better equipped to understand party behavior in the future.

Conclusion

Authoritarianism as Tragedy

The fact that the criminal, who only succumbed to the superior power of fate, was *punished* all the same—this was the recognition of human freedom, an *honor* owed to freedom. It was by *allowing* its hero to *fight* against the superior power of fate that Greek tragedy honored human freedom.

—FRIEDRICH SCHELLING, *PHILOSOPHICAL LETTER ON DOGMATISM AND CRITICISM*

The End of the Democratic Journey

In recent years, the metaphor of the democratic journey has faded from *al-'Alam* and other Istiqlali texts. In its place are terms like *democratization* (*al-damaqraṭa*) that less clearly organize the moral relationships among past, present, and future and newer metaphors—the skirmish, for example—that emphasize conflict without linear progress. In December 2014 I met with Istiqlal's spokesman for a wide-ranging conversation about the country's political situation. He favored the terms *democratic reform* (*al-iṣlāḥ al-dimuqrāṭī*), *democratization* (*al-damaqraṭa*), and *democratic transition* (*al-intiqāl al-dimuqrāṭī*) as he described the party's aspirations. While *transition* evokes a liminal state in a way that *reform* and *democratization* do not, none of these three terms implies or summons a Romantic narrative of necessary sacrifice followed by ultimate vindication. He was not convinced that the 2011 constitution was a step forward: "The constitution is gray, it's murky," he told me. "It can be read any way, depending on the person in power." Even if victories were achieved, they might subsequently be lost: "If we don't push [for more powers], if there is no contest over purviews [*al-ikhtiṣāṣāt*], the regime will take things back." The contemporary political situation, he explained, is a "cat and mouse game" (*karr wa farr*), an expression often used to describe skirmishes between police and protesters in other contexts: "we go forward, and we step back." These metaphors are still spatial, but they lack progressive, gradualist, or teleological connotations.

Other party members have ventured similar re-emplotments of political life.[1] In a dramatic redeployment of a metaphor of motion—the country as vehicle—another prominent Istiqlali, asked whether being in the cabinet damaged the party's image, replied, "That's in the nature of the system. The king is the basic mover, and we are the shock absorbers. He's the motor, and we are what gets hit in a crash."[2] In this metaphor, the direction of the car's movement and its eventual destination go unmentioned because they are irrelevant. In 2017 a member of the party's executive committee explained his own evolving thinking on political reform. Arranging two sugar packets on a café table in central Rabat, he said, "You think that it's going to be like this," and drew a straight line with his finger between the two. "But," he explained, tracing his finger in seemingly random loops, "in the end it's like this, and there are so many forces pushing you back to the first point."[3]

Although the party has not yet offered a formal re-emplotment of politics, its members' shifts away from Romantic metaphors are instances of a broader phenomenon. David Scott argues that as postcolonial utopias have failed to arrive, political actors have shaken off future-oriented, Romantic narratives and adopted Tragic ones in their place.[4] The collapse of the Soviet Union and the repeated failures of leftist politics have robbed many once-communists of their faith in teleological Marxian progress. Authoritarianism, neocolonialism, and neoliberalism have tarnished anticolonial aspirations to total independence. And in the Arabic-speaking world, the wave of authoritarian retrenchments and civil wars that emerged out of the 2011 uprisings have led many to question whether even revolution can offer a way out of the perpetual present. In Istiqlal's case, a unified Tragic narrative has not yet emerged. New ways of talking about politics that emphasize obscurity, confusion, and conflict without progress, however, contain within them the seeds of a Tragic vision.[5]

Authoritarian Politics as Tragedy

I began this project as a longtime activist trying to settle a perennial debate: is it better to destabilize the system from the outside or try to change it from the inside? In the spirit of *crescat scientia, vita excolatur*, I thought that exhaustive study might yield concrete guidelines for opposition actors. How could such groups—how could I—avoid the traps into which the Wafd and the Istiqlal have fallen?

A decade later, I do think this project has yielded actionable insights and a conceptual vocabulary that can facilitate better conversations about cooptation. But I am increasingly convinced that my original goal was misguided. I share with many scholars of authoritarianism a deep and personal antipathy to tyrannical regimes; I find them consistently inimical to human flourishing and long for a world in which they are fewer and weaker. My work began with a simple aim: seek out "optimal" antiauthoritarian strategies and explain how opposition groups might be induced to employ them. I was answering what Martha Nussbaum calls "the obvious question: 'what shall we we do?'"[6] Should groups incorporate or not? What are the pros and cons? How can we balance the benefits against the costs? A strategic approach to authoritarianism, however, rests on what I now see as a fundamentally Romantic conceit: the "moral aspiration to rational self-sufficiency."[7] Strategy assumes consistent relationships between cause and effect; it assumes that there are "right" and "wrong" choices; and it claims that the right choices will be rewarded and the wrong ones punished. With the increasing prevalence of formal modeling, strategic thinking lies at the heart of most scholarship on authoritarianism. But, as anyone who has spent any time near an authoritarian regime knows, such consistent patterns simply do not hold in the real world.

One of the key lessons of this book is that co-optative neutralization requires an audience. We, as scholars, are very much a part of that audience; our power as witnesses to co-optation is much greater than we usually imagine. We must choose how we interpret co-optation (and authoritarian politics more broadly)—and, crucially, our choices can change co-optation's effects. I suggest that, under such circumstances, we should choose to emplot authoritarian politics as Tragedy.[8] Tragedy's definition, meaning, and political consequences have, of course, been debated for at least 2,500 years. Here, in calling for Tragic emplotments, I emphasize three distinct features of Tragedy: first, that crucial decisions are made in a state of heightened ignorance about their consequences; second, that Tragic actors face impossible choices that put them "at the same time in the right and wrong";[9] and finally, that Tragedy draws our attention to "that which is wasted" in the struggle against a superior force.[10]

Authoritarian Unknowns

As Jean-Pierre Vernant and Pierre Vidal-Naquet argue in their work on the Greek dramatic form, action in a tragic world necessarily involves "weighing up the pros and cons, foreseeing as accurately as possible the means and the ends," and then nevertheless also "placing one's stake on what is unknown and incomprehensible, risking oneself on a terrain that remains impenetrable, entering into a game with supernatural forces, not knowing . . . whether they will bring success or doom."[11] The Tragic protagonist brings about her own demise through her own actions; she is responsible for her own fall but could not have known that in advance (nor, as I discuss later, made any better choice).

Scholars have long recognized that the obscurity attending authoritarianism poses severe challenges for both rulers and ruled. The ruled are likely to falsify their preferences out of fear, which complicates rulers' ability to predict how their decisions will be received by their subjects.[12] Meanwhile, it is difficult to determine whether rulers will make good on their promises, which hinders strategic planning for the ruled.[13] Such obscurity puts all actors at risk of specifically Tragic miscalculations. Recent work has begun to take this endemic uncertainty as an endemic—and irresolvable—feature of authoritarian politics. In his synthetic theory of authoritarian rule, *The Politics of Uncertainty*, Andreas Schedler argues that "structural opacity" of authoritarian regimes, driven primarily by their denial of basic rights and liberties, produces situations in which all actors "face irredeemable epistemic uncertainties: basic political facts are uncertain, their general significance is uncertain, and their causal relationships are uncertain."[14] Without full confidence in causal relationships, and with prior events open to particularly wide interpretive ranges, human actions are especially likely to have consequences other than those their initiators might have intended. Choosing a course of action under these circumstances, in which the stakes of politics are high and dire consequences are imaginable but not particularly predictable, seems to invite Tragedy in.

Impossible Choices

Another key feature of Tragedy, especially in its more Hegelian forms, is that it presents its heroes with impossible choices. Opposition activists have very good reasons to judge one another's choices harshly: life and death are at stake, and people unsure about the moral rightness of their own actions can be unforgiving in their assessments of others'. Judgment does not require good reasons though: distant observers, themselves not versed in the reality of life under authoritarianism, are often quick to condemn opposition groups for "selling out," among many other sins. Tragedy, however, can break us out of these cycles of blame. As Scott explains, "We may be essentially good people, have good characters, but acting in the world necessarily presents us with situations that are anomalous or that make conflicting and incommensurable demands on us. . . . We choose; and in being obliged to choose between impossible actions we sometimes choose badly."[15] Peter Szondi goes even further, explaining that the "pathos [of the Tragic hero] puts him at the same time in the right and wrong and . . . he thus incurs guilt precisely through his ethical life."[16] The twin stories of the Wafd and the Istiqlal can be emplotted as Tragedy precisely because all the options before them were right and wrong at the same time. Incorporating could lend credibility to brutal regimes, but it also offered the chance to make parliaments into meaningful political arenas. Staying out of the system would signal disapproval, but it also meant abandoning formal politics, allowing legislatures to become purely clientelistic or theatrical. Both choices were right *and* wrong, and the parties had to choose. Their choices to incorporate and to narrate incorporation in a particular way brought about their own declines. But it is not immediately obvious, in either case, that another choice would have produced a better outcome.

In such a telling, the system and its constraints take the place that fate or the gods might have played in earlier Tragedies. Bad things happen to people not because they are bad people or because they make the wrong choices but because the system presents them with only wrong choices—and then forces them to choose. A Tragic perspective on authoritarianism thus shifts the focus away from the morality of opposition actors toward the world in which they operate. We must ask, in Nussbaum's terms, the "tragic question"—"whether any of the alternatives available . . . are morally acceptable"[17]—and then go one step further, to ask why.

CONCLUSION

What Is Wasted, and Why

Emplotting authoritarianism as Tragedy has powerful moral weight. In his lectures on Shakespearean tragedy, A. C. Bradley outlines what he takes to be the affective impact of a tragic play. "A Shakespearean tragedy," he writes,

> is never, like some miscalled tragedies, depressing. No one ever closes the book with the feeling that man is a poor mean creature. He may be wretched and he may be awful, but he is not small. His lot may be heart-rending and mysterious, but it is not contemptible . . . Everywhere, from the crushed rocks beneath our feet to the soul of man, we see power, intelligence, life and glory, which astound us and seem to call for our worship. And everywhere we see them perishing, devouring one another and destroying themselves, often with dreadful pain, as though they came into being for no other end.[18]

Tragedy highlights "the worth of that which is wasted."[19] It draws our attention to the expenditures of time, thought, effort, action, and life that have led to so little hoped-for change. And it refocuses our attention away from the bad choices of those who have nothing but bad choices to make and onto the ultimate source of that waste: the authoritarian system itself.

As I write, authoritarian regimes and authoritarian movements are resurgent in many parts of the world. Perhaps nowhere is this resurgence more keenly felt than in Southwest Asia and North Africa, where those uprisings that were not transformed into devastating wars have, for the most part, given way to even fiercer forms of authoritarianism. Across the region, arguments against authoritarianism are under pressure on multiple fronts. Rulers fearmonger about "terrorism," "radical Islamism," and civil war while positioning themselves as the only guardians of national sovereignty, integrity, and anticolonialism.[20] Meanwhile, critiques of authoritarianism are tarred by their association with American and European pathologies, aggressions, and hypocrisy.

Emplotting—and critiquing—authoritarianism as Tragedy draws its normative power not from comparison with a "democratic West" or from promises of a specific future whose disappointment will invalidate the entire enterprise. Instead, it reminds us what authoritarianism wastes: lives of civic engagement confounded by the badness of every possible choice; decades of organization-building that bleed away with hardly any notice; the energy and dynamism of entire generations faced with political systems that see them only as threats. A Tragic critique can therefore be immanent to a political community's own experience; it needs no outside referent or utopian ideal. Such a critique, moreover, need not be purely negative. Telling a story in which citizens face only bad choices involves explaining why those choices are so constrained in the first place. A model of what non-authoritarian politics might look like can be derived from an attentiveness to what is wasted, and why.

Notes

Introduction

1. Hayden White, *Metahistory: The Historical Imagination in Nineteenth-Century Europe* (Baltimore: Johns Hopkins University Press, 1973); and David Scott, *Conscripts of Modernity: The Tragedy of Colonial Enlightenment* (Durham, N.C.: Duke University Press, 2004).
2. Interview, Wafd member, Imbaba, October 2013.
3. George Lakoff and Mark Johnson, *Metaphors We Live By* (Chicago: University of Chicago Press, 1980); and Raymond W. Gibbs Jr., *Metaphor Wars: Conceptual Metaphors in Human Life* (Cambridge: Cambridge University Press, 2017).
4. Jennifer Gandhi and Adam Przeworski, "Authoritarian Institutions and the Survival of Autocrats," *Comparative Political Studies* 40:11 (2007), 1279–1301; and Ellen Lust, *Structuring Conflict in the Arab World: Incumbents, Opponents, and Institutions* (Cambridge: Cambridge University Press, 2005).
5. On anticolonial movements that became ruling parties, see, for example, Benjamin Smith, "Life of the Party: The Origins of Regime Breakdown and Persistence Under Single-Party Rule," *World Politics* 57, no. 3 (2005), 421–451; and Steven Levitsky and Lucan A. Way, *Competitive Authoritarianism: Hybrid Regimes After the Cold War* (Cambridge: Cambridge University Press, 2010).
6. The human subjects research that contributed to this book was carried out with the approval of Institutional Review Boards at the University of Chicago and Bryn Mawr College. Protocol details will be happily provided upon request.
7. Theda Skocpol and Margaret Somers, "The Uses of Comparative History in Macrosocial Inquiry," *Comparative Studies in Society and History* 22, no. 2 (April 1980): 174–197.
8. Skocpol and Somers, "The Uses of Comparative History," 176.

9. Erica S. Simmons and Nicholas Rush Smith, "Comparison with an Ethnographic Sensibility," *PS: Political Science & Politics* 50, no. 1 (2017): 126–130.
10. Maarten Asscher, *Apples and Oranges: In Praise of Comparisons*, trans. by Brian Doyle-Du Breuil (San Francisco: Four Winds, 2015), 11.
11. Matt Buehler, *Why Alliances Fail: Islamists and Leftist Coalitions in North Africa* (Syracuse, N.Y.: Syracuse University Press, 2018). See also Matt Buehler, "Continuity Through Co-optation: Rural Politics and Regime Resilience in Morocco and Mauritania," *Mediterranean Politics* 20, no. 3 (2015): 364–385.
12. Suad Joseph, "Gender and Relationality Among Arab Families in Lebanon," *Feminist Studies* 19, no. 3 (1993), 465–486.
13. "Endemic uncertainty" is Andreas Schedler's term. Andreas Schedler, *The Politics of Uncertainty: Sustaining and Subverting Electoral Authoritarianism* (Oxford: Oxford University Press, 2013).

1. The Wafd and the Istiqlal

1. Marius Deeb, *Party Politics in Egypt: The Wafd and Its Rivals* (London: Ithaca Press, 1979), 162.
2. Deeb, *Party Politics in Egypt*, 126. The same usage reoccurs with the Istiqlal in Morocco.
3. Cited in Janice J. Terry, *The Wafd, 1919–1952: Cornerstone of Egyptian Political Power* (London: Third World Centre for Research and Publishing, 1982), 218.
4. Shaun T. Lopez, "Madams, Murders, and the Media: *Akhbar al-Hawadith* and the Emergence of a Mass Culture in 1920s Egypt," in *Re-envisioning Egypt 1919–1952*, ed. Arthur Goldschmidt, Amy J. Johnson, and Barak A. Salmoni (New York: American University in Cairo Press, 2005), 388.
5. See Marius Deeb, "Labour and Politics in Egypt, 1919–1939," *International Journal of Middle East Studies* 10:2 (1979), 187–203.
6. Joel Gordon, "The False Hopes of 1950: The Wafd's Last Hurrah and the Demise of Egypt's Old Order," *International Journal of Middle East Studies* 12 (1989): 209.
7. Zuhair Mardini, *Al-ladudan: al-wafd wal-ikhwan* (Cairo: Dar Iqra,' 1984), 158.
8. Deeb, *Party Politics in Egypt*, 154.
9. This professional class is sometimes referred to as a "middle class," but it was only truly a middle class in relationship to (largely foreign) big capitalists and the Ottoman-connected royal court. Deeb, *Party Politics in Egypt*, 26. As far as most Egyptians were concerned, urban *effendiyya* were wealthy.
10. Deeb, *Party Politics in Egypt*, 69.
11. Deeb, *Party Politics in Egypt*, 183, 185.
12. Deeb, *Party Politics in Egypt*, 153.
13. Some observers blame this change on Zaynab al-Wakil, Nahhas's wife, who was less than half his age and hailed from a major landholding family. For such an analysis, see Terry, *The Wafd*. While Zaynab's purchasing habits would have made any populist uncomfortable, the way in which she is depicted as a nefarious

influence on the innocent Nahhas is too similar to the contemporary scapegoating of Suzanne Mubarak to be entirely credible as fact.

14. Gordon, "The False Hopes of 1950."
15. Gordon, "The False Hopes of 1950."
16. Deeb, *Party Politics in Egypt*, 345.
17. For a sensibly critical take on generational lenses in the historiography of the colonial era, see Gordon, "The False Hopes of 1950."
18. Deeb, *Party Politics in Egypt*, 254.
19. Gordon, "The False Hopes of 1950," 195.
20. Terry, *The Wafd*, 301.
21. Nancy Reynolds, *A City Consumed: Urban Commerce, the Cairo Fire, and the Politics of Decolonization in Egypt* (Stanford, Calif.: Stanford University Press, 2012), 182.
22. Terry, *The Wafd*, 308.
23. Terry, *The Wafd*, 303.
24. Terry, *The Wafd*, 307.
25. Mardini, *Al-ladudan*, 181–182.
26. Mardini, *Al-ladudan*, 188.
27. Mardini, *Al-ladudan*,195.
28. Mardini, *Al-ladudan*, 196. Among other things, this platform also called for a minimum-wage, mandatory religious education, and a ban on the sale of alcohol.
29. Terry, *The Wafd*, 211.
30. Mardini, *Al-ladudan*, 164.
31. Interview, former Wafd member and political analyst, November 2013; and Yunan Labib Rizq, *Tarikh al-ahzab al-masriya* (Cairo: Al-hi'a al-'ulia lil-kitab, 1997).
32. Mardini, *Al-ladudan*, 198–199.
33. Ibrahim al-Baathi, "*Fu'ad Siraj al-din yatakallam ba'd samt tawil,*" *al-Musawwar*, June 2, 1977, reprinted in Fu'ad Sirag al-Din, *Limatha al-hizb al-jadid?* (Cairo: Dar al-Shorouk, 1977).
34. Mardini, *Al-ladudan*, 201–202. Mardini reports that Sirag al-Din was in fact rather successful at defending his reputation during the trial, primarily by emphasizing his nationalist credentials. One of the facts that became public during the process was that he had personally loaned Egypt money to cover budget shortfalls (205).
35. Hassanayn Karam, "*Shakhsiyat fu'ad siraj al-din,*" in *Tarikh al-Wafd*, by Gamal Bedawy and Lami'i al-Miti'i (Cairo: Dar al-Shorouk, 2004), 719.
36. My thanks to Tarek Masoud for suggesting this second interpretation.
37. The term "administered mass organizations" is Kasza's. Gregory James Kasza, *The Conscription Society: Administered Mass Organizations* (London: Yale University Press, 1995).
38. Although the placement of the government-identified minbar in the "center" may seem initially to accord with Greene's assumption that authoritarian ruling parties occupy the center range of a unidimensional political spectrum, it is worth noting that "left," "right," and "center" in these cases were all construed primarily in economic terms; on highly salient issues such as foreign

policy, the military's political status, or the role of religion in society, there is no indication that the *manābīr* were supposed to differ from one another at all, or from government positions that are difficult to characterize as "centrist." For a more extensive discussion of Greene's theory and how it relates to the Wafd and the Istiqlal, see chapter 4 and Kenneth Greene, *Why Dominant Parties Lose: Mexico's Democratization in Comparative Perspective* (Cambridge: Cambridge University Press, 2007).

39. Although Sadat may have been intending to completely replace the Egypt Party with the NDP, the Egypt Party's leadership refused to disband, and the party remains legal but inactive.

40. Mohamed Ali Shita, "*Hizb al-wafd al-jadid*," in *Tarikh al-Wafd*, by Gamal Bedawy and Lami'i al-Miti'i, 634.

41. Fu'ad Sirag al-Din and others made much of the differences between the New Wafd and its predecessors during the late 1970s and early 1980s, when too much continuity might have been grounds for banning the new party. But by the 1990s Wafdists preferred to refer to the episode as the "return of the Wafd." Fu'ad Sirag al-Din himself declared in an interview in the 1990s that he "did not recognize" the word "new" in the party's legal name. Interview with Tariq Habib, YouTube, posted October 13, 2013, http://www.youtube.com/watch?v=RkivToNE7_o.

42. Shita, "*Hizb al-wafd al-jadid*," 641.

43. There are rumors that the Wafd was offered legal status and even cabinet seats in exchange for dropping Sirag al-Din as its leader. If such offers were in fact made, they were obviously declined. See Samia Seragaldin, *The Cairo House: A Novel* (Syracuse, N.Y.: Syracuse University Press, 2000), 107.

44. Karam, "Shakhsiyat fu'ad' siraj al-din," 732–733.

45. Rizq, *Tarikh al-ahzab al-masriya*; and Mardini, *Al-ladudan: al-wafd wal-ikhwan*.

46. Terry, *The Wafd*, 312–313.

47. Mona el-Ghobashy, "Egypt's Paradoxical Elections," *Middle East Report* 36 (2005): 238, 378; and Ninette S. Fahmy, *The Politics of Egypt: State-Society Relationship* (London: Routledge, 2002).

48. Karam, "Shakhsiyat fu'ad siraj al-din," 721.

49. The total number of votes cast was 5,323,086; the Wafd won 15.1 percent. Vote totals in this paragraph come from the International Parliamentary Union.

50. This came out to about 10 percent of the total 7,207,467 votes cast.

51. International Parliamentary Union.

52. Other prominent defectors over the Brotherhood alliance include Ibrahim Talaat, Lewis Awad, and Muhammad Anis. Fouda, of course, is better known because he was declared an apostate by Azhari clerics later in the decade and assassinated in 1992 by members of the hardline Islamist group al-Gama'a al-Islamiyya.

53. The constitution matters because Egypt had (at least until 2013) an unusually independent ("arbitrary" may be a better word) judiciary, which rarely hesitated to rule against incumbents, especially in defense of its own institutional interests. See Mona el-Ghobashy, "Taming Leviathan: Constitutionalist Contention in Contemporary Egypt" (PhD dissertation, Columbia University, New

York, 2009); and Tamir Moustafa, *The Struggle for Constitutional Power: Law, Politics, and Economic Development in Egypt* (Cambridge: Cambridge University Press, 2007).

54. See el-Ghobashy, "Egypt's Paradoxical Elections."

55. I discuss this moment in more detail in chapter 2.

56. This has not kept some scholars of the region, animated perhaps by the Wafd's landowning origins, from holding the party responsible for laws passed during this period; see, for example, Timothy Mitchell, *Rule of Experts: Egypt, Technopolitics, Modernity* (Berkeley: University of California Press, 2002), 264.

57. *Al-Wafd*, November 29, 1995.

58. *Al-Wafd*, November 30, 1995.

59. For colorful descriptions of Goumaa by other Wafdists, see Eric Trager, " 'Trapped' and 'Untrapped': Egypt's Wafd Party and the January Revolt," paper prepared for presentation at the Annual Conference of the American Political Science Association, Seattle, Washington, August 31–September 4, 2011.

60. Interview, Wafd member, January 2014.

61. Gamal Bedawi and Lami'i al-Miti'i, eds. *Tarikh al-wafd* (Cairo: Dar al-Shorouk, 2003), 747. This edition of the party's history—which overwhelmingly focuses on the colonial era—was replaced after Goumaa's ouster with a new version that did not include the admiring portrait of Goumaa found in the 2004 edition. I was given several copies of the new edition by people within the Wafd but was able to locate the older version at a commercial bookstore.

62. Nihal Shukry, "Fi awal hiwar ma' al-daktur nu'man juma' ra'is hizb al-wafd: tarshihi huwwa qarar al-aghlabiya bil-hizb wa laysa radd fa'il li-tarshish ayman nur," *al-Ahram*, August 26, 2005.

63. Human Rights Watch, "From Plebiscite to Contest? Egypt's Presidential Election," Briefing Paper (2005): 3.

64. Human Rights Watch, "From Plebiscite to Contest?," 7.

65. "Egypt Party Rivals Clash in Cairo," BBC News, April 1, 2006.

66. Interview, Wafd member, October 2013.

67. "Hukumat al-thill al-wafdiyya tu'ayyid qarar ra'is al-wafd bil-insihab min al-intikhabat," statement reprinted in *Duniya al-Watan*, December 7, 2010.

68. Interview, Wafd member, January 2014.

69. Carrie Rosefsky Wickham, *The Muslim Brotherhood: Evolution of an Islamist Movement* (Princeton, N.J.: Princeton University Press, 2013), 292. Wickham considers the Wafd "secular," a description I would refute (true secularists are rare in Egyptian politics). I suggest "ecumenical" instead.

70. Wickham, *The Muslim Brotherhood*, 293.

71. Interviews, Wafd vice president and senior adviser to el-Badawy, November 2013.

72. Hossam Bahgat, "Anatomy of an Election," *Mada Masr*, March 14, 2016.

73. Fadi al-Sawy, "Lamees al-hadidi tushayyid bi-mawqif hizb al-wafd min ittfaqiyat tiran wa sanafir," *al-Wafd*, June 11, 2017.

74. This term can also mean "cardboard party," that is, one that is only a facade or a hastily constructed substitute for the real thing.

75. Susan Gilson Miller, *A History of Modern Morocco* (Cambridge: Cambridge University Press, 2012), loc. 2521, Kindle.

76. The categories Amazigh and Arab are not always fixed in contemporary Morocco; to the extent that it is possible to sort people into these two categories, it is done on a linguistic basis (do you speak an Amazigh language or *darija* at home?). For a detailed account of the controversy over the "Berber *ḍahir*" and its consequences, see Jonathon Wyrtzen, *Making Morocco: Colonial Intervention and the Politics of Identity* (Ithaca, N.Y.: Cornell University Press, 2015).

77. For more on the civil service college, including a discussion of Amazigh Moroccans' participation in the nationalist movement, see Mohamed Benhlal, *Le collêge d'Azrou: une élite berbère civile et militaire au Maroc (1927–1959)* (Paris: Éditions Karthala, 2005). On the trend of "free schools," see Mustapha El Qadéry, "Les Berbères entre le myth colonial et la négacion national: Le cas du Maroc," *Revue d'histoire moderne et contemporaine* 45, no. 2 (April–June 1998).

78. Miller, *A History of Modern Morocco*, loc. 2996. The link between the nationalist movement—especially the Istiqlal—and the organizational traditions of Moroccan Sufism has not gone unnoticed. Several Moroccan scholars have suggested that Moroccan political life imported its authoritarian and hierarchical tendencies from these early Sufi models. See Abdellah Hammoudi, *Master and Disciple: The Cultural Foundations of Moroccan Authoritarianism* (Chicago: University of Chicago Press, 1997); and Said Jaafar, *Al-zawiya wal-hizb bil-maghrib: usul al-istibdad al-siyasi* (Casablanca: Al-Najah al Jadida, 2014).

79. Adria Lawrence, *Imperial Rule and the Politics of Nationalism: Anti-Colonial Protest in the French Empire* (Cambridge: Cambridge University Press, 2013).

80. Lawrence, *Imperial Rule*, 59–60.

81. Lawrence, *Imperial Rule*, 61.

82. Miller, *A History of Modern Morocco*, loc. 3327.

83. My thanks to Adria Lawrence for pushing me to clarify this point. Kutla demands in 1934 and 1936 did not include the continuation of the monarchy. Lawrence, *Imperial Rule*, 59.

84. John Waterbury, *The Commander of the Faithful: The Moroccan Political Elite: A Study in Segmented Politics* (London: Weidenfeld and Nicholson, 1970), 173. As Waterbury correctly notes, the notion of Allal al-Fassi as the unquestioned leader of the Istiqlal is a product of the post-1959 era (175).

85. Miller, *A History of Modern Morocco*, loc. 3327.

86. Daniel Zisenwine, *The Emergence of Nationalist Politics in Morocco: The Rise of the Independence Party and the Struggle Against Colonialism After World War II* (New York: I. B. Tauris, 2010).

87. Miller, *A History of Modern Morocco*, loc. 3378.

88. Zisenwine, *The Emergence of Nationalist Politics*, 104–105.

89. Waterbury surmises that al-Fassi crafted the speech to ingratiate himself with his new July Regime hosts. Waterbury, *The Commander of the Faithful*, 174.

90. Miller, *A History of Modern Morocco*, loc. 3498–3504.

91. The classic account of this process is Remy Leveau's *Le fellah marocain, defenseur du trône* (Paris: Presses de la Fondation Nationale des Sciences Politiques, 1985).

92. Miller, *A History of Modern Morocco*, loc. 155.

93. Waterbury, *The Commander of the Faithful*, 254–256. Waterbury translates *munsajima* as "homogeneous," which gives it a rather more ominous tone.

94. Waterbury, *The Commander of the Faithful*, 180.
95. See, for example, Ellen Lust and Amaney Jamal, "Rulers and Rules: Reassessing the Influence of Regime Type on Electoral Law Formation," *Comparative Political Studies* 35 (2002): 337–366.
96. Waterbury, *The Commander of the Faithful*, 171.
97. Waterbury, *The Commander of the Faithful*, 172.
98. For more on Istiqlal's resistance to schism, see chapters 5 and 6.
99. Douglas Ashford, *Perspectives of a Moroccan Nationalist* (Totowa, N.J.: Bedminster, 1964).
100. Waterbury, *The Commander of the Faithful*, 193.
101. Muhammad Shaqir, *Tatawwur al-dawla fil-maghrib: Ishkaliyat al-takawwun wal-tamarkaz wal haymana min al qarn al-thalith qabl al-milad ila al-qarn al'ishrin* (Casablanca: Ifriqiya al-Sharq, 2006), 138.
102. "*Limatha ayyidna al-dustur,*" *al-ʿAlam*, January 6, 1963.
103. Waterbury, *The Commander of the Faithful*, 259.
104. Waterbury, *The Commander of the Faithful*, 263. The Moroccan constitution, like Agamben, uses the term *exception* (*istithnāʾ*) rather than *emergency*.
105. For an excellent treatment of this shift, see Muhammad Radwani, *Al-tanmiyya al-siyasiyya fi al-maghrib: Tashakkul al-sulta al-tanfidhiyya wa mumarisatiha min sanat 1956 ila sanat 2000* (Rabat: Al-Maʾarif Al-Jadida, 2011).
106. *Al-ʿAlam*, July 20, 1970.
107. Interview, married couple of Istiqlal activists, northern Morocco, February 2014.
108. *Al-ʿAlam*, February 19, 1972.
109. *Al-ʿAlam*, April 6, 1972.
110. Abdelkarim Ghellab, *Mahammad busitta al-diblomasi al-hakim* (Rabat: Dar Abi Raqraq lil-Tabaa wal-Nashr, 2017), 46.
111. The title "president" was retired in Allal al-Fassi's honor; all future leaders of the party would be referred to as "secretary-general" (*al-amīn al-ʿām*). Ghellab, *Mahammad busitta al-diblomasi al-hakim*, 43.
112. Pierre Vermeren, *Histoire du maroc depuis l'indépendance* (Paris: La Découverte, 2010), 83.
113. Ghellab, *Mahammad busitta al-diblomasi al-hakim*, 7.
114. "Ijtima' wafd min al-fariq al-istiqlali ma' al-sayyid al-wazir al-awil," *al-ʿAlam*, June 6, 1981.
115. "La idrab fi waqt ma'rakat al-sahra'" *al-ʿAlam*, June 20, 1981.
116. Vermeren, *Histoire du maroc depuis l'indépendance*, 83.
117. Muhammad Nabil Muleen, *Fikrat al-dustur fil-maghrib: Watha'iq wa nusus (1901–2011)* (Casablanca: TelQuel Media, 2017), 184.
118. Muleen, *Fikrat al-dustur fil-maghrib*, 184.
119. Muhammad Dreef, *Al-haql al-siyasi al-maghribi: Al-as'ila al hadira wal al-ajwiba al-ghu'iba* (Rabat: Al-Majella al-Maghribiyya li-'Ilm al-Ijtima' al-Siyasi, 1998), 136.
120. Muleen, *Fikrat al-dustur fil-maghrib*, 184.
121. Muleen, *Fikrat al-dustur fil-maghrib*, 196.
122. Dreef, *Al-haql al-siyasi al-maghribi*, 9.
123. Ali Ouasri, *Min wahm al-intiqal al-dimuqrati ila mutahat al-tahawwul al-mujtama'i ba'd 20 febrair* (Rabat: Top Press, 2012), 13.

124. The head of Istiqlal's human rights organization, Muhammad al-Zahari, was known to be active in the protests, for example. Interview, member of Istiqlal's executive committee, December 2015.
125. Moroccan Constitution of 2011, article 19.
126. Maâti Monjib, "Lopsided Struggle for Power in Morocco," *Sada Middle East Analysis*, January 15, 2017.
127. Interview, member of Istiqlal Executive Committee, July 2017; and interview, member of the Daughters of the Renaissance (Istiqlal's young women's organization), July 2017.
128. I take this question up explicitly in chapter 6.
129. For example, Jennifer Gandhi and Adam Przeworski, "Cooperation, Cooptation, and Rebellion Under Dictatorship," *Economics and Politics* 18, no. 1 (2006): 1–26; Gandhi and Przeworski, "Authoritarian Institutions"; and Michael J. Willis, "Political Parties in the Maghrib: The Illusion of Significance," *Journal of North African Studies* 7, no. 2 (2002), 1–22.
130. On programmatic orientation, see, for example, Greene, *Why Dominant Parties Lose*. On legal status, see, for example, Ellen Lust, *Structuring Conflict in the Arab World: Incumbents, Opponents, and Institutions* (Cambridge: Cambridge University Press, 2005).
131. For more on why this is a problem, see chapter 2.
132. Beatriz Magaloni, *Voting for Autocracy: Hegemonic Party Survival and Its Demise in Mexico*, Cambridge Studies in Comparative Politics, (Cambridge: Cambridge University Press, 2008); Greene, *Why Dominant Parties Lose*; and Milan Svolik, *The Politics of Authoritarian Rule* (Cambridge: Cambridge University Press, 2012).
133. Note the difference here between a ruling party and a palace party. Palace parties may be more common in monarchical regimes in which there is no ruling party, but they can be found even in dominant-party regimes. The Egypt Party is a good example of this latter phenomenon.
134. Buehler's account is a primarily transactional one. His conclusions, however, also suggest that there is much more ambivalence to co-optative processes than is typically assumed. Matt Buehler, *Why Alliances Fail: Islamist and Leftist Coalitions in North Africa* (Syracuse, N.Y.: Syracuse University Press, 2018); and Matt Buehler, "Continuity Through Cooptation: Rural Politics and Regime Resilience in Morocco and Mauritania," *Mediterranean Politics* 20, no. 3: 364–385.
135. For example, Lust, *Structuring Conflict*; and Jennifer Gandhi, *Political Institutions Under Dictatorship* (Cambridge: Cambridge University Press, 2008).

2. Conceptualizing Co-optation

1. My approach is centered on nonruling actors rather than on regimes. As a result, an "authoritarian regime" for my purposes is any regime that a given nonruling actor *experiences* as authoritarian—that is, as limiting basic human agency in a way that needs to be fundamentally unsettled, regardless of its institutional character. Regimes that most scholars would label democratic

based on their procedural or institutional features could thus be authoritarian in the sense that I mean the term.

2. For example, Ronald Wintrobe, *The Political Economy of Dictatorship* (Cambridge: Cambridge University Press, 2000); and Milan Svolik, *The Politics of Authoritarian Rule* (Cambridge: Cambridge University Press, 2012).

3. For example, Eva Bellin, "Coercive Institutions and Coercive Leaders," in *Authoritarianism in the Middle East*, ed. by Marsha Pripstein Posusney and Michele Penner Angrist (Boulder, Colo.: Lynne Rienner, 2005), 21–38; Diane E. Davis and Anthony W. Pereira, eds. *Irregular Armed Forces and Their Role in Politics and State Formation* (Cambridge: Cambridge University Press, 2003); and Dina Rashed, "The Resurrection of the Ministry of the Interior Under Sadat: Junta Threat and Presidential Power," paper presented at the *Middle East Studies Association Annual Meeting*, Washington D.C., November 22–25, 2014.

4. For example, Lisa Wedeen, *Ambiguities of Domination: Politics, Rhetoric and Symbols in Contemporary Syria* (Chicago: University of Chicago Press, 1999); and Michael Albertus, Sofia Fenner, and Dan Slater, *Coercive Distribution* (Cambridge: Cambridge University Press, 2018).

5. For example, Christian Davenport, Hank Johnston, and Carol McClurg Mueller, eds., *Mobilization and Repression* (Minneapolis: University of Minnesota Press, 2005).

6. On authoritarian institutions, see, for example, Ellen Lust, *Structuring Conflict in the Arab World: Incumbents, Opponents, and Institutions* (Cambridge: Cambridge University Press, 2005); Jennifer Gandhi and Adam Przeworski, "Cooperation, Cooptation, and Rebellion Under Dictatorship," *Economics and Politics* 18, no. 1 (2006): 1–26; Jennifer Gandhi and Adam Przeworski, "Authoritarian Institutions and the Survival of Autocrats," *Comparative Political Studies* 40, no. 11 (2007): 1279–1301; Beatriz Magaloni, *Voting for Autocracy: Hegemonic Party Survival and Its Demise in Mexico. Cambridge Studies in Comparative Politics* (Cambridge: Cambridge University Press, 2008); Jason Brownlee, *Authoritarianism in an Age of Democratization* (Cambridge: Cambridge University Press, 2007); Kenneth Greene, *Why Dominant Parties Lose: Mexico's Democratization in Comparative Perspective* (Cambridge: Cambridge University Press, 2007); and Gandhi, *Political Institutions Under Dictatorship* (Cambridge: Cambridge University Press, 2008). On electoral authoritarianism, see, for example, Andreas Schedler, "The Nested Game of Democratization by Elections," *International Political Science Review* 23, no. 1 (2002): 103–122; Andreas Schedler, *The Politics of Uncertainty: Sustaining and Subverting Electoral Authoritarianism* (Oxford: Oxford University Press, 2013); Jennifer Gandhi and Ellen Lust, "Elections Under Authoritarianism," *Annual Review of Political Science* 12 (2006), 403–422; Ellen Lust and Amaney Jamal, "Rulers and Rules: Reassessing the Influence of Regime Type on Electoral Law Formation," *Comparative Political Studies* 35 (2002): 337–366; and Steven Levitsky and Lucan A. Way, *Competitive Authoritarianism: Hybrid Regimes After the Cold War* (Cambridge: Cambridge University Press, 2010). On authoritarian distribution, see, for example, Bruce Bueno de Mesquita, Alastair Smith, Randolph M. Siverson, and James D. Morrow, *The Logic of Political Survival* (Cambridge, Mass.: MIT Press, 2003); Daron Acemoglu and James A. Robinson, *Economic Origins of Dictatorship*

and Democracy (Cambridge: Cambridge University Press, 2006); and Svolik, *The Politics of Authoritarian Rule.*

7. A possible exception to this status quo is the literature on elections, which has embraced elections' ambiguous and transformative effects in recent years; see, for example, Schedler, *The Politics of Uncertainty.* Such studies, however, tend to focus on the specific capacities of elections rather than on electoral participation as a subset of or an occasion for incorporation.

8. This definition suggests correctly that I do not engage with more atmospheric understandings of co-optation, such as those that ask how individuals and others are interpellated into diffuse political-economic systems. Louis Althusser, "Ideology and Ideological State Apparatuses (Notes Towards an Investigation)" (1970), in *Cultural Theory: An Anthology*, ed. by Imre Szeman and Timothy Kaposy, 204–222 (Malden, Mass.: Wiley, 2010). To what extent does an individual's interpellation into a saturating political-economic world (say, global neoliberal capitalism) truly parallel her assumption of a government post? Both do imply a shouldering of some sort of moral responsibility as a participant in and beneficiary of a given system. Indeed, a number of scholars have recognized the ways in which ordinary people serve as essential pillars of support for systems of authoritarian control. For example, Václav Havel, *The Power of the Powerless: Citizens Against the State in Central-eastern Europe*, Routledge Revivals (Abingdon, Oxon: Routledge Press, 2009); Timur Kuran, "Now out of Never: The Element of Surprise in the East European Revolutions of 1989," *World Politics* 44:1 (1991), 7–48; and Wedeen, *Ambiguities of Domination.* Yet many citizens of authoritarian regimes would *perceive* a difference between the kind of participation exemplified by Havel's greengrocer, for example, and that exemplified by a former dissident who becomes the head of a state-sponsored labor union— even if it might be fair to speak of both as co-opted in some sense. Most fundamentally, the greengrocer's type and level of participation is often unavoidable, or avoidable only at great personal cost. More active participation in more prominent positions, however, usually involves a process that can more meaningfully be thought of as a choice. To some extent, the distinction between what looks more like interpellation and what looks more like formal incorporation is captured by Selznick's distinction between "formal" co-optation, which involves explicit agreements and rules, and "informal co-optation," which occurs without being announced publicly and in a less institutionalized fashion. Philip Selznick, *TVA and the Grass Roots: A Study of Politics and Organization* (Berkeley: University of California Press, 1953). However, in Selznick's account, it is ordinary citizens who are formally co-opted and influential societal elites who are informally co-opted. In global comparative perspective, I suspect it is more often the other way around.

9. "Co-opt," *Oxford English Dictionary Online*, accessed March 31, 2013.

10. "Co-opt," *Oxford English Dictionary Online*, accessed March 31, 2013.

11. There is no single Arabic term that contains both of these meanings in the way that *co-optation* does in English. The most common direct translation, istiʾnās, concerns only neutralization and is best translated as "domestication." It cannot, I would argue, be used as a synonym for *co-optation. Co-optation* is also

increasingly used as a synonym for *appropriation*, denoting the adoption of an idea, practice, or cause by a group or actor other than its originator. While I treat the incorporative and neutralizing senses of *co-optation* as irreducible and inevitable components of the term, I do not consider the sense of the term captured by phrases such as, "The regime co-opted the opposition's slogan." The incorporation of nonactors—slogans, arguments, colors, hairstyles, and so on—are acts of appropriation and should be described as such. That co-optation involves bringing a potentially hostile and agentive *actor* into a system is what makes it an interesting and indeterminate process in a way that appropriation rarely is.

12. It should be noted, however, that the OED still does not recognize this latter meaning. Nor does *Merriam Webster*, although it recognizes *appropriate* and *assimilate* as potential synonyms.

13. On distributive practices such as patronage and social spending, see, for example, Gandhi and Przeworski, "Cooperation, Cooptation, and Rebellion"; Gandhi and Przeworski, "Authoritarian Institutions"; and Svolik, *The Politics of Authoritarian Rule*.

14. Michael Lacy, "The United States and American Indians: Political Relations," in *American Indian Policy in the Twentieth Century*, ed. by Vine Deloria Jr. (Norman: Oklahoma University Press, 1985), 83. I came across Lacy's work later than I would have liked, but his agnosticism about co-optation's effects complements and has informed my own.

15. Excellent work has been done on co-optation (usually of social movements) in democracies, including Frances Fox Piven and Richard A. Cloward, *Poor People's Movements: How They Succeed, Why They Fail*, 2nd ed. (New York: Vintage, 1979). In large part, however, this work is based on an understanding of co-optation as the "extension of established procedures to new groups" (795), which does not comport well with the cases at hand, or with authoritarian dynamics more broadly. It is certainly true that offers of cabinet participation to Istiqlal and other parties in the 1970s, 1990s, and 2000s were "reforms with which . . . [the regime] had experience" (795), but in other instances this was not the case. When the Egyptian regime grudgingly allowed the Wafd into the political system, meaningful party politics was not something with which the July Regime had prior experience; a multiparty system went far beyond both "established procedures" and the apparent intentions of President Anwar Sadat (see discussion in chapter 1). Nor is the steady expansion of the Moroccan parliament's powers—an expansion which has repeatedly served as an occasion for the (re)integration of Istiqlal and other opposition parties into institutional politics—necessarily self-limiting. Indeed, although successive constitutional reforms fall far short of what would be needed to make the country meaningfully democratic, scholars of monarchical reform elsewhere in the region have noted that even minor changes in the relationship between king and parliament can produce dramatic and unanticipated results. Michael Herb, "Princes and Parliaments in the Arab World," *Middle East Journal* 58, no. 3 (2004), 367–384. Bringing in new actors (or old ones who had left) has often meant empowering parliament, raising the real risk that while opposition

parties may be contained within parliament, parliament itself will become more difficult to contain. Thus, co-optation in authoritarian regimes is a riskier proposition (from a regime standpoint) than co-optation in procedural democracies; the very introduction of pluralism into the formal structures of the regime threatens the autocratic logic of the regime itself.

16. On transactional models, see, for example, Gandhi and Przeworski, "Cooperation, Cooptation, and Rebellion"; Gandhi and Przeworski, "Authoritarian Institutions"; Matt Buehler, *Why Alliances Fail: Islamist and Leftist Coalitions in North Africa* (Syracuse, N.Y.: Syracuse University Press, 2018); Gandhi, *Political Institutions Under Dictatorship*; and, to some extent, Lust, *Structuring Conflict*. Lust's 2005 argument, impressive in its attempt to address multiple ways in which co-optation works on the co-opted, includes elements of acculturation arguments as well.

17. Gandhi, *Political Institutions Under Dictatorship*.

18. It is important to note that Lust's theory depends heavily on these benefits being unavailable to illegal opposition. In Egypt (one of Lust's own cases) an illegal group—the Muslim Brotherhood—was long able to access the benefits of incorporation. Lust's broader point that the letter of authoritarian law does matter is a salutary one, but legal status—while important—is not determinative of access to benefits.

19. Lust, *Structuring Conflict*.

20. On the incorporation of Islamist groups, see, for example, Carrie Rosefsky Wickham, *Mobilizing Islam: Religion, Activism and Political Change in Egypt* (New York: Columbia University Press, 2002); Carrie Rosefsky Wickham, *The Muslim Brotherhood: Evolution of an Islamist Movement* (Princeton, N.J.: Princeton University Press, 2013); Jillian Schwedler, *Faith in Moderation: Islamist Parties in Jordan and Yemen* (Cambridge: Cambridge University Press, 2006); Nathan Brown, *When Victory Is Not An Option: Islamist Movements in Arab Politics* (Ithaca, N.Y.: Cornell University Press, 2012); Shadi Hamid, *Temptations of Power: Islamists and Illiberal Democracy in A New Middle East* (New York: Oxford University Press, 2014). Most works have suggested some moderating effect, although Hamid has argued that it is authoritarian repression, not electoral participation, that produces Islamist moderation. Hamid, *Temptations of Power*. The applicability of findings related to Islamist moderation for the broader study of co-optation is unclear: an Islamist group that "moderates" and becomes committed to democracy has by no means moderated its position vis-à-vis an incumbent authoritarian regime.

21. Wickham, *The Muslim Brotherhood*; and Schwedler, *Faith in Moderation*.

22. Lust, *Structuring Conflict*, 82–83.

23. Following J. L. Austin, I consider speech acts to be a form of action. John Langshaw Austin, *How to Do Things with Words* (Oxford: Oxford University Press, 1975).

24. The following argument also holds for shifts in party position in transactional accounts.

25. Lust, *Structuring Conflict*, 7–11.

26. Lust, *Structuring Conflict*, 8–9.

27. William H. Sewell Jr. *Logics of History: Social Theory and Social Transformation*, Electronic (Chicago: University of Chicago Press, 2005), loc. 1274.

28. Interview, high-ranking Wafd official, December 2013.
29. See, for example, Samuel Huntington, *Political Order in Changing Societies* (New Haven, Conn.: Yale University Press, 1968); and Levitsky and Way, *Competitive Authoritarianism.*
30. For an example from Jordan, see "Intilaq hamlat al-sha'b yurid islah al-nizam fil-'umla" *AmmanNet*, July 18, 2011. http://ar.ammannet.net/news/116712. For an example from a protest in Tangier, Morocco, see "Tanga 11 shatambir 2011: al-sha'b yurid isqat al-fasad," YouTube, September 11, 2011, https://www.youtube.com/watch?v=3flIFuH7ixA.
31. Of course, some Istiqlalis have privately gone further. But my concern throughout is not so much what individuals truly believe but rather what the party chooses to say aloud.
32. Interview, member of Istiqlal Executive Committee, February 2014.
33. My thanks to an anonymous reviewer for pushing me to clarify this point.
34. Interview, member of Istiqlal Executive Committee, March 2013.
35. Allal al-Fassi, *Al-naqd al-thati*, 6th ed., (Rabat: Al-Risala, 1999), 126–127.
36. Al-Fassi, *Al-naqd al-thati*, 126–127.
37. Al-Fassi, *Al-naqd al-thati*, 127.
38. Interview, member of the Istiqlal Executive Committee, March 2014.
39. See, for example, John Waterbury, *The Commander of the Faithful: The Moroccan Political Elite; A Study in Segmented Politics* (London: Weidenfeld and Nicholson, 1970); and Lust and Jamal, "Rulers and Rules." For a robust and insightful discussion of the Moroccan monarchy's legitimation strategies, see Patrick Snyder, "Red Lines: Legitimation and Dissent in Contemporary Morocco" (Ph.D. dissertation, University of Minnesota, Minneapolis, 2022).
40. See chapter 1 for an explanation of this alliance. Fu'ad Sirag al-Din may have thought the Wafd would garner votes from the MB base when he agreed to the alliance, but it is anachronistic to assume that the Wafd has always had the weak popular base that it has now.
41. Yunan Labib Rizq, *Tarikh al-ahzab al-masriya* (Cairo: Al-hi'a al-'ulia lil-kitab, 1997), 47.
42. Farag Fouda, *Al-wafd wal-mustaqbal* (Cairo: Al-Mu'allif, 1984), 68.
43. Fouda, *Al-wafd wal-mustaqbal*, 104.
44. Interview, Wafd official, Cairo, January 2014.
45. For one example of Egyptian Islamists as traitors or foreign agents, which depicts the Brotherhood's post-2013 activities as "an initiative of traitors," see Muhammad Tharwat, "Bayan al-khawana yufaddih tawatu' al-ikhwan ma' al-irhab fi sina,'" *al-Wafd*, July 1, 2015. One aspect of the Wafd's commitments to liberal rights and freedoms *does* seem to have changed over time. Fu'ad Sirag al-Din's commitment to free speech was deep; in his speech "Why the New Party?" in August 1977, he fondly recalled the days of the final Wafd government in 1950–1951, when he was minister of the interior and allowed members of his own ministry to call for his removal. Fu'ad Sirag al-Din, *Limatha al-hizb al-jadid?* (Cairo: Dar al-Shorouk, 1977), 60. Contemporary Wafdists are much more likely to frame free speech as something that naturally comes with constraints. As one Wafd activist told me, in a representative formulation, "I believe

in freedom of expression, with religious and ethical restrictions." Interview, Wafd activist, Cairo, January 2014. Whether this shift is one that has come from the top (i.e., been encouraged by the incorporation of elites) or whether it is more of a grassroots shift in Egyptian opinions more broadly is unclear.

46. My thanks to Lisa Wedeen for raising this possibility.

47. Fouda, *Al-wafd wal-mustaqbal*, 63, 54.

48. "Fu'ad Sirag al-Din: Lan nu'id al-wafd al-qadim bal nunshi' hizban jadidan," *Al-Hawadith* (Beirut), July 1, 1977.

49. That said, Istiqlal did experience a major split in 1959, which altered its programmatic commitments by removing some of the more socialist-inclined leaders—first among them, Mehdi Ben Barka—from the party. Thus, when speaking of change over time in Istiqlal's positions, it probably makes the most sense to consider the party's ideological trajectory since 1959 rather than since its founding in 1944.

50. Al-Fassi, *Al-naqd al-thati*, 129. Al-Fassi's analysis is ambitious but often confusing. In one passage—written in 1949—he suggests that Moroccans could "take from the Soviet system the idea of voter oversight over their elected representatives, one way or another" (132). As 1949 was the peak of the Stalinist period, it is unclear to what practices al-Fassi might be referring.

51. Al-Fassi, *Al-naqd al-thati*, 133.

52. Al-Fassi, *Al-naqd al-thati*, 128.

53. Al-Fassi, *Al-naqd al-thati*, 130.

54. See chapter 3, especially the discussion of a 1975 editorial, "A New Morocco . . . and Elections" in Istiqlal's *al-'Alam* newspaper.

55. Interviews, Wafd activist and high-ranking Wafd official, Cairo, January 2014.

56. Interview, Wafd vice-president, Cairo, December 2013.

57. Interview, Wafd vice-president, Cairo, January 2014.

58. The correlation between cabinet participation and refusal to engage in contentious strikes is particularly dramatic; this may explain why Lust, who focuses on such strikes as her main indicator of opposition's willingness to challenge the regime, finds an automatic relationship between incorporation and neutralization. Lust, *Structuring Conflict*).

59. Muhammad al-Ta'ia', *'Abd al-rahman al-yussufi wal-tanawwub al-dimuqrati al-mujhad* (Rabat: Imprimerie Négoce com, 2013), 30–31.

60. The Democratic Bloc consisted of Istiqlal, the USFP, and several smaller progressive parties.

61. Muhammad Dreef, *Al-haql al-siyasi al-maghribi: Al-as'ila al hadira wal al-ajwiba al-gha'iba* (Rabat: Al-Majella al-Maghribiyya li-'Ilm al-Ijtima' al-Siyasi, 1998), 136.

62. Dreef, *Al-haql al-siyasi al-maghribi*, 136.

63. Muhammad Nabil Muleen, *Fikrat al-dustur fil-maghrib: Watha'iq wa nusus 1901–2011* (Casablanca: TelQuel Media, 2017), 184.

64. Dreef, *Al-haql al-siyasi al-maghribi*, 11.

65. Dreef, *Al-haql al-siyasi al-maghribi*, 11.

66. Muleen, *Fikrat al-dustur fil-maghrib*, 196.

67. al-Ta'ia', *'Abd al-rahman al-yussufi wal-tanawwub al-dimuqrati al-mujhad*, 28.

68. Dreef, *Al-haql al-siyasi al-maghribi*, 9.

69. Muhammad al-Taʾiaʾ, "Il était une fois l'alternance," *TelQuel*, February 19, 2013, p. 43.
70. Several USFP candidates won seats in 1998 that they were not expected to win, especially over Islamist opponents. Two of the most prominent were Muhammad Hafidh, a member of the USFP youth wing, and Muhammad Adeeb, a USFP labor activist. Hafidh himself denounced the rigging that produced his victory. al-Taʿiaʿ, "Il était une fois l'alternance," 30.
71. Dreef, *Al-haql al-siyasi al-maghribi*, 9.
72. al-Taʾiaʾ, "Il était une fois l'alternance," 45.
73. One of the most commonly mentioned examples of parliamentary perks in Morocco is that parliamentarians (apparently) have access not just to cars but to Mercedes-Benzes.
74. Interview, Istiqlal member of parliament, December 2014.
75. Interview, Wafd member, Cairo, October 2013.
76. Buehler, *Why Alliances Fail*.
77. Samer S. Shehata, *Shop Floor Culture and Politics in Egypt* (Albany: SUNY Press, 2009).
78. Ellen Lust, "Competitive Clientelism in the Middle East," Journal of Democracy 20:3 (2009), 122–135; and Lisa Blaydes, *Elections and Distributive Politics in Mubarak's Egypt* (Cambridge: Cambridge University Press, 2010).
79. Interview, high-ranking Istiqlal member, March 2013.
80. Because Morocco has no ruling party, a large number of parties (currently, around thirty-five) in comparison to other authoritarian regimes, and (at least until recently) an electoral law favorable to independent candidates, it is unheard of for a single party to win an outright majority of the seats.
81. Douglas Ashford, *Political Change in Morocco* (Princeton, N.J.: Princeton University Press, 1961).
82. World Values Survey, waves 4 (2001, question v220: "If there were a national election tomorrow, for which party on this list would you vote?"), 5 (2007, question v231: "If there were a national election tomorrow, for which party on this list would you vote? If you are uncertain, which party appeals to you most?"), and 6 (2011, question v228: "If there were a national election tomorrow, for which party on this list would you vote?").
83. World Values Survey, wave 4 (2001, question v222: "Is there any party on this list that you would never vote for?").
84. Ashford, *Political Change in Morocco*, 220.
85. Susan Gilson Miller, *A History of Modern Morocco* (Cambridge: Cambridge University Press, 2012), loc. 3541, Kindle.
86. Nina Kozlowski and Abdellah Tourabi, "Game of Thrones: Version Marocaine," *TelQuel*, December 26, 2014–January 6, 2015.
87. Rizq, *Tarikh al-ahzab al-masriya*, 226.
88. I choose not to use voter turnout data because registration rules have changed dramatically during the period in question, rendering turnout percentages incomparable.
89. Shaqir, *Tatawwur al-dawla fil-maghrib*, 140–141.
90. Shaqir, *Tatawwur al-dawla fil-maghrib*, 141.

91. Cited in "Al-ahzab al-siyasiya fi al-maghrib," episode of *Malaf Niqash*, October 21, 2014. Available on YouTube, https://www.youtube.com/watch?v=pwQiz1GM2Vs.
92. World Values Survey, wave 6, question V29, "Now I am going to read off a list of voluntary organizations. For each organization, could you tell me whether you are an active member, an inactive member, or not a member of that type of organization?"
93. Note the difference here between a ruling party and a palace party. Palace parties may be more common in monarchical regimes in which there is no ruling party, but they can be found even in dominant-party regimes.
94. Buehler finds that co-optation of individual politicians out of leftist parties into palace ones does, in fact, work on a largely transactional basis. Buehler, *Why Alliances Fail*; and Buehler, "Continuity through Co-optation."

3. Co-optation as Interpretative Dilemma: Istiqlal's Democratic Journey

1. For an example of such an analysis, see Maye Kassem, *Egyptian Politics: The Dynamics of Authoritarian Rule* (Boulder, Colo.: Lynne Rienner, 2004).
2. This same assumption is at the heart of acculturational approaches as well.
3. Interview, Wafd member, Cairo, October 2013.
4. Hayden White, *Metahistory: The Historical Imagination in Nineteenth-Century Europe* (Baltimore: Johns Hopkins University Press, 1973).
5. For an excellent account of the development of Morocco's newspaper industry, see Jonathan Smolin, *Moroccan Noir: Police, Crime, and Politics in Popular Culture* (Bloomington: Indiana University Press, 2013).
6. Istiqlal also produces a French-language newspaper, *L'Opinion*, with similar but not identical coverage (the contemporary *L'Opinion* is more focused on economic news than the contemporary al-ʿAlam). For linguistic reasons, *L'Opinion* is more often referenced in French- and English-language scholarship, and there have certainly been times when *L'Opinion* had particularly combative editors or faced censorship for its political statements. However, Arabic (whether colloquial Moroccan *darija* in informal settings or standard Arabic in formal ones) has always been the primary language of party work (conferences, for example, mostly take place in Arabic, with some inevitable code-switching). I focus on Istiqlal's Arabic-language public face both to correct the overrepresentation of *L'Opinion* in international scholarship and because it is more proximate to the language in which Moroccan politics overwhelmingly takes place.
7. The notion of "publicly available transcripts" is, of course, James Scott's; see his *Domination and the Arts of Resistance: Hidden Transcripts* (New Haven, Conn.: Yale University Press, 1990).
8. That said, there are several populations that would probably not have access to the scripts I discuss here—especially people (mostly in rural areas) who only speak Amazigh languages or who have only very limited *darija*.

9. That there was no such moment does not, as we shall see, keep scholars from claiming that there was one.

10. It is true, however, that the metaphor has become less common in party sources since 2011 (or even 2012, when I began my field research). I return to this development in the book's conclusion.

11. Václav Havel, *The Power of the Powerless: Citizens Against the State in Central-Eastern Europe*, Routledge Revivals (Abingdon, Oxon: Routledge Press, 2009). My understanding of Havel is informed by Lisa Wedeen's analysis in *Ambiguities of Domination: Politics, Rhetoric and Symbols in Contemporary Syria* (Chicago: University of Chicago Press, 1999).

12. Havel, *The Power of the Powerless*, 7.

13. Havel, *The Power of the Powerless*, 10.

14. I do not mean to imply that such lying is normatively undesirable. On the contrary, it may well be that deceiving ourselves about certain realities is an eminently salutary political behavior.

15. In doing so, I align myself with much of conceptual metaphor theory, as initially introduced by George Lakoff and Mark Johnson in *Metaphors We Live By* (Chicago: University of Chicago Press, 1980).

16. See Lisa Wedeen, *Authoritarian Apprehensions: Ideology, Judgment, and Mourning in Syria* (Chicago: University of Chicago Press, 2019), chap. 3, for a discussion of the relationship between ideology and hesitance to act in Syria.

17. By *regime* in the Moroccan context, I mean both the monarchy and the *makhzen*, the coterie of loyalists and advisers who surround the king and retain much informal power. Much of what is said in this section also applies to Istiqlal's socialist counterpart (and splinter), the UNFP/USFP. It is customary to treat the "nationalist parties" (Istiqlal and the USFP) as a coherent bloc—they were, after all, in a formal alliance for much of the 1970s and 1990s. However, I choose to separate their stories because there is reason to believe that the two parties' readings of incorporation were shaped by different factors. The UNFP/USFP and its leaders faced far more and more intense repression than their Istiqlali counterparts between 1959 and 1975, which makes it difficult to rule out the possibility that securing immediate physical security was a central USFP priority. See discussion of challenger parties in chapters 1 and 2. The USFP also operates in a distinctly Marxian discursive mode that opens (and forecloses) different logical avenues than those opened up by Istiqlal's nationalism.

18. Such calls have always been illegal in independent Morocco, but even the more scandalous rumors about Istiqlal leaders' private statements concern individual kings, not the institution as a whole. Contemporary Istiqlalis often argue that a symbolic monarchy is critical to holding Morocco's diverse society together.

19. For an excellent treatment of this shift, see Muhammad Radwani, *Al-tanmiyya al-siyasiyya fi al-maghrib: Tashakkul al-sulta al-tanfidhiyya wa mumarisatiha min sanat 1956 ila sanat 2000* (Rabat: Al-Ma'arif Al-Jadida, 2011).

20. The Green March and the entire issue of the Sahara are part of Istiqlal's story, but they are part of other stories as well. My concern here is not with what has actually occurred in the area—much of which has been horrific—but with how

this particular nationalist party and the regime narrated a particular set of events. There are unquestionably better, fuller, and more equitable treatments of this issue, but what matters for understanding Istiqlal's co-optation is how the party read the moment. I therefore restrict myself to their readings here. Another oft-mentioned factor spurring Istiqlal into a more conciliatory stance vis-à-vis the monarchy was the prospect of military rule raised by two attempted coups against the King in 1971 and 1972. The coups may well explain why King Hassan II was willing to change his policy of relying on military allies and invite the parties back into the political process. They do not, however, explain why the parties were willing to play along. Istiqlal rejected the king's proposed constitutional amendments after the coup in 1972; when Istiqlal members were invited to join the cabinet that year, the party refused on the grounds that their "conditions for participation were not on offer"; the party wanted "comprehensive," not "partial," change (al-'Alam, 6 and 7 April 1972). It was only after the Green March and the 1976 and 1977 elections that Istiqlal was willing to enter the cabinet.

21. For a thoughtful account of the Green March's role as an unresolved, recurrent issue in Moroccan politics, see Susan Gilson Miller, *A History of Modern Morocco* (Cambridge: Cambridge University Press, 2012), Kindle. While the Green March did result in Spain's relinquishing control over the Sahara, Morocco's dispute with Sahrawi separatists who did not see themselves as belonging to the Moroccan nation is still ongoing, with disastrous consequences for the territory's inhabitants.

22. Miller, *A History of Modern Morocco*, loc. 4026.

23. Ellen Lust, *Structuring Conflict in the Arab World: Incumbents, Opponents, and Institutions* (Cambridge: Cambridge University Press, 2005), 58.

24. Jennifer Gandhi and Adam Przeworski, "Cooperation, Cooptation, and Rebellion Under Dictatorship," *Economics and Politics* 18, no. 1 (2006): 14.

25. Radwani, *Al-tanmiyya al-siyasiyya fi al-maghrib*, 67.

26. In outlining Istiqlal's "democratic journey" discourse, I draw upon party documents spanning more than five decades, including public speeches and interviews, the documents that resulted from national party conferences, and individually and collectively authored editorials in *al-'Alam*. I gathered archival materials at the National Archives, the National Center for Documentation, the Istiqlal Party library, and the archives of *al-'Alam*. I am immensely grateful to the staff of these four institutions, who are of course not responsible for my interpretations of the material they so generously made available.

27. Istiqlal's "democratic journey" is but one of many anticolonial and postcolonial narratives of gradual, teleological "marches" toward progress found around the world in the middle of the twentieth century, a point to which I return in the epilogue. By focusing on the political work done by this particular journey metaphor, I am able to derive portable analytical tools with which to study these and other forms of metaphor across diverse authoritarian contexts. Moreover, I am able to examine the role of anticolonial modernist teleologies as *oppositional* ideological formations; in much of the postcolonial world, the bearers of such ideologies came to power at independence, and their narratives of linear

progress—whether anticolonial, modernist, or Marxist—were deployed from positions of rule, relatively unconcerned with questions of co-optation. Attention to those nationalist movements that failed to come to power at independence helps complete our understanding of the role of progressive teleologies in the postcolonial world.

28. Allal al-Fassi, opening address, Second National Conference of the Istiqlal Party, January 1959. Al-Fassi took a deep, public interest in the issue of the Western Sahara. In the 1950s he served as the editor-in-chief of *Morocco's Sahara* (*Sahra' al-Maghrib*), a periodical that emphasized the Alawite dynasty's historical claims to sovereignty over the area in articles such as "Morocco's Desert Character and the Interaction of the Desert and the Atlas Mountains in Forming the Moroccan Nation" ("Tab'iyat al-maghrib al-sahrawiyya wa tafa'ul al-sahra' wal-atlas fi takwin al-watan al-maghribi," *Sahra' al-Maghrib*, no 2, [March 13, 1957]).

29. The title of the "Call from Kuwait" echoes al-Fassi's famous "Call from Cairo" (*nidā' al-qāhira*), one of the central texts of Morocco's nationalist movement in which al-Fassi condemned the exile of then-sultan Muhammad V at the hands of French authorities and launched the all-out struggle for Moroccan independence. Interview, former Istiqlal mayor; interview, Istiqlal party and syndicate activist, northern Morocco, March 2014.

30. After 'Allal al-Fassi's death, the party retired the term *president*. All subsequent party leaders have been referred to by the title *secretary-general*.

31. Ahmed bin Idriss al-Youssoufi, *al-'Alam*, October 7, 1975.

32. al-Youssoufi, *al-'Alam*, October 7, 1975.

33. Interview reprinted in *al-'Alam*, October 24, 1975.

34. al-Youssoufi, *al-'Alam*, October 7, 1975.

35. "Maghrib jadid . . . wal-intikhabat," *al-'Alam*, November 22, 1975.

36. "Maghrib jadid . . . wal-intikhabat."

37. White, *Metahistory*, 5.

38. Abd al-Qadir al-Alami, "Al-musalsal al-dimuqrati," *al-'Alam*, January 21, 1997. For other representative articles citing 1976 or thereabouts as the beginning of the democratic journey, see "Ma'na tahdhirat al-majlis al-watani," *al-'Alam*, December 14, 1983; and "Ahamiat al-intikhabat al-qadima fil-musalsal al-dimuqrati," *al-'Alam*, December 3, 1983.

39. White, *Metahistory*, 5.

40. M'hamed Boucetta, "Programmatic Report," Tenth General Conference of the Istiqlal Party, April 1978, 21–23.

41. I do not mean to imply that a constitutional monarchy necessarily meets the criteria that political theorists—or even procedural comparativists—might lay out for democracy. I refer to such a regime as democratic here because to the vast majority of Istiqlal's members and according to the party's official organs, monarchy is not only compatible with democracy but, in Morocco at least, a necessary condition for it to thrive. See discussion of party ideology in chapter 2.

42. White, *Metahistory*; and David Scott, *Conscripts of Modernity: The Tragedy of Colonial Enlightenment* (Durham, N.C.: Duke University Press, 2004).

43. White, *Metahistory*, 7.

3. ISTIQLAL'S DEMOCRATIC JOURNEY

44. This is why, although discourse in the real world often mixes and shifts among genres, it is not possible to truly combine the two genres under consideration here—Tragedy and Romance—because their endings are fundamentally incompatible.
45. Hayden White, *The Content and the Form: Narrative Discourse and Historical Representation* (Baltimore: Johns Hopkins University Press, 1978), 23.
46. Paul Ricoeur. "Narrative Time," *Critical Inquiry* 7, no. 1 (1980), 1809.
47. Reinhart Koselleck, *Futures Past: On the Semantics of Historical Time* (New York: Columbia University Press, 1985).
48. One way of thinking about the grammatic difference between Koselleck's use of the term and mine is to note their differing plurals. Koselleck's are "futures past"; mine are "future pasts."
49. "Wa yastamirr al-rihan 'ala al-dimuqratiyya," *al'-Alam*, September 15, 1984.
50. Scott, *Conscripts of Modernity*, 83.
51. Abdelkrim Ghellab, *Mahammad busitta al-diblomasi al-hakim* (Rabat: Dar Abi Raqraq lil-Tabaa wal-Nashr, 2017), 5.
52. Philip Selznick, *TVA and the Grass Roots: A Study of Politics and Organization* (Berkeley: University of California Press, 1953), 14.
53. Interview, woman in her twenties, Rabat, July 2017.
54. Abd al-Latif Husni, "Fi ritha' al-ahzab al-siyyasiyya al-maghribiyya," *Wijhat Nazar*, no. 36–37 (Spring–Summer 2008), 2.
55. Husni, "Fi ritha' al-ahzab al-siyyasiyya al-maghribiyya," 13.
56. Husni, "Fi ritha' al-ahzab al-siyyasiyya al-maghribiyya," 14.
57. "Shabab fi ma'rakat al-dimuqratiyya," *al-'Alam*, May 22, 1993.
58. Ali Ouasri, *Min wahm al-intiqal al-dimuqrati ila mutahat al-tahawwul al-mujtama'i ba'd 20 febrair* (Rabat: Top Press, 2012), 14.
59. Ouasri, *Min wahm al-intiqal*, 13, 21.
60. Interview, woman in her twenties, Casablanca, July 2017.
61. See "Wathiqa musarriba li-amwal yasmina badu al-muharriba li-shira' shuquq baris . . . wal-istiqlal yatahadi binkiran wa yutajih lil-qada' " *Al-Su'al*, January 3, 2014, http://laquestion.ma/archives/456; and "Binkiran: shuquq yasmina badu fi baris (fidyu)" *Kifache*, December 31, 2013, http://www.kifache.com/56453.
62. Interview, man in his fifties, outside Casablanca, July 2017.
63. Cited in "Al-ahzab al-siyasiya fi al-maghrib," episode of *Malaf Niqash*, October 21, 2014, available on YouTube, https://www.youtube.com/watch?v=pwQiz1GM2Vs.
64. National Democratic Institute, "Youth Perceptions in Morocco: Political Parties and Reforms" (2011), 11.
65. National Democratic Institute, "Youth Perceptions in Morocco," The translation is the NDI's.
66. Interview, man in his thirties, Rabat, July 2017.
67. Interview, man in his twenties, Rabat, July 2017.
68. Interview, man in his sixties, Rabat, December 2014.
69. Ronald Wintrobe, *The Political Economy of Dictatorship* (Cambridge: Cambridge University Press, 2000); and Andreas Schedler, *The Politics of Uncertainty: Sustaining and Subverting Electoral Authoritarianism* (Oxford: Oxford University Press, 2013).

70. Istiqlal, as I discuss in detail in part 3, did withdraw from the cabinet in 2013; whether that action was "in protest over regime policies" is a complicated question.

71. Scott, *Conscripts of Modernity*, 70.

72. Consider, for example, the literature that has sprung up around why opposition forces do not coalesce to oppose incumbents—the assumption being that a broader opposition coalition is better for overthrowing regimes—and under what conditions they might be induced to co-operate. See, for example, Nicolas Van de Walle, "Tipping Games: When do Opposition Parties Coalesce?" in *Electoral Authoritarianism: The Dynamics of Unfree Competition*, ed. by Andreas Schedler (Boulder, Colo.: Lynne Rienner, 2006); Jillian Schwedler, *Faith in Moderation: Islamist Parties in Jordan and Yemen* (Cambridge: Cambridge University Press, 2006); Janine A. Clark, "Threats, Structures, and Resources: Cross-Ideological Coalition Building in Jordan," *Comparative Politics* 43, no. 1 (2010); and Jennifer Gandhi and Grant Buckles, "Opposition Unity and Cooptation in Hybrid Regimes," paper presented at the *Annual Midwest Political Science Association Conference*, Chicago, Illinois, April 7–10, 2016.

73. Paul Pierson, "Increasing Returns, Path Dependence, and the Study of Politics," *APSR* 94, no. 2 (2000), 252.

74. Alberto Simpser, Dan Slater, and Jason Wittenberg, "Dead but Not Gone: Contemporary Legacies of Communism, Imperialism, and Authoritarianism," *Annual Review of Political Science* 21 (2018): 419–439.

75. For the original account of metaphor's centrality, see Lakoff and Johnson, *Metaphors We Live By*. An updated overview of the debate around conceptual metaphor theory can be found in Raymond W. Gibbs Jr., *Metaphor Wars: Conceptual Metaphors in Human Life* (Cambridge: Cambridge University Press, 2017).

76. Gibbs, *Metaphor Wars*, 4.

77. Hannah Pitkin, *Fortune Is a Woman: Gender and Politics in the Thought of Niccolo Machiavelli* (Chicago: University of Chicago Press, 1984).

78. Pitkin, *Fortune Is a Woman*, 291.

79. Diane Vaughan, *The Challenger Launch Decision* (Chicago: University of Chicago Press, 1996), loc. 1769.

80. Vaughan, *The Challenger Launch Decision*, loc. 1769.

81. Vaughan, *The Challenger Launch Decision*, loc. 105.

82. The five Istiqlal members named in 1977 were party secretary-general M'hamed Boucetta (minister of state for foreign affairs and cooperation), Mohamed Douiri (minister of resources and national development), future party secretary-general Abbas El Fassi (minister of housing and planning), Abderrahmane Baddou (secretary of state for foreign affairs), and Abdelhak Tazi (secretary of state for cadre training). In the November 1981 shuffle, Abdelkrim Ghellab was nominated to the position of minister delegate to the prime minister, taking Abderrahmane Baddou's place. In November 1983 Istiqlal retained five positions, but several more titles were changed. To foreshadow my argument in the coming chapters, it is worth noting that, except for Boucetta, all of these cabinet members were either the parents or children of other Istiqlalis who had or would go on to serve in the cabinet or parliament.

83. "Fi hadith al-akh muhammad busitta al-amin al-'am li-hizb al-istiqlal lil-majalla: tadakhkhul al-jihaz al-idari la yumakkin min ma'rifat al-quwwa al-haqiqiyya lil-ahzab, hunak quwwat daght tataharrak li-ijhad kul tawajuh dimuqrati," *al-'Alam*, September 15, 1984.

84. The reason that front-page, above-the-fold headlines are important is that they reach a much broader audience than other parts of the paper. It has long been a Moroccan tradition, at least in cities, to stop and read the front pages of various newspapers on display at a sidewalk stand before—or instead of—buying.

85. "Min mahzelat 10 yunio 83 ila mahzalat 14 shatanbar 1984: al-hadaf tasfiyat al-dimuqratiyya wa iqamat mu'assasat bila musdaqiyya/hizb al-istiqlal ikhtar al-dimuqratiyya li-jihadihi wa lan yataraji'" *al'-Alam*, September 17, 1984.

86. "Min mahzelat 10 yunio 83 ila mahzalat 14 shatanbar 1984."

87. "Min mahzelat 10 yunio 83 ila mahzalat 14 shatanbar 1984."

88. "Min mahzelat 10 yunio 83 ila mahzalat 14 shatanbar 1984."

89. Scott, *Conscripts of Modernity*, 70.

90. "Wa yastamirr al-rihan 'ala al-dimuqratiyya," *al-'Alam*, September 16, 1984.

91. "Wa yastamirr al-rihan 'ala al-dimuqratiyya."

4. Co-optation as Interpretive Dilemma: The Wafd at War

1. Michael J. Willis, "Political Parties in the Maghrib: The Illusion of Significance," *Journal of North African Studies* 7, no. 2 (2002): 5.

2. Although the placement of the government-identified *minbar* in the center may seem initially to accord with Greene's assumption that authoritarian ruling parties occupy the center range of a unidimensional political spectrum, "left" / "right" / "center" here were all construed in primarily economic terms, and entirely within a left-socialist orientation. On highly salient issues such as foreign policy, the military's political status, or the role of religion in public life, there is no indication that the *manābīr* were supposed to differ from one another at all, or from government positions that are difficult to characterize as "centrist." For a more extensive discussion of Greene's theory and how it relates to the Wafd and the Istiqlal, see chapter 5.

3. It was not until the January 1977 bread riots tarnished the Egypt Party's reputation that Sadat created the National Democratic Party and named himself as its president. In a classically Egyptian twist, the Egypt Party refused to disband; it remained legal but inactive. For a searing critique of these events, see Farag Fouda, *Al-wafd wal-mustaqbal* (Cairo: Al-Mu'allif, 1984).

4. Mohamed Ali Shita, "*Hizb al-wafd al-jadid*," In *Tarikh al-wafd*, by Gamal Bedawy and Lami'i al-Miti'i (Cairo: Dar al-Shourouk, 2003), 534–635.

5. Shita, "*Hizb al-wafd al-jadid*," 637.

6. Those with criminal convictions could still be banned from politics. Although five of the founding members had been accused of crimes, none had ever been convicted. Shita, "*Hizb al-wafd al-jadid*," 637.

7. This lobbying was primarily carried out by Farag, Sirag al-Din, and 'Abd al-Fattah Hussein. See Raymond A. Hinnebusch, "The Reemergence of the Wafd Party: Glimpses of a Liberal Opposition in Egypt," *International Journal of Middle East Studies* 16, no. 1 (March 1984): 103.
8. Marius Deeb, *Party Politics in Egypt: The Wafd and Its Rivals* (London: Ithaca Press, 1979), 26.
9. That non-lawyer was pharmaceutical executive El-Sayyid el-Badawy Shehata.
10. Yunan Labib Rizq, *Tarikh al-ahzab al-masriya* (Cairo: Al-hi'a al-'ulia lil-kitab, 1997), 230.
11. Hinnebusch, "The Reemergence of the Wafd Party," 107.
12. Shita, "*Hizb al-wafd al-jadid,*" 638.
13. Shita, "*Hizb al-wafd al-jadid,*" 637.
14. This fact remains true at the time of writing (2021).
15. Hassanayn Karam, "*Shakhsiyat fu'ad siraj al-din,*" in *Tarikh al-wafd,* by Gamal Bedawy and Lami'i al-Miti'i (Cairo: Dar al-Shourouk, 2003), 734.
16. Karam, "*Shakhsiyat fu'ad siraj al-din,*" 734.
17. Karam, "*Shakhsiyat fu'ad siraj al-din,*" 734.
18. For an excellent account of the relationship between the legal profession and politics in pre-1952 Egypt, see Donald Reid, *Lawyers and Politics in the Arab World, 1880–1960* (Minneapolis: Bibliotheca Islamica, 1981). For the definitive account of the decline of Egypt's legal profession during the twentieth century, see Amr al-Shalakany, *Izdihar wa inhiyar al-nukhba al-qanuniyya fi misr, 1805–2005* (Cairo: Dar al-Shorouk, 2013).
19. Tamir Moustafa, *The Struggle for Constitutional Power: Law, Politics, and Economic Development in Egypt* (Cambridge: Cambridge University Press, 2007), 111.
20. Al-Shalakany, *Izdihar wa inhiyar,* 26.
21. Moustafa, *The Struggle for Constitutional Power.*
22. Moustafa, *The Struggle for Constitutional Power,* loc. 875.
23. Moustafa, *The Struggle for Constitutional Power,* loc. 85.
24. Shita, "Hizb al-wafd al-jadid," 652.
25. August 23 is the anniversary of Mustafa Nahhas's death in 1965, so the selection of this day was not an accident. See chapter 5 for a fuller discussion of Nahhas's funeral and its importance to the Wafd.
26. Magdi Mehanna, "Dirasat al-wafd: Ma'rakat ithbat al-wujud bayn al-wafd wal-hukuma," *al-Wafd,* April 5, 1984.
27. Shita, "Hizb al-wafd al-jadid," 653.
28. Mehanna, "Dirasat al-wafd."
29. "Egyptian Court Rehabilitates Two Opposition Party Leaders," *New York Times,* February 13, 1984.
30. "Nujum al-wafd fil-barlaman al-jadid," *al-Wafd,* April 10, 1987.
31. "Nujum al-wafd."
32. Mehanna, "Dirasat al-Wafd." All quotations in this paragraph are from this piece unless otherwise noted.
33. Mehanna, "Dirasat al-Wafd."
34. Ahmed Aboul Foutouh, "Limatha al-Wafd?" *al-Wafd,* March 22, 1984.
35. Wahid Ra'fat, "*Masr al-ghad: 'An al-intikhabat al-qadima,*" *al-Wafd,* March 22, 1984.

36. Ra'fat, "Masr al-ghad." The Umma Party was legalized in 1983 by a court decision. Abd al-Ghaffar Shukr, Emad Siyam, and Mustafa Magdy Al-Gamal, *Al-ahzab al-siyasiya wa azmat al-ta'adudiya fi masr* (Cairo: Jazirat al-Ward, 2010), 57.
37. Ibrahim Dessouqi Abaza, "La taqta' al-amal," *al-Wafd*, May 9–18, 1984.
38. This system was not "pure" PR since it also honored the 1971 constitution's requirement that half of the seats go to candidates designated as "workers" or "peasants." This requirement created a baffling system of contingencies that misrepresented voter preference without guaranteeing representation since "worker" or "peasant" status often bore a tenuous relationship to reality. On the complexities of this system, see Sahar F. Aziz, "Revolution Without Reform: A Critique of Egypt's Election Laws," *George Washington International Law Review* 45, no. 1 (2013): 27–28.
39. Aziz, "Revolution Without Reform," 28.
40. Interview with constitutional scholar Dr. Mohsin Khalil, *al-Wafd*, October 3, 1990.
41. Interview with constitutional scholar Dr. Mohsin Khalil, *al-Wafd*, October 3, 1990.
42. The Muslim Brotherhood's surprise performance in the 2005 elections finally brought opposition representation back to (indeed, beyond) pre-1990 levels.
43. For examples of such claims, see interview with Fu'ad Sirag al-Din, *al-Wafd*, April 5, 1984; and coverage of Sirag al-Din at a rally in Minya, *al-Wafd*, April 7, 1987.
44. Fu'ad Sirag al-Din, "Ra'i al-wafd," *al-Wafd*, March 22, 1984.
45. I use *actual* here to acknowledge—within the constraints of a language steeped in an action/speech binary—that both metaphor and other action are real.
46. Mustafa Sherdy, "Al-intikhabat: Al-wa'd wal-haqiqa," *al-Wafd*, May 31, 1984.
47. Michael Lowy and Robert Sayre, *Romanticism Against the Tide of Modernity*, trans. by Catherine Porter (Durham, N.C.: Duke University Press, 2002), 11. In making this point about Romanticism's "dual nature," Lowy and Sayre are indebted to Jan Fischer.
48. Ibrahim Farag, "Azmat al-hurriyat hiyya sabab al-nakasat," *al-Wafd*, February 5, 1987.
49. Sherdy, "Al-intikhabat: Al-wa'd wal-haqiqa."
50. Sherdy, "Al-intikhabat: Al-wa'd wal-haqiqa."
51. Gamal Bedawy, "Mustaqbal al-mu'arada fi zill al-ta'adud al-hizbi," *al-Wafd*, June 7, 1984.
52. Mustafa Sherdy, "Hata nibda' . . . al-bidaya al-sahiha," *al-Wafd*, June 7, 1984.
53. Mustafa Sherdy, "Sawtak sayf fi-yadd al-umma," *al-Wafd*, April 6, 1984.
54. White, *Metahistory*, 7.
55. Gamil Hana Masiha, "Wa wada't al-harb awzariha," *al-Wafd*, June 4, 1984.
56. The SCC would confirm Sherdy's claim some three years later.
57. This and subsequent quotes from "Your Vote Is a Sword in the Hand of the Nation" are from Mustafa Sherdy, "Sawtak sayf fi-yadd al-umma."
58. Qur'an 2:226, interpretation based on Sahih International with my amendments.
59. Ibrahim Dessouqi Abaza, "Lam nafqad al-amal . . . ba'd," *al-Wafd*, April 7, 1987.
60. Mustafa Sherdy, "Idfinu hadha al-mayyit: Raham allah mawtakum . . !" *al-Wafd*, April 7, 1984.

61. Sherdy, "Idfinu hadha al-mayyit."
62. Abaza, "Lam nafqad."
63. Abaza, "Lam nafqad."
64. Abdelkrim Ghellab, M'hammad busitta al-diblomasi al-hakim (Rabat: Dar Abi Raqraq lil-Tabaa wal-Nashr, 2017), 5.
65. Abaza, "Lam nafqad."
66. The Wafd also boycotted the Consultative Council elections of 1989. The Consultative Council, created in 1980, is a partially elected body with two-thirds of its members chosen by popular vote and the remaining one-third appointed by the president. The council's powers are limited; it has never been a major arena of struggle between regime and opposition. The council was ultimately abolished by the 2014 constitution, although Egypt now has a senate that is entirely elected, half via individual constituencies and half via closed-party-list PR. The only party listed on the ballot for the senate's inaugural 2020 elections was the proto-ruling-party Mustaqbal Watan.
67. Mustashar Mustafa al-Tawil, "Al-hall huwwa al-hall," al-Wafd, January 22, 1987.
68. Interview with Dr. Muhsin Khalil, al-Wafd, October 3, 1990.
69. Al-Wafd, October 18, 1990. The HEC also decided that night to expel any member who did not honor the boycott, leading to the expulsion of thirty-two members in November 1990 and more later. The names of the expelled were listed on the front page of al-Wafd on November 4, 1990. The most prominent expellee was Mona Makram-Ebeid, who accepted one of parliament's ten appointed seats from President Mubarak.
70. Gamal Bedawy, "Mughalitat intikhabiyya," al-Wafd, October 21, 1990.
71. Sherdy, "Sawtak sayf fi-yadd al-umma."
72. "Fi nadwat al-wafd bil-daqhiliyya: al-wafd yuqati' al-intikhabat li-yakhudh ma'rakat al-dimuqratiyya," al-Wafd, October 21, 1990.
73. Badr al-Din Hassan, "Fu'ad badrawi fi bur sa'id: qararna muqati'at al-intikhabat.. wa khawdh ma'rakat al-dimuqratiyya min ajl al-sha'b," al-Wafd, November 2, 1990.
74. "Madha ba'd muqata' al-intikhabati," al-Wafd, October 20, 1990.
75. Four matching headlines led four stories on the cover of an opposition paper I bought in the summer of 2010 in Cairo. At the time, the headlines did not seem like harbingers, which is why I did not keep the page or record the name of the newspaper. As 2011 unfolded, however, I thought of it often: a reminder of how unthinkable change had seemed just a few months earlier.
76. World Values Survey, Egypt, 2008, question V231: 6.1 percent of Egyptians reported in the same survey that they would never vote for the Wafd Party under any circumstances (World Values Survey, Egypt, 2008, question V233). Illegal organizations, like the Muslim Brotherhood, were not included among the poll's options, although there were many options for "don't know," "no preference," "no response," and so on.
77. Osama Heikal, "Intikhabat laysat kal-intikhabat," Al Masry Al Youm, June 5, 2010. Interestingly, the party made similar claims in the early 2000s about the "election" of Goumaa—claims that disappeared once Goumaa proved polarizing. See,

for example, the now-omitted chapter on Goumaa in the original edition of *Tarikh al-wafd*.

78. For those following along with the typology of opposition parties offered in chapter 2, the coalition included one holdover party (the Wafd), one palace party gone somewhat rogue (Tagammu⁣ᶜ), and two challenger parties—although one, the Nasserists, was based on the ideology of a prior regime leader. These parties were of different ages, had different backgrounds, and were animated by different organizational needs. Approaches that lump all opposition parties together ignore these diverse trajectories.

79. "I'tilaf al-mu'arada al-misriyya yutlaw hamla did al-tawari,'" *al-Jarida*, April 14, 2010.

80. Hibba al-Sharqawi, "Al-mu'aradad tabhath 'at aliyat mukhtalifa lil-muwajiha," *al-Mal*, May 12, 2010.

81. Diaa Rashwan, "Muqtarahat li-ta'dil wa taf'il wathiqat damanat al-intikhabat," *al-Shorouk*, August 2, 2010.

82. Yehya Gamal, "Al-wafd . . . wal-ikhwan..wal-intikhabat," *Al Masry Al Youm*, September 20, 2010.

83. Al-Daragli, "Al-wafd yuqarir yakhudh al-intikhabat wa yudfa' bil-ajrudi did sabbahi," *Al Masry Al Youm*, October 30, 2010.

84. Marwa al-A'sar, "Activists Call on Al-Wafd Party to Boycott PA Elections," *Daily News Egypt*, September 20, 2010.

85. Al-A'sar, "Activists Call on Al-Wafd."

86. Osama El Ghazaly Harb, "Na'm . . . khadhal al-wafd al-umma," *Al Masry Al Youm*, October 3, 2010.

87. Shadi Hamid, "Why Not Boycott? The Egyptian Opposition and the November Elections," *Up Front* (blog), Brookings Institution, July 22, 2010.

88. Harb, "Na'm . . . khadal al-wafd."

89. Harb, "Na'm . . . khadal al-wafd."

90. All quotations in this paragraph are from Harb, "Na'm . . . khadal al-wafd."

91. ᶜAmmar ᶜAli Hassan, "Ammar ali hassan yakshif: Safqa bayn al-watani wal-wafd 'ala hisab al-barada'i wa li-tahjim al-ikhwan," *Al Masry Al Youm*, March 14, 2010. The irony of these rumors is that the liberal Egyptian commentators who repeated them had little interest in allowing the Brotherhood to take its proportional place in power. Widespread support among this group for the 2013 military coup, which ended Egypt's democratic transition in order to cripple the Brotherhood, suggests that their pearl-clutching about NDP deals was something less than sincere. For an excellent dissection of Egyptian liberals in the Morsi era, see Dalia Fahmy and Daanish Faruqi, *Egypt and the Contradictions of Liberalism: Illiberal Intelligentsia and the Future of Egyptian Democracy* (London: Oneworld, 2017).

92. Hassan, "Ammar ali hassan yakshif."

93. Interview with El-Sayyid el-Badawy Shehata, *al-Watani*, September 26, 2010.

94. "Jaridat al-dustur al-misriyya ila ayna," *France24 Arabic*, October 6, 2010.

95. Interview, adviser to el-Badawy, Cairo, October 2013.

96. Al-Daragli, "Al-wafd yuqarir khawd al-intikhabat."

97. "Misr al-nahar da bahth i'alanat hizb al wafd bil-tilifisyun 2010-10-31," YouTube, November 1, 2010, https://www.youtube.com/watch?v=8bCs0j1DQNI&t=1s.
98. "I'alanat hizb al-wafd al-intikhabiyya," YouTube, November 6, 2010, https://www.youtube.com/watch?v=Tij8gVnH3Ls.
99. "I'alanat hizb al-wafd al-intikhabiyya."
100. The *masir* in *masirnā hanawṣal* comes from the same m-y-r root that gives us *masira*, "journey."

5. Party-as-Family

1. See discussion in chapter 2.
2. Interview, Istiqlal Executive Committee (EC) member, Rabat, March 2013.
3. Kenneth Greene, *Why Dominant Parties Lose: Mexico's Democratization in Comparative Perspective* (Cambridge: Cambridge University Press, 2007), 176.
4. Greene, *Why Dominant Parties Lose*, 182.
5. The World Values Survey does ask such questions (for reasons of comparability with other regions), but the results further demonstrate their inapplicability to Southwest Asian and North African politics. In the 2011 wave, for example, 82.6 percent of Moroccans surveyed answered "don't know" or "no answer" to a question asking them to place themselves on a unidimensional left–right spectrum.
6. Suad Joseph, "Gender and Relationality among Arab Families in Lebanon," *Feminist Studies* (1993): 465–486.
7. I owe the formulation of ideologies as unevenly saturating to Lisa Wedeen. See Wedeen, *Authoritarian Apprehensions: Ideology, Judgment, and Mourning in Syria* (Chicago: University of Chicago Press, 2019), chap. 1.
8. Max Weber, *Economy and Society*, ed. G. Roth and C. Wittich (Berkeley: University of California Press, 1968), 954, 1006.
9. Weber, *Economy and Society*, 956.
10. Weber, *Economy and Society*, 956–957.
11. Weber, *Economy and Society*, 958, 1011.
12. Weber, *Economy and Society*, 1026.
13. Weber, *Economy and Society*, 1029.
14. On patrimonial state apparatuses, see Eva Bellin, "Reconsidering the Robustness of Authoritarianism in the Middle East: Lessons from the Arab Spring," *Comparative Politics* 44, no. 2 (2012): 127–149; Peter Evans, *Embedded Autonomy: States and Industrial Transformation* (Cambridge: Cambridge University Press, 1995); Steffan Hertog, *Princes, Brokers, and Bureaucrats: Oil and the State in Saudi Arabia* (Ithaca, N.Y.: Cornell University Press, 2010); and Atul Kohli, *State-Directed Development: Political Power and Industrialization in the Global Periphery* (Cambridge: Cambridge University Press, 2004). On family businesses, see Euysung Kim, "The Impact of Family Ownership and Capital Structures on Productivity Performance of Korean Manufacturing Firms: Corporate Governance

and the 'Chaebol Problem,'" *Journal of the Japanese and International Economies* 20, no. 2 (2006): 209–233; Eun Mee Kim, "The Industrial Organization and Growth of the Korean Chaebol: Integrating Development and Organizational Theories," *Asian Business Networks* 64 (1996): 231.

15. James C. Scott, *Seeing Like A State: How Certain Schemes to Improve the Human Condition Have Failed* (New Haven, Conn.: Yale University Press, 1998); Michael Herb, *All in the Family: Absolutism, Revolution, and Democracy in the Middle Eastern Monarchies* (Albany: State University of New York Press, 1999); and Julia Adams, *The Familial State: Ruling Families and Merchant Capitalism in Early Modern Europe* (Ithaca, N.Y.: Cornell University Press, 2005).

16. Ellen Lust, "Competitive Clientelism in the Middle East," *Journal of Democracy* 20, no. 3 (2009): 127. Lust notes but does not fully explore the consequences of the fact that even if opposition parties had platforms, they are usually in no position to implement them, no matter how many votes they win. Morocco and Kuwait may be partial exceptions.

17. Michael J. Willis, "Political Parties in the Maghrib: The Illusion of Significance," *Journal of North African Studies* 7, no. 2 (2002): 13.

18. Aida Seif al-Dawla, quoted in Fatemah Farag, "What Lies Beneath," *Al-Ahram Weekly*, May 5–11, 2005.

19. "'Abbas al-fassi kan wafiyan li-majlis al-'a'ila fa-wazzar al-ashar wa atlal amr wuzara' ahl fas," *al-Sabah*, January 5, 2013.

20. Hisham Sharabi, *Neopatriarchy: A Theory of Distorted Change in Arab Society* (Oxford: Oxford University Press, 1988), 7–8. Another classic example of this line of argumentation is Hammoudi Abdellah's *Master and Disciple: The Cultural Foundations of Moroccan Authoritarianism* (Chicago: University of Chicago Press, 1997).

21. Jason Brownlee, ". . . And Yet They Persist: Explaining Survival and Transition in Neopatrimonial Regimes," *Studies in Comparative International Development* 37, no. 3 (2002): 35–63; Eva Bellin, "Coercive Institutions and Coercive Leaders" in *Authoritarianism in the Middle East*, ed. by Marsha Pripstein Posusney and Michele Penner Angrist, 21–38 (Boulder, Colo.: Lynne Rienner, 2005); Holger Albrecht and Oliver Schlumberger, "'Waiting for Godot': Regime Change Without Democratization in the Middle East," *International Political Science Review* 25, no. 4 (2004): 371–392; Lust, "Competitive Clientelism"; Bellin, "Reconsidering the Robustness of Authoritarianism"; and Kenneth M. Pollack, *Armies of Sand: The Past, Present, and Future of Arab Military Effectiveness* (Oxford: Oxford University Press, 2019).

22. Raymond A. Hinnebusch, "Authoritarian Persistence, Democratization Theory, and the Middle East: An Overview and Critique," *Democratization* 13, no. 3 (2006): 376.

23. See Hannah Arendt, "Ideology and Terror: A Novel Form of Government," *Review of Politics* 15, no. 3 (1953): 303–327.

24. Donald Reid, "Fu'ad Siraj al-Din and the Egyptian Wafd," *Journal of Contemporary History* 15, no. 4 (October 1980): 725.

25. Eric Trager, "'Trapped' and 'Untrapped': Egypt's Wafd Party and the January Revolt." Paper prepared for presentation at the Annual Conference of the

American Political Science Association. Seattle, Washington, August 31–September 4, 2011, 48.

26. Mona Makram-Ebeid was expelled for taking an appointed seat in parliament offered to her by President Hosni Mubarak in 1990. She later rejoined the party only to leave it again in 2004 to join Ayman Nour's al-Ghad Party. She then joined the Wafd *again* in 2011 and left it again to become a member of the new Egyptian Social Democratic Party. See Rahma Diaa, "Muna makram 'ibid rihalat al-ahzab tastaqil min al-wafd wa tandumm lil-masry al-dimuqrati," *Al-Doustour al-Asly*, September 14, 2011.

27. Sayyid 'Abd al-'Ati, "Al-daktur numa'n juma'a al-ra'is al-rabi' lil-wafd," in *Tarikh al-Wafd*, by Gamal Bedawy and Lami'i al-Miti'i (Cairo: Dar Al Shorouk, 2003), 737. In later editions of this book, given to me by Wafd members rather than purchased in bookstores, this largely sympathetic chapter on Goumaa is absent.

28. Interview, Wafd member, Imbaba, October 2013; and interview, former Wafd member, Cairo, November 2013.

29. Yunan Labib Rizq, *Tarikh al-ahzab al-masriya* (Cairo: Al-hi'a al-'ulia lil-kitab, 1997), 229–230.

30. Rizq, *Tarikh al-ahzab al-masriya*, 234.

31. "Ra'is hizb al-wafd wa ra'is al-hi'a al-barlamaniyya li-hizb al-wafd," Abu Shoka's personal website, www.bahaaabushoka.com, accessed September 30, 2019.

32. Interview, Wafd activist, Imbaba, October 2013.

33. Wafd rally, January 2014; and interview, Giza, December 2013.

34. Al-Fassis use various names and transliterations, including Fassi, Fassi Fihri, and al-Fassi al-Fihri.

35. For an example of such misidentification, see Samia Errazouki, "The Façade of Political Crises in Morocco," *Jadaliyya*, May 12, 2013.

36. For a dramatic example of what happens when contemporary Wafdists were invited to share their suspicions about Gomaa, see Trager, "'Trapped' and 'Untrapped.'"

37. Interview, government official, Rabat, November 2014.

38. Mohammed Boudarham, "Chiba Mae El Ainine, numéro 3 de l'Istiqlal par consensus," *TelQuel*, April 24, 2018.

39. Jassim Ahdani, "Hamdi Ould Errachid: Faiseur et défaiseur de leaders," *TelQuel*, October 12, 2017.

40. Ahdani, "Hamdi Ould Errachid."

41. Interview, party librarian, Rabat, December 2014.

42. As China's one-child policy and Soviet attempts to remake the bourgeois family illustrate, some authoritarian regimes (perhaps especially those with totalitarian aspirations and relatively high coercive or surveillance capacity) do intervene directly in family matters. Egyptian and Moroccan authoritarians, however, have never had either the capacity or much of an interest in reshaping the basics of family life.

43. The terms are of course Hirschman's. Albert O. Hirschman, *Exit, Voice, and Loyalty: Responses to Decline in Firms, Organizations, and States* (Cambridge, Mass.: Harvard University Press, 1970).

44. "Mustafa Nahas, Egyptian Leader: Foe of British Dies at 86—Superseded by Nasser," *New York Times*, August 24, 1965; and "Nahas Supporters Fight Police After His Funeral," *New York Times*, August 25, 1965.
45. Reid, "Fu'ad Siraj al-Din," 740.
46. Farag Fouda, *Al-wafd wal-mustaqbal* (Cairo: Al-Mu'allif, 1984), 47.
47. Ninette S. Fahmy, *The Politics of Egypt: State-Society Relationship* (London: Routledge, 2002), 77. The Wafd may not keep central membership lists; if party leaders know how many members they actually have, they are not interested in sharing that information. The most common explanation offered for their reluctance to disclose membership totals is that it might hurt the party's electoral chances. It is also possible that a total count does not exist.
48. Interview, adviser to Wafd president, Dokki, November 2013.
49. Sirag al-Din, *Limatha al-hizb al-jadid?* (Cairo: Dar al-Shorouk, 1977), 24–25.
50. Ahmed, dissatisfied with the Wafd's position on secularism, eventually found a political home in the al-Ghad Party, led by another Wafd defector (more properly, an expellee), Ayman Nour.
51. Interview, former Wafd member, Cairo, October 2013.
52. Interview, Fuad Badrawi, Cairo, November 2013.
53. Mohamed Ali Shita, "*Hizb al-wafd al-jadid*," in *Tarikh al-wafd*, by Gamal Bedawy and Lami'i al-Miti'i (Cairo: Dar al Shourouk, 2003), 732.
54. Fouda, *Al-wafd wal-mustaqbal*, 56.
55. Interview, Wafd member, Dokki, December 2013.
56. Interview, Wafd member, Imbaba, October 2013.
57. Yitzhak Oron, ed., *Middle East Record*, vol. 2 (Jerusalem: Tel Aviv University, 1961), 579.
58. Interview, Fuad Badrawi, Dokki, November 2013.
59. Samia Seragaldin, *The Cairo House: A Novel* (Syracuse, N.Y.: Syracuse University Press, 2000), 88.
60. Samar Nabih, "Tajdid bayt al-umma lil-mara al-rabia' min 'sudu' al-tarikh'" *Al-Watan*, July 10, 2018.
61. Interview, Wafd vice-president, Dokki, December 2013.
62. While Istiqlal's headquarters are not family property, there are certainly homes across Morocco that serve as meeting places for the party and its affiliate union. As Hamid Chabat's wife, Fatima Tariq, describes their home, "we didn't have, at many times, a private life in the traditional sense. The house was essentially a second headquarters for the union and the party, where we constantly had meetings, nearly every day, and this is the climate our kids grew up in, and are still in—even the grandkids, now." Muhammad Bilqasim, "Shabat wa tariq . . . tafasil zawaj 'kubil' siyasi turwa li-awal marra," *Hespress*, June 30, 2015.
63. "Al-wazira al-maghrebia yasmina badu: Al-siyasi haramitni min al-matbakh," *Al-Sharq Al-Awsat*, January 23, 2003. The article's title translates as "Moroccan minister Yasmina Baddou: Politics Kept Me Out of the Kitchen."
64. Bilqasim, "Shabat wa tariq."

65. Scholars of American politics may initially find this unsurprising. However, what is being inherited here is not "party identification" but "party identity," and—thanks to authoritarianism—that carries responsibilities and risks far beyond those entailed by checking a box on a voter registration form.
66. The so-called Berber *Ẓahir* was a controversial 1930 colonial decree separating "Berbers" from "Arabs" for judicial purposes.
67. In the context of 1990s Morocco, being "left" implied a preference for a more thoroughgoing transformation of the political (and therefore economic system).
68. Interview, member of Istiqlal's EC, Rabat, January 2014.
69. Interview, member of Istiqlal's EC, Rabat, December 2014.
70. Interview, high-ranking Shabiba official, December 2014.
71. Interview, Wafd activist, Cairo, January 2014.
72. Group interview, Qasr al-Sayyid activists, January 2014.
73. Interview, Fuad Badrawi, Cairo, November 2013.
74. Interview, Istiqlal activist, Rabat, December 2014.
75. John Waterbury, *The Commander of the Faithful: The Moroccan Political Elite; A Study in Segmented Politics* (London: Weidenfeld and Nicholson, 1970).
76. Ellen Lust and Amaney Jamal, "Rulers and Rules: Reassessing the Influence of Regime Type on Electoral Law Formation." *Comparative Political Studies* 35 (2002): 337–366.
77. Ellen Lust, *Structuring Conflict in the Arab World: Incumbents, Opponents, and Institutions* (Cambridge: Cambridge University Press, 2005).
78. Abd al-Ghaffar Shukr, Emad Siyam, and Mustafa Magdy Al-Gamal, *Al-ahzab al-siyasiya wa azmat al-ta'adudiya fi masr* (Cairo: Jazirat al-Ward, 2010); Fahmy, *The Politics of Egypt*; and Joshua Stacher, "Parties Over: The Demise of Egypt's Opposition Parties," *British Journal of Middle Eastern Studies* 31, no. 2 (2004): 215–233.
79. I am indebted for the idea of focusing on processes rather than outcomes to Erica Simmons and Nick Smith's notion of "comparison with an ethnographic sensibility." See Erica S. Simmons and Nicholas Rush Smith, "Comparison with an Ethnographic Sensibility," *PS: Political Science & Politics* 50, no. 1 (2017): 126–130.
80. Suad Joseph, "Gender and Relationality Among Arab Families in Lebanon," *Feminist Studies* (1993): 467.
81. Joseph, "Gender and Relationality," 482.
82. Joseph, "Gender and Relationality," 467.
83. Marcia Inhorn, *Infertility and Patriarchy: The Cultural Politics of Gender and Family Life in Egypt* (Philadelphia: University of Pennsylvania Press, 1996), 8.
84. Joseph, "Gender and Relationality," 467.
85. Joseph, "Gender and Relationality," 480.
86. Allal al-Fassi, *La Hawada* (Rabat: Al-Risala, 1972); and interview, Istiqlal MP, Rabat, December 2014.
87. Interview, member of Istiqlal EC, Rabat, December 2014.
88. Bilqasim, "Shabat wa tariq."
89. Bilqasim, "Shabat wa tariq."

90. al-Fassi, *La Hawada*.
91. "Istiqlal. Chabat vire El Fassi," *TelQuel*, December 21, 2013.
92. Jassim Ahdani, " '*L'unité istiqlalieene' malmeneé par des scenes de bagarres à l'overture du 17e congrès*," *TelQuel*, September 30, 2017.
93. According to Eric Trager, Goumaa expelled four of the party's seven members of parliament during his tenure in office. See Trager, " 'Trapped' and 'Untrapped.' "
94. For video of this moment, see "Al-fa'iz al-yawm huwwa al-wafd," April 26, 2014, YouTube, https://www.youtube.com/watch?v=C6jWrDiPgs0.
95. "Fasl fu'ad badrawi min al-wafd wa kafat tashkilihi," *Bawab al-Wafd*, June 24, 2014.
96. "Fasl fu'ad badrawi min al-wafd wa kafat tashkilihi."
97. Amin Saleh, "Fu'ad badrawi ya'tadhar lil-wafd..wal-badawi: nuqtat da'afi anaka hafidh fu'ad siraj al-din," *Al-Yom al-Sebaa*, September 9, 2014.
98. As discussed in chapter 1, the Wafd performed better than any other non-Islamist party in the 2011–2012 parliamentary elections. Although its "ground game" is somewhat feeble, it still has an organizational advantage over the plethora of new parties formed immediately after the uprising.
99. Prominent security establishment figures who have joined the Wafd since 2011, like retired general Safir Nour, have not drawn nearly as much criticism as NDP-linked figures.
100. At the time, parliamentary elections were scheduled for March 2015; these elections were eventually canceled after the electoral law organizing them was declared unconstitutional by the country's Supreme Constitutional Court.
101. Ashraf Shaaban, "Tafaqum al-sira' dakhil hizb al-wafd bil-buhaira," *Al-Bawaba News*, December 26, 2014.
102. Shaaban, "Tafaqum al-sira' dakhil hizb al-wafd bil-buhaira."
103. Magdy al-Safqi, "Mu'aridu al-badawi yirfudun al-ikhwan wal-fulul," *Al Watan* (Kuwait), December 31, 2014.
104. Ashraf Shaaban, "Ba'd faslihi min al-wafd . . . abu al-rish fi hiwar lil-bawaba niuz: lan nasmah bi-an yakun bayt al-umma makhaba' lil-anthima al-sabiqa," *Al-Bawaba News*, December 30, 2014.
105. Ahmed Behnis, " 'ulia al-wafd tuqarar fasl qiyadat al-hizb al-mu'tasimin bi-damanhur," *Al-Bawaba News*, December 28, 2014.
106. For a discussion of continued internal contestation in the Wafd, see Sofia Fenner, "Why Egypt's Oldest Opposition Party Isn't Challenging President Sissi," *Washington Post*, February 7, 2018.

6. Generation After Generation: Making Sense of Confrontational Turns

1. These characteristics are drawn from the work of Asef Bayat and Samuel Huntington, whose arguments about youth I address in more detail later in the chapter.

2. Panel discussion on the Shabiba's 12th General Conference framing document, Bibliotheque National du Royaume du Maroc, Rabat, December 26, 2014.

3. Intriguingly, Istiqlal's sixty-seat performance was an improvement of eight seats over the 2007 elections—but because the party lost its plurality, the elections were considered a defeat.

4. Mohammed Boudarham, "Istiqlal: Chabat boucle la boucle," *TelQuel*, January 22, 2013.

5. Muhammad Bouharid, "Chabat: Hizb al-istiqlal lan yataraji 'an al-insihab min al-hukuma," *Al-Anadol*, June 30, 2013.

6. Mahmoud Maarouf, "Insihab hizb al-istiqlal min al-hukuma wa qararuhu bil-taraja' mu'aqatan yuthir al-jadal bayn al-maghariba," *Al-Quds al-Arabi*, May 13, 2013.

7. Maarouf, "Insihab hizb al-istiqlal."

8. Personal communication, Jamila Ghazi, October 2019.

9. Muhammad Bilqasim, "Shabat: al-malik ya yuqarrir makanina . . . wa insihab al-istiqlal qa'im," *Hespress*, June 28, 2013.

10. Interview, Istiqlal spokesman, Rabat, December 2014.

11. See Michael Hoffman and Amaney Jamal, "The Youth and the Arab Spring: Cohort Differences and Similarities," *Middle East Law and Governance* 4, no. 1 (2012): 168–188; and Mohammad al-Momani, "The Arab 'Youth Quake:' Implications on Democratization and Stability," *Middle East Law and Governance* 3, no. 1–2 (2011): 159–170.

12. For example, Dan LaGraffe, "The Youth Bulge in Egypt: An Intersection of Demographics, Security, and the Arab Spring," *Journal of Strategic Security* 5, no. 2 (2012): 65–80. For a critique of this approach, see Charles Kurzman, "The Arab Spring Uncoiled," *Mobilization* 17, no. 4 (2012): 377–390.

13. For excellent entry points into this literature, see Marc Lynch, "How the Media Trashed the Transitions," *Journal of Democracy* 26, no. 4 (2015): 90–99; Miryam Aouragh and Anne Alexander, "The Egyptian Experience: Sense and Nonsense of the Egyptian Revolution," *International Journal of Communication* 5 (2011): 1344–1358; and Manuel Castells, *Networks of Outrage and Hope: Social Movements in an Internet Age* (Hoboken, N.J.: Wiley, 2012).

14. Asef Bayat, *Life as Politics: How Ordinary People Change the Middle East,* 2nd ed., (Palo Alto, Calif.: Stanford University Press, 2013), chap. 6.

15. Samuel Huntington, *The Clash of Civilizations and the Remaking of World Order* (New York: Simon and Schuster, 1996), 117.

16. Karl Mannheim, "The Problem of Generations," in *Karl Mannheim: Essays on Sociology and Social Psychology*, ed. Paul Kecskemeti (London: Routledge and Kegan Paul, 1953), 290.

17. Mannheim, "The Problem of Generations," 296.

18. Mannheim, "The Problem of Generations," 303.

19. Mannheim, "The Problem of Generations," 309.

20. Tahar Abu Farah, "Abdelkader El Kihel: De Tarbia wa takhiyme au comité exécutif de l'Istiqlal, 33 ans de militantisme," *La Vie ECO*, June 8, 2012.

21. Muhammad Bilqasim, "*Shabat wa tariq . . . tafasil zawaj 'kubil' siyasi turwa li-awal marra,*" *Hespress*, June 30, 2015.

22. The term is, of course, Stuart Hall's. See Stuart Hall, "The Toad in the Gardens: Thatcherism Among the Theorists," in *Marxism and the Interpretation of Culture*, ed. by Cary Nelson and Lawrence Grossberg (Urbana: University of Illinois Press, 1988), 44.
23. Bilqasim, "*Shabat wa tariq.*"
24. All quotations in this paragraph are from my interview with Brahim, December 2014.
25. See discussion of al-Fassi's ideological commitments in chapter 2.
26. Hannah Arendt, *The Human Condition* (Chicago: University of Chicago Press, 1958), 247.
27. The name translates to English as the Moroccan League for the Defense of Human Rights.
28. Interview, member of the EC, Salé, December 2014.
29. Video of these comments, from September 12, 2017, is available at YouTube, https://www.youtube.com/watch?v=mACjR5oi1h8&feature=emb_title.
30. Interview, Wafd activist, Giza, November 2013.
31. Ellen Lust, *Structuring Conflict in the Arab World: Incumbents, Opponents, and Institutions* (Cambridge: Cambridge University Press, 2005), 126.
32. "Al-ahzab fi 'yawm al-ghadab:' al-wafd wal-jabha yusharikan . . . wal-tagammu' yirfud . . . wal-nasiri mughlaq," *Al Shorouk*, January 25, 2011.
33. Abdel Latif El-Menawy, *Tahrir: The Last Days of Mubarak: An Insider's Account of the Uprising in Egypt* (Cairo: Gilgamesh 2012), 69.
34. Wagdi Zayn al-Din, "Dhikriyat wafiyya fi 2 yanair," *al-Wafd*, January 23, 2017.
35. The information in this paragraph is drawn from minute-by-minute coverage from *BBC Arabic*, *Al-Jazeera*, *Al-Jazeera English*, and the Egyptian newspaper *al-Doustour* in January and February 2011.
36. See Hind Adil, "Ta'jil intikhabat ri'asat lagnat shabab al-wafd bil-gharbiyya," *Al-Yom al-Sebiaa*, July 9, 2010.
37. Jadaliyya/Al-Ahram, "Al-Wafd Party," November 18, 2011.
38. Interview, adviser to El-Sayyid el-Badawy Shehata, Giza, October 2013.
39. Video of this event can be found at "Tawthiq musharakit al-wafd fi thawrat 25 yanair," YouTube, October 12, 2011, https://www.youtube.com/watch?v=G77j3Ig1x8Y. Ellipsis in original.
40. Zayn al-Din, "Dhikriyat wafdiyya fi 25 yanair."
41. Zayn al-Din, "Dhikriyat wafdiyya fi 25 yanair."
42. Zayn al-Din, "Dhikriyat wafdiyya fi 25 yanair." Other named participants include Muhammad 'Abd al-'Alim Dawud (an MP), High Council members Ayman 'Abd al-'Aal and Hussayn Mansour, and prominent youth Muhammad Fu'ad Sharif 'Arif, Sami al-Tarawi, Gamal Abu Hamila, Nabil al-Rifa'i, Abdallah al-Gabari, and Walim Zaki.
43. Asma' Subhi, "Hussam al-khawli . . . al-rajal al-thani fi hizb al-wafd . . . brufail," *Al-Arabiya News*, n.d.
44. Ahmed Said, "Fu'ad badrawi: tarikh al-shabab al-wafdi yartabit bi-kafah al-sha'b al-masry mundhu thawrat 1919," *Al-Ahram*, September 27, 2019.
45. Mannheim, "The Problem of Generations," 304.

Conclusion: Authoritarianism as Tragedy

Epigraph: Quoted and translated in Peter Szondi, *An Essay on the Tragic*, trans. Paul Fleming (Stanford: Stanford University Press, 2002), 7.

1. Perhaps "de-emplotments" is more apt.
2. Interview, high-ranking Istiqlal member, December 2014.
3. Interview, member of the Istiqlal executive committee, July 2014.
4. David Scott, *Conscripts of Modernity: The Tragedy of Colonial Enlightenment* (Durham, N.C.: Duke University Press, 2004), 7–8.
5. I understand Romance and Tragedy as two genres with fundamentally incompatible plots and temporal structures; although in reality all genres can be combined, Romance and Tragedy cannot be, in the sense that I mean them, *coherently* combined. A Tragic ending is not redemptive and does not justify suffering along the way; a Romantic ending does.
6. Martha Nussbaum, "The Costs of Tragedy: Some Moral Limits of Cost-Benefit Analysis," *Journal of Legal Studies* 29, no. 52 (June 2000): 1005.
7. Scott, *Conscripts of Modernity*, 185.
8. Although I am writing at what seems to be a particularly bleak global political moment, I do not mean that the existence or resurgence of authoritarianism is a Tragedy. Instead, I advocate for emplotting our analyses of authoritarian politics (that is, regime-subject dynamics) as Tragedies.
9. Peter Szondi, *An Essay on the Tragic*, trans. Paul Fleming (Stanford, Calif.: Stanford University Press, 2002), 19.
10. Andrew Cecil Bradley, *Shakespearean Tragedy* (New York: Penguin Putnam, 1991), 38.
11. Jean-Pierre Vernant and Pierre Vidal-Naquet, *Mythe et tragédie en la Grèce ancienne* (Paris: Éditions la Découverte), cited in Scott, *Conscripts of Modernity*, 13.
12. For example, Timur Kuran, "Now out of Never: The Element of Surprise in the East European Revolutions of 1989," *World Politics* 44, no. 1 (1991): 7–48; and Ronald Wintrobe, *The Political Economy of Dictatorship* (Cambridge: Cambridge University Press, 2000).
13. For example, Jennifer Gandhi and Adam Przeworski, "Cooperation, Cooptation, and Rebellion Under Dictatorship," *Economics and Politics* 18, no. 1 (2006): 1–26; Jennifer Gandhi, *Political Institutions Under Dictatorship* (Cambridge: Cambridge University Press, 2008); and Milan Svolik, *The Politics of Authoritarian Rule* (Cambridge: Cambridge University Press, 2012).
14. Andreas Schedler, *The Politics of Uncertainty: Sustaining and Subverting Electoral Authoritarianism* (Oxford: Oxford University Press, 2013), 28, 37. He acknowledges that similar circumstances might occur in procedurally democratic regimes, hinting at a deeper epistemological reality: "as human action is by definition indeterminate," he writes, "social actions are by definition indeterminate" (23). Yet he—and I—remain convinced that "profound differences exist between the relative transparency of democratic regimes and the structural opacity of authoritarian regimes" (38).

15. Scott, *Conscripts of Modernity*, 185.

16. Szondi, *An Essay on the Tragic*, 19.

17. Nussbaum, "The Costs of Tragedy," 1007.

18. Bradley, *Shakespearean Tragedy*, 37–38.

19. Bradley, *Shakespearean Tragedy*, 38.

20. Wedeen, *Authoritarian Apprehensions: Ideology, Judgment, and Mourning in Syria* (Chicago: University of Chicago Press, 2019).

Bibliography

'Abd al-'Ati, Sayyid. *"Al-daktur numa'n juma'a al-ra'is al-rabi' lil-wafd."* In *Tarikh al-Wafd* by Gamal Bedawy and Lami'i al-Miti'i. Cairo: Dar Al Shorouk, 2003.

Acemoglu, Daron, and James A. Robinson. *Economic Origins of Dictatorship and Democracy.* Cambridge: Cambridge University Press, 2006.

Adams, Julia. *The Familial State: Ruling Families and Merchant Capitalism in Early Modern Europe.* Ithaca, N.Y.: Cornell University Press, 2005.

Albertus, Michael, Sofia Fenner, and Dan Slater. *Coercive Distribution.* Cambridge: Cambridge University Press, 2018.

Albrecht, Holger, and Oliver Schlumberger. " 'Waiting for Godot': Regime Change Without Democratization in the Middle East." *International Political Science Review* 25, no. 4 (2004): 371–392.

Althusser, Louis. "Ideology and Ideological State Apparatuses (Notes Towards an Investigation)" (1970). In *Cultural Theory: An Anthology*, ed. by Imre Szeman and Timothy Kaposy, 204–222. Malden, Mass.: John Wiley, 2010.

Aouragh, Miryam, and Anne Alexander. "The Egyptian Experience: Sense and Nonsense of the Egyptian Revolution." *International Journal of Communication* 5 (2011): 1344–1358.

Arendt, Hannah. *The Human Condition.* University of Chicago Press, 1958.

——. "Ideology and Terror: A Novel Form of Government." *Review of Politics* 15, no. 3 (1953): 303–327.

Ashford, Douglas. *Perspectives of a Moroccan Nationalist.* Totowa, N.J.: Bedminster Press, 1964.

——. *Political Change in Morocco.* Princeton, N.J.: Princeton University Press, 1961.

Asscher, Maarten. *Apples and Oranges: In Praise of Comparisons.* Trans. by Brian Doyle-de Breuil. San Francisco: Four Winds, 2015.

Austin, John Langshaw. *How to Do Things with Words.* Oxford: Oxford University Press, 1975.

Aziz, Sahar F. "Revolution Without Reform: A Critique of Egypt's Election Laws." *George Washington International Law Review* 45, no. 1 (2013): 27–28.

Bayat, Asef. *Life as Politics: How Ordinary People Change the Middle East.* 2nd ed. Palo Alto, Calif.: Stanford University Press, 2013.

Bedawi, Gamal, and Lami'i al-Miti'i. eds. *Tarikh al-wafd.* Cairo: Dar al-Shorouk, 2003.

Bellin, Eva. "Coercive Institutions and Coercive Leaders." In *Authoritarianism in the Middle East,* ed. by Marsha Pripstein Posusney and Michele Penner Angrist, 21–38. Boulder, Colo.: Lynne Rienner, 2005.

——. "Reconsidering the Robustness of Authoritarianism in the Middle East: Lessons from the Arab Spring." *Comparative Politics* 44, no. 2 (2012): 127–149.

Benhlal, Mohamed. *Le collège d'Azrou: une élite berbère civile et militaire au Maroc (1927–1959).* Paris: Éditions Karthala, 2005.

Blaydes, Lisa. *Elections and Distributive Politics in Mubarak's Egypt.* Cambridge: Cambridge University Press, 2010.

Boucetta, M'hamed. "Programmatic Report." Tenth General Conference of the Istiqlal Party, April 1978, 21–23.

Bradley, Andrew Cecil. *Shakespearean Tragedy.* New York: Penguin Putnam, 1991.

Brownlee, Jason. ". . . And Yet They Persist: Explaining Survival and Transition in Neopatrimonial Regimes." *Studies in Comparative International Development,* 37, no. 3 (2002): 35–63.

——. *Authoritarianism in an Age of Democratization.* Cambridge: Cambridge University Press, 2007.

Brown, Nathan. *When Victory Is Not An Option: Islamist Movements in Arab Politics.* Ithaca, N.Y.: Cornell University Press, 2012.

Buehler, Matt. "Continuity Through Co-optation: Rural Politics and Regime Resilience in Morocco and Mauritania." *Mediterranean Politics* 20, no. 3: 364–385.

——. *Why Alliances Fail: Islamist and Leftist Coalitions in North Africa.* Syracuse, N.Y.: Syracuse University Press, 2018.

Bueno de Mesquita, Bruce, Alastair Smith, Randolph M. Siverson, and James D. Morrow. *The Logic of Political Survival.* Cambridge, Mass.: MIT Press, 2003.

Castells, Manuel. *Networks of Outrage and Hope: Social Movements in the Internet Age.* Hoboken, N.J.: Wiley, 2012.

Clark, Janine A. "Threats, Structures, and Resources: Cross-Ideological Coalition Building in Jordan." *Comparative Politics* 43, no. 1 (2010): 101–120.

Davenport, Christian, Hank Johnston, and Carol McClurg Mueller, eds. *Mobilization and Repression.* Minneapolis: University of Minnesota Press, 2005.

Davis, Diane E., and Anthony W. Pereira, eds. *Irregular Armed Forces and Their Role in Politics and State Formation.* Cambridge: Cambridge University Press, 2003.

Deeb, Marius. "Labour and Politics in Egypt, 1919–1939." *International Journal of Middle East Studies* 10, no. 2 (1979): 187–203.

——. *Party Politics in Egypt: The Wafd and Its Rivals.* London: Ithaca Press, 1979.

Dreef, Muhammad. *Al-haql al-siyasi al-maghribi: Al-as'ila al hadira wal al-ajwiba al-gha'iba.* Rabat: Al-Majella al-Maghribiyya li-'Ilm al-Ijtima' al-Siyasi, 1998.

Evans, Peter. *Embedded Autonomy: States and Industrial Transformation.* Cambridge: Cambridge University Press, 1995.

Fahmy, Dalia, and Daanish Faruqi. *Egypt and the Contradictions of Liberalism: Illiberal Intelligentsia and the Future of Egyptian Democracy.* London: Oneworld, 2017.

Fahmy, Ninette S. *The Politics of Egypt: State-Society Relationship*. London: Routledge, 2002.

Fassi, Allal al-. *Al-naqd al-thati*, 6th ed. Rabat: Al-Risala, 1999.

——. *La Hawada*. Rabat: Al-Risala, 1972.

Fouda, Farag. *Al-wafd wal-mustaqbal*. Cairo: Al-Mu'allif, 1984.

Gandhi, Jennifer. *Political Institutions Under Dictatorship*. Cambridge: Cambridge University Press, 2008.

Gandhi, Jennifer, and Grant Buckles. "Opposition Unity and Cooptation in Hybrid Regimes." Paper presented at the *Annual Midwest Political Science Association Conference*. Chicago, Illinois, April 7–10, 2016.

Gandhi, Jennifer, and Ellen Lust. "Elections Under Authoritarianism." *Annual Review of Political Science* 12 (2006), 403–422.

Gandhi, Jennifer, and Adam Przeworski. "Authoritarian Institutions and the Survival of Autocrats." *Comparative Political Studies* 40, no. 11 (2007): 1279–1301.

——. "Cooperation, Cooptation, and Rebellion Under Dictatorship." *Economics and Politics* 18, no. 1 (2006): 1–26.

Ghellab, Abdelkrim. *Mahammad busitta al-diblomasi al-hakim*. Rabat: Dar Abi Raqraq lil-Tabaa wal-Nashr, 2017.

Ghobashy, Mona, el-. "Egypt's Paradoxical Elections." *Middle East Report* 36 (2005): 238.

——. "Taming Leviathan: Constitutionalist Contention in Contemporary Egypt." PhD dissertation, Columbia University, New York, 2009.

Gibbs, Raymond W., Jr. *Metaphor Wars: Conceptual Metaphors in Human Life*. Cambridge: Cambridge University Press, 2017.

Gordon, Joel. "The False Hopes of 1950: The Wafd's Last Hurrah and the Demise of Egypt's Old Order." *International Journal of Middle East Studies* 12 (1989): 193–214.

Greene, Kenneth. *Why Dominant Parties Lose: Mexico's Democratization in Comparative Perspective*. Cambridge: Cambridge University Press, 2007.

Hall, Stuart. "The Toad in the Gardens: Thatcherism Among the Theorists." In *Marxism and the Interpretation of Culture*, ed. by Cary Nelson and Lawrence Grossberg. Urbana: University of Illinois Press, 1988.

Hamid, Shadi. *Temptations of Power: Islamists and Illiberal Democracy in A New Middle East*. New York: Oxford University Press, 2014.

——. "Why Not Boycott? The Egyptian Opposition and the November Elections." *Up Front* (blog), Brookings Institution, July 22, 2010.

Hammoudi, Abdellah. *Master and Disciple: The Cultural Foundations of Moroccan Authoritarianism*. Chicago: University of Chicago Press, 1997.

Havel, Václav. *The Power of the Powerless: Citizens Against the State in Central-Eastern Europe*. Routledge Revivals. Abingdon, Oxon: Routledge Press, 2009.

Herb, Michael. *All in the Family: Absolutism, Revolution, and Democracy in the Middle Eastern Monarchies*. Albany: State University of New York Press, 1999.

——. "Princes and Parliaments in the Arab World." *Middle East Journal* 58, no. 3 (2004): 367–384.

Hertog, Steffan. *Princes, Brokers, and Bureaucrats: Oil and the State in Saudi Arabia*. Ithaca, N.Y.: Cornell University Press, 2010.

Hinnebusch, Raymond A. "Authoritarian Persistence, Democratization Theory, and the Middle East: An Overview and Critique." *Democratization* 13, no. 3 (2006): 373–395.

——. "The Reemergence of the Wafd Party: Glimpses of a Liberal Opposition in Egypt." *International Journal of Middle East Studies*, March 16, no. 1 (1984).

Hirschman, Albert O. *Exit, Voice, and Loyalty: Responses to Decline in Firms, Organizations, and States.* Cambridge, Mass.: Harvard University Press, 1970.

Hoffman, Michael, and Amaney Jamal. "The Youth and the Arab Spring: Cohort Differences and Similarities." *Middle East Law and Governance* 4, no. 1 (2012): 168–188.

Human Rights Watch. "From Plebiscite to Contest? Egypt's Presidential Election." Briefing Paper, 2005.

Huntington, Samuel. *The Clash of Civilizations and the Remaking of World Order.* New York: Simon and Schuster, 1996.

——. *Political Order in Changing Societies.* New Haven, Conn.: Yale University Press, 1968.

Husni, ʿAbd al-Latif. "Fi ritha' al-ahzab al-siyyasiyya al-maghribiyya." *Wijhat Nazar*, no. 36–37 (Spring–Summer 2008).

Inhorn, Marcia. *Infertility and Patriarchy: The Cultural Politics of Gender and Family Life in Egypt.* Philadelphia: University of Pennsylvania Press, 1996.

Jaafar, Said. *Al-zawiya wal-hizb bil-maghrib: Usul al-istibdad al-siyasi.* Casablanca: Al-Najah al Jadida, 2014.

Joseph, Suad. "Gender and Relationality Among Arab Families in Lebanon." *Feminist Studies* (1993): 465–486.

Karam, Hassanayn. "Shakhsiyat fu'ad siraj al-din." In *Tarikh al-wafd*, by Gamal Bedawy and Lami'i al-Miti'i. Cairo: Dar al-Shourouk, 2003.

Kassem, Maye. *Egyptian Politics: The Dynamics of Authoritarian Rule.* Boulder, Colo.: Lynne Rienner, 2004.

Kasza, Gregory James. *The Conscription Society: Administered Mass Organizations.* London: Yale University Press, 1995.

Kim, Eun Mee. "The Industrial Organization and Growth of the Korean Chaebol: Integrating Development and Organizational Theories." *Asian Business Networks* 64 (1996): 231.

Kim, Euysung. "The Impact of Family Ownership and Capital Structures on Productivity Performance of Korean Manufacturing Firms: Corporate Governance and the 'Chaebol Problem.' " *Journal of the Japanese and International Economies* 20, no. 2 (2006): 209–233.

Kohli, Atul. *State-Directed Development: Political Power and Industrialization in the Global Periphery.* Cambridge: Cambridge University Press, 2004.

Koselleck, Reinhart. *Futures Past: On the Semantics of Historical Time.* New York: Columbia University Press, 1985.

Kuran, Timur. "Now out of Never: The Element of Surprise in the East European Revolutions of 1989." *World Politics* 44, no. 1 (1991): 7–48.

Kurzman, Charles. "The Arab Spring Uncoiled." *Mobilization* 17, no. 4 (2012): 377–390.

Lacy, Michael G. "The United States and American Indians: Political Relations." In *American Indian Policy in the Twentieth Century*, ed. by Vine Deloria Jr., 83–104. Norman: Oklahoma University Press, 1985.

LaGraffe, Dan. "The Youth Bulge in Egypt: An Intersection of Demographics, Security, and the Arab Spring." *Journal of Strategic Security* 5, no. 2 (2012): 65–80.

Lakoff, George, and Mark Johnson. *Metaphors We Live By*. Chicago: University of Chicago Press, 1980.

Lawrence, Adria. *Imperial Rule and the Politics of Nationalism: Anti-Colonial Protest in the French Empire*. Cambridge: Cambridge University Press, 2013.

Leveau, Remy. *Le fellah marocain, defenseur du trône*. Paris: Presses de la Fondation Nationale des Sciences Politiques, 1985.

Levitsky, Steven, and Lucan A. Way. *Competitive Authoritarianism: Hybrid Regimes After the Cold War*. Cambridge: Cambridge University Press, 2010.

Lopez, Shaun T. "Madams, Murders, and the Media: *Akhbar al-Hawadith* and the Emergence of a Mass Culture in 1920s Egypt." In *Re-envisioning Egypt 1919-1952*, ed by Arthur Goldschmidt, Amy J. Johnson, and Barak A. Salmoni, 371–397. New York: American University in Cairo Press, 2005.

Lowy, Michael, and Robert Sayre. *Romanticism Against the Tide of Modernity*. Trans. by Catherine Porter. Durham, N.C.: Duke University Press, 2002, 11.

Lust, Ellen. "Competitive Clientelism in the Middle East." *Journal of Democracy* 20, no. 3 (2009): 122–135.

——. "Elections Under Authoritarianism: Preliminary Lessons from Jordan." *Democratization* 13, no. 3 (2006): 456–471.

——. *Structuring Conflict in the Arab World: Incumbents, Opponents, and Institutions*. Cambridge: Cambridge University Press, 2005.

Lust, Ellen, and Amaney Jamal. "Rulers and Rules: Reassessing the Influence of Regime Type on Electoral Law Formation." *Comparative Political Studies* 35 (2002): 337–366.

Lynch, Marc. "How the Media Trashed the Transitions." *Journal of Democracy* 26, no. 4 (2015): 90–99.

Magaloni, Beatriz. *Voting for Autocracy: Hegemonic Party Survival and Its Demise in Mexico*. Cambridge Studies in Comparative Politics. Cambridge: Cambridge University Press, 2008.

Mannheim, Karl. "The Problem of Generations." In *Karl Mannheim: Essays on Sociology and Social Psychology*, ed. Paul Kecskemeti. London: Routledge and Kegan Paul, 1953.

Mardini, Zuhair. *Al-ladudan: Al-wafd wal-ikhwan*. Cairo: Dar Iqra,' 1984.

Masoud, Tarek. *Counting Islam: Religion, Class, and Elections in Egypt*. Cambridge: Cambridge University Press, 2014.

Menawy, Abdel Latif el-. *Tahrir: The Last 18 Days of Mubarak: An Insider's Account of the Uprising in Egypt*. Cairo: Gilgamesh, 2012.

Miller, Susan Gilson. *A History of Modern Morocco*. Cambridge: Cambridge University Press, 2012. Kindle.

Mitchell, Timothy. *Rule of Experts: Egypt, Techno-politics, Modernity*. Berkeley: University of California Press, 2002.

Momani, Mohammad al-. "The Arab 'Youth Quake:' Implications on Democratization and Stability." *Middle East Law and Governance* 3, no. 1-2 (2011): 159–170.

Monjib, Maâti. "Lopsided Struggle for Power in Morocco." *Sada Middle East Analysis*, January 15, 2017.

Montabes Pereira, Juan, and Maria A. Parejo Fernandez. "Morocco." In *Elections in Africa: A Data Handbook*, ed. by Dieter Nohlen, Michael Krennerich, and Bernard Thibaut, 630–637. Oxford: Oxford University Press, 1999.

Moustafa, Tamir. *The Struggle for Constitutional Power: Law, Politics, and Economic Development in Egypt.* Cambridge: Cambridge University Press, 2007.

Muleen, Muhammad Nabil. *Fikrat al-dustur fil-maghrib: Watha'iq wa nusus 1901–2011.* Casablanca: TelQuel Media, 2017.

National Democratic Institute. "Youth Perceptions in Morocco: Political Parties and Reforms." 2011.

Nussbaum, Martha. "The Costs of Tragedy: Some Moral Limits of Cost-Benefit Analysis." *Journal of Legal Studies* 29, no. 52 (June 2000).

Oron, Yitzhak, ed. *Middle East Record*, vol. 2. Jerusalem: Tel Aviv University, 1961.

Ouasri, Ali. *Min wahm al-intiqal al-dimuqrati ila mutahat al-tahawwul al-mujtama'i ba'd 20 febrair.* Rabat: Top Press, 2012.

Pierson, Paul. "Increasing Returns, Path Dependence, and the Study of Politics." *APSR* 94, no. 2 (2000): 252.

Pitkin, Hannah. *Fortune Is a Woman: Gender and Politics in the Thought of Niccolo Machiavelli.* Chicago: University of Chicago Press, 1984.

Piven, Frances Fox, and Richard A. Cloward. *Poor People's Movements: How They Succeed, Why They Fail*, 2nd ed. New York: Vintage, 1979.

Pollack, Kenneth M. *Armies of Sand: The Past, Present, and Future of Arab Military Effectiveness.* Oxford: Oxford University Press, 2019.

Qadéry, Mustapha El. "Les Berbères entre le myth colonial et la négacion national: Le cas du Maroc." *Revue d'histoire moderne et contemporaine* 45, no. 2 (April–June 1998).

Radwani, Muhammad. *Al-tanmiyya al-siyasiyya fi al-maghrib: Tashakkul al-sulta al-tanfidhiyya wa mumarisatiha min sanat 1956 ila sanat 2000.* Rabat: Al-Ma'arif Al-Jadida, 2011.

Rashed, Dina. "The Resurrection of the Ministry of the Interior Under Sadat: Junta Threat and Presidential Power." Paper presented at the Middle East Studies Association Annual Meeting, Washington D.C., November 22–25, 2014.

Reid, Donald. "Fu'ad Siraj al-Din and the Egyptian Wafd." *Journal of Contemporary History* 15, no. 4 (October 1980).

——. *Lawyers and Politics in the Arab World, 1880–1960.* Minneapolis: Bibliotheca Islamica, 1981.

Reynolds, Nancy. *A City Consumed: Urban Commerce, the Cairo Fire, and the Politics of Decolonization in Egypt.* Stanford, Calif.: Stanford University Press, 2012.

Ricoeur, Paul. "Narrative Time." *Critical Inquiry* 7, no. 1 (1980): 169–190.

Ries, Matthias. "Egypt." In *Elections in Africa: A Data Handbook*, ed. by Dieter Nohlen, Michael Krennerich, and Bernard Thibaut, 337–344. Oxford: Oxford University Press, 1999.

Rizq, Yunan Labib. *Tarikh al-ahzab al-masriya.* Cairo: Al-hi'a al-'ulia lil-kitab, 1997.

Schedler, Andreas. "The Nested Game of Democratization by Elections." *International Political Science Review* 23, no. 1 (2002): 103–122.

——. *The Politics of Uncertainty: Sustaining and Subverting Electoral Authoritarianism.* Oxford: Oxford University Press, 2013.

Schwedler, Jillian. *Faith in Moderation: Islamist Parties in Jordan and Yemen.* Cambridge: Cambridge University Press, 2006.

Scott, David. *Conscripts of Modernity: The Tragedy of Colonial Enlightenment.* Durham, N.C.: Duke University Press, 2004.

Scott, James C. *Seeing Like A State: How Certain Schemes to Improve the Human Condition Have Failed*. New Haven, Conn.: Yale University Press, 1998.

——. *Domination and the Arts of Resistance: Hidden Transcripts*. New Haven, Conn.: Yale University Press, 1990.

Selznick, Philip. *TVA and the Grass Roots: A Study of Politics and Organization*. Berkeley: University of California Press, 1953.

Seragaldin, Samia. *The Cairo House: A Novel*. Syracuse, N.Y.: Syracuse University Press, 2000.

Sewell, William H., Jr. *Logics of History: Social Theory and Social Transformation*. Chicago: University of Chicago Press, 2005.

Shalakany, Amr al-. *Izdihar wa inhiyar al-nukhba al-qanuniyya fi misr, 1805–2005*. Cairo: Dar al-Shorouk, 2013.

Shaqir, Muhammad. *Tatawwur al-dawla fil-maghrib: Ishkaliyat al-takawwun wal-tamarkaz wal haymana min al qarn al-thalith qabl al-milad ila al-qarn al'ishrin*. Casablanca: Ifriqiya al-Sharq, 2006.

Sharabi, Hisham. *Neopatriarchy: A Theory of Distorted Change in Arab Society*. Oxford: Oxford University Press, 1988.

Shehata, Samer S. *Shop Floor Culture and Politics in Egypt*. Albany: State University of New York Press, 2009.

Shita, Mohamed Ali. "*Hizb al-wafd al-jadid*." In *Tarikh al-wafd*, by Gamal Bedawy and Lami'i al-Miti'i. Cairo: Dar al Shourouk, 2003.

Shukr, Abd al-Ghaffar, Emad Siyam, and Mustafa Magdy Al-Gamal. *Al-ahzab al-siyasiya wa azmat al-ta'adudiya fi masr*. Cairo: Jazirat al-Ward, 2010.

Simmons, Erica S., and Nicholas Rush Smith. "Comparison with an Ethnographic Sensibility." *PS: Political Science & Politics* 50, no. 1 (2017): 126–130.

Simpser, Alberto, Dan Slater, and Jason Wittenberg. "Dead but Not Gone: Contemporary Legacies of Communism, Imperialism, and Authoritarianism." *Annual Review of Political Science* 21 (2018): 419–439.

Sirag al-Din, Fu'ad. *Limatha al-hizb al-jadid?* Cairo: Dar al-Shorouk, 1977.

Skocpol, Theda, and Margaret Somers. "The Uses of Comparative History in Macrosocial Inquiry." *Comparative Studies in Society and History* 22, no. 2 (1980): 174–197.

Smith, Benjamin. "Life of the Party: The Origins of Regime Breakdown and Persistence Under Single-Party Rule." *World Politics* 57, no. 3 (2005): 421–451.

Smolin, Jonathan. *Moroccan Noir: Police, Crime, and Politics in Popular Culture*. Bloomington: Indiana University Press, 2013.

Snyder, Patrick. "Red Lines: Legitimation and Dissent in Contemporary Morocco." Ph.D. dissertation, University of Minnesota, Minneapolis, 2022.

Stacher, Joshua. "Parties Over: The Demise of Egypt's Opposition Parties." *British Journal of Middle Eastern Studies* 31, no. 2 (2004).

Svolik, Milan. *The Politics of Authoritarian Rule*. Cambridge: Cambridge University Press, 2012.

Szondi, Peter. *An Essay on the Tragic*. Trans. by Paul Fleming. Stanford, Calif.: Stanford University Press, 2002.

Ta'ia', Muhammad al-. *'Abd al-rahman al-yussufi wal-tanawwub al-dimuqrati al-mujhad*. Rabat: Imprimerie Négoce com, 2013.

Terry, Janice J. *The Wafd, 1919-1952: Cornerstone of Egyptian Political Power*. London: Third World Centre for Research and Publishing, 1982.

Trager, Eric. " 'Trapped' and 'Untrapped': Egypt's Wafd Party and the January Revolt." Paper prepared for presentation at the Annual Conference of the American Political Science Association. Seattle, Washington, August 31–September 4, 2011.

Van de Walle, Nicolas. "Tipping Games: When do Opposition Parties Coalesce?" In *Electoral Authoritarianism: The Dynamics of Unfree Competition*, ed. by Andreas Schedler. Boulder, Colo.: Lynne Rienner, 2006.

Vaughan, Diane. *The Challenger Launch Decision*. Chicago: University of Chicago Press, 1996.

Vermeren, Pierre. *Histoire du maroc depuis l'indépendance*. Paris: La Découverte, 2010.

Vernant, Jean-Pierre, and Pierre Vidal-Naquet. *Mythe et tragedie en grèce ancienne*. 2 vols. Paris: Editions la Découverte, 1986.

Waterbury, John. *The Commander of the Faithful: The Moroccan Political Elite; A Study in Segmented Politics*. London: Weidenfeld and Nicholson, 1970.

Weber, Max. *Economy and Society*. Ed. by G. Roth and C. Wittich. 3 vols. Berkeley: University of California Press, 1968.

——. *The Protestant Ethic and the Spirit of Capitalism*. 1930. Reprint, New York: Routledge, 2001.

Wedeen, Lisa. *Ambiguities of Domination: Politics, Rhetoric and Symbols in Contemporary Syria*. Chicago: University of Chicago Press, 1999.

——. *Authoritarian Apprehensions: Ideology, Judgment, and Mourning in Syria*. Chicago: University of Chicago Press, 2019.

White, Hayden. *The Content and the Form: Narrative Discourse and Historical Representation*. Baltimore: Johns Hopkins University Press, 1978.

——. *Metahistory: The Historical Imagination in Nineteenth-Century Europe*. Baltimore: Johns Hopkins University Press, 1973.

Wickham, Carrie Rosefsky. *Mobilizing Islam: Religion, Activism and Political Change in Egypt*. New York: Columbia University Press, 2002.

——. *The Muslim Brotherhood: Evolution of an Islamist Movement*. Princeton, N.J.: Princeton University Press, 2013.

Willis, Michael J. "Political Parties in the Maghrib: The Illusion of Significance." *Journal of North African Studies* 7, no. 2 (2002): 1–22.

Wintrobe, Ronald. *The Political Economy of Dictatorship*. Cambridge: Cambridge University Press, 2000.

Wyrtzen, Jonathan. *Making Morocco: Colonial Intervention and the Politics of Identity*. Ithaca, N.Y.: Cornell University Press, 2015.

Zisenwine, Daniel. *The Emergence of Nationalist Politics in Morocco: The Rise of the Independence Party and the Struggle Against Colonialism After World War II*. New York: I. B. Tauris, 2010.

Index

GPSR Authorized Representative: Easy Access System Europe, Mustamäe tee
50, 10621 Tallinn, Estonia, gpsr.requests@easproject.com

www.ingramcontent.com/pod-product-compliance
Lightning Source LLC
Chambersburg PA
CBHW032122020426
42334CB00016B/1037

9 780231 208598